Recent Photo of the Author

旋法至極

佛法無邊

法輪常轉

This Falun Emblem is the miniature of the universe.
It also has its own form of existence and process of
evolution in all other dimensions. Therefore, I call
it a world.

Li Hongzhi

這個法輪圖形是宇宙的縮影，他在其他各個空間也有
他存在的形式、演化過程，所以我說是一個世界。

— 李洪志

ZHUAN FALUN

(ENGLISH VERSION)

LI HONGZHI

Copyright © 1999 by Li, Hongzhi

For information, write:
The Universe Publishing Company
P.O. Box 2026
New York, NY 10013

ISBN: 1-58613-101-X

Third Translation Edition (December, 1999. USA)

Published by The Universe Publishing Company

Printed in the United States of America

LUNYU[1]

"The Buddha Fa"[2] is most profound; among all the theories in the world, it is the most metaphysical and extraordinary science. In order to explore this domain, humankind must fundamentally change its conventional thinking. Otherwise, the truth of the universe will forever remain a mystery to humankind, and everyday people will forever crawl within the boundary delimited by their own ignorance.

Then, what exactly is "the Buddha Fa"? Is it a religion? Is it a philosophy? That is only the understanding of the "modernized Buddhist scholars," who merely study theories. They regard it as a philosophical category for critical studies and so-called research. Actually, "the Buddha Fa" is not only the tiny portion documented in the scriptures, for that is simply "the Buddha Fa" at an elementary level. "The Buddha Fa" is an insight into all mysteries. It encompasses everything and leaves out nothing—from particles and molecules to the universe, from the even smaller to the even greater. It is an exposition of the characteristic of the universe, "Zhen-Shan-Ren,"[3] expressed at different levels with different layers of meaning. It is also what the Tao School calls the "Tao,"[4] or what the Buddha School calls the "Fa."[5]

---

[1] Lunyu (loon-yew)—statement; comment.

[2] the Buddha Fa—the universal principles and law; the way of the universe.

[3] Zhen-Shan-Ren (jhun-shahn-ren)—Zhen (truth, truthfulness); Shan (compassion, benevolence, kindness); Ren (forbearance, tolerance, endurance).

[4] Tao—1. also known as "Dao," Taoist term for "the Way of nature and the universe"; 2. enlightened being who has achieved this Tao.

[5] Fa (fah)—law and principles in the Buddha School.

As advanced as the present human science has become, it is still only part of the mysteries of the universe. Whenever we mention specific phenomena of "the Buddha Fa," someone will claim: "This is already the electronic age, and science is very advanced. Spaceships have already flown to other planets, yet you still bring up these outdated superstitions." To put it frankly, no matter how advanced a computer is, it is still no match for the human brain, which to this day remains an unfathomable enigma. However far a spaceship may fly, it cannot travel beyond this physical dimension in which our human race exists. What can be understood with modern human knowledge is extremely shallow and tiny; it is far from truly coming to terms with the truth of the universe. Some people even dare not face, touch upon, or admit the facts of phenomena that objectively exist, because they are too conservative and unwilling to change their conventional thinking. Only through "the Buddha Fa," can the mysteries of the universe, time-space, and the human body be completely unveiled. It is able to truly distinguish what is righteous from evil, good from bad, and eliminate all misconceptions while providing what is correct.

The guiding ideology for today's human science is confined only to this physical world in its research and development, as a subject will not be studied until it is recognized—it follows such a path. As for phenomena that are intangible and invisible in our dimension, but objectively exist and are reflected into our physical dimension as concrete manifestations, people dare not approach them, dismissing them as unknown phenomena. Opinionated people groundlessly try to reason that they are natural phenomena, while those with ulterior motives, against their own conscience, simply label all of them as superstition. Those who are indifferent simply stay away from the issue with the excuse that science is not yet advanced enough. If human beings are able to take a fresh look at themselves as well as the universe and change their rigid mentalities, humankind will make a leap forward. "The Buddha Fa" enables humankind to understand the immeasurable and boundless world. Throughout the ages, only "the Buddha Fa" has been able to perfectly provide a clear exposition of humanity, every dimension of material existence, life, and the entire universe.

CONTENTS

LECTURE ONE

Genuinely Bringing People Toward Higher Levels

Throughout the entire course of my lectures on the Fa and cultivation practice, I have been responsible to society and practitioners. The results we have received have been good, and their impact upon the entire society has also been quite good. A few years ago there were many qigong[1] masters who taught qigong. All of what they taught belonged to the level of healing and fitness. Of course, I am not saying that their ways of practice were not good. I am only pointing out that they did not teach anything at a higher level. I also know the qigong situation in the entire country. At present, I am the only person genuinely teaching qigong towards higher levels at home and abroad. Why has no one done such a thing as teaching qigong towards higher levels? It is because this relates to questions of major concerns, profound historical reasons, a wide range of issues, and very serious matters. It is not something that an everyday person can teach, for it involves the practices of many qigong schools. In particular, many of our practitioners who study one practice today and another tomorrow have already messed up their own bodies. Their cultivation is bound to fail. While others advance by taking the main road in cultivation, these people are on the side roads. If they practice one way, the other way will interfere. If they practice the other way, this practice will interfere. Everything is interfering with them, and they can no longer succeed in cultivation practice.

---

[1] *qigong* (chee-gong)—a form of traditional Chinese practice which cultivates qi or "vital energy."

1

We will straighten out all these matters and, by preserving the good part and removing the bad part, ensure that you are able to practice cultivation later. However, you must be here to genuinely study this Dafa.[2] If you hold various attachments and come to gain supernormal capabilities, have illnesses cured, listen to some theories, or come with some ill intentions, that will not work at all. As I have mentioned, this is because I am the only person who is doing such a thing. There are not many opportunities for something like this, and I will not teach this way forever. I think that those who can listen to my lectures in person, I would say, honestly... you will realize in the future that this period of time is extremely precious. Of course, we believe in predestined relationship. Everyone sits here all because of a predestined relationship.

Think about it, everyone: What matter is it to teach qigong toward higher levels? Isn't this offering salvation to humankind? Offering salvation to humankind means that you will be truly practicing cultivation, and not just healing illness and keeping fit. Accordingly, genuine cultivation practice has a higher *xinxing*[3] requirement for practitioners. Everyone sits here to learn this Dafa, so you must here conduct yourselves as true practitioners, and you must give up attachments. If you come to learn the practice and this Dafa with various pursuits, you will not learn anything. To tell you the truth, the entire cultivation process for a practitioner is one of constantly giving up human attachments. In ordinary human society, people compete with, deceive, and harm each other for a little personal gain. All of these mentalities must be

---

[2] Dafa (dah-fah)—"Great law"; principles.

[3] *xinxing* (sheen-shing)—mind or heart nature; moral character.

given up. Especially for people who are studying the practice today, these mentalities should be given up even further.

I do not talk about healing illness here, nor will we heal illness. As a genuine practitioner, however, you cannot practice cultivation with an ill body. I will purify your body. The body purification will be done only for those who come to truly learn the practice and the Fa. We emphasize one point: If you cannot relinquish the attachment or concern for illness, we cannot do anything and will be unable to help you. Why is this? It is because there is such a principle in the universe: Ordinary human affairs, according to the Buddha School, all have predestined relationships. Birth, old age, illness, and death exist as such for ordinary people. Due to karma resulting from past wrongdoings, one has illnesses or tribulations; suffering is repaying a karmic debt, and thus nobody can casually change this. Changing it means that one does not have to repay the debt after being in debt, and this cannot be done at will. Doing otherwise is the same as committing a bad deed.

Some people think that treating patients, curing their illnesses, and improving their health are good deeds. In my view, they have not really cured the illnesses. Instead of removing them, they have either postponed or transformed the illnesses. To really dispel such tribulations, karma must be eliminated. If one could truly cure an illness and completely remove such karma, one's level would have to be quite high. One would have already seen a fact: The principles of ordinary human society cannot be casually violated. In the course of cultivation practice, a practitioner, out of his or her compassion, can do some good deeds by helping treat diseases and heal others' illnesses, or maintain their health—these are permitted. However, one cannot completely heal other

3

people's illnesses. If the cause of an ordinary person's illness is indeed removed, a non-practitioner will walk away without any illness. Once this person steps outside this door, he will remain an everyday person. He will still compete for personal profit like ordinary people. How can his karma be casually eliminated? That is absolutely prohibited.

Why can this be done for a practitioner, then? It is because a practitioner is most precious, for he or she wants to practice cultivation. Therefore, developing this thought is most precious. In Buddhism, people talk about Buddha-nature. When a person's Buddha-nature emerges, the enlightened beings are able to help him. What does this mean? If you ask me, since I am teaching the practice at higher levels, it involves the principles of higher levels as well as issues of great importance. We see that in this universe a human life is not created in ordinary human society; the creation of one's actual life is in the space of the universe. Because there is a lot of matter of various kinds in this universe, such matter can, through its interactions, produce life. In other words, a person's earliest life comes from the universe. The space of the universe is benevolent to begin with and embodies the characteristic of Zhen-Shan-Ren. At birth, one is assimilated to the characteristic of the universe. Yet, as the number of lives increases, a collective form of social relations develops in which some people may develop selfishness and gradually their level will be lowered. If they cannot stay at this level, they must drop down further. At that level, however, they may again become not so good and not be able to stay there, either. They will continue to descend further until, in the end, they reach this level of human beings.

The entire human society is on the same level. From the

4

perspective of supernormal capabilities or of the great enlightened beings, these lives should have been destroyed upon falling to this level. Out of their benevolent compassion, however, the great enlightened beings gave them one more chance and constructed this special environment and unique dimension. All of the lives in this dimension are different from those in other dimensions of the universe. The lives in this dimension cannot see the lives in other dimensions or the truth of the universe. Thus, these human beings are actually lost in a maze. In order to cure illness or eliminate tribulations and karma, these people must practice cultivation and return to their original, true selves. This is how all the different cultivation schools view it. One should return to one's original, true self; this is the real purpose of being human. Therefore, once a person wants to practice cultivation, his or her Buddha-nature is considered to have come forth. Such a thought is most precious, for this person wants to return to his or her original, true self and transcend the ordinary human level.

Perhaps, everyone has heard this statement in Buddhism: "When one's Buddha-nature emerges, it will shake 'the world of ten directions.'"[4] Whoever sees it will come to give a hand and help this person out unconditionally. In providing salvation to humankind, the Buddha School does not attach any condition or seek returns, and it will help unconditionally. Accordingly, we can do many things for practitioners. But for an everyday person who just wants to be an everyday person and to cure his or her illness, it will not work. Some people may think, "I'll practice cultivation after my illness is cured." There is no precondition for practicing cultivation, and one should practice cultivation if one wants to. Yet, some people's bodies have illnesses, and some

---

[4] "the world of ten directions"—Buddhist conception of the universe.

people carry disorderly messages in their bodies. Some people have never practiced qigong. There are also people who have practiced it for several decades and still wander about at the level of *qi*,[5] but without making progress in cultivation.

What should be done about this? We will purify their bodies and enable them to practice cultivation toward higher levels. There is a transition at the lowest level of cultivation practice, and this is to purify your body completely. All of the bad things on your mind, the karmic field surrounding your body, and the elements that make your body unhealthy will be cleaned out. If they are not cleaned out, how can you, with such an impure, dark body and a filthy mind, practice cultivation toward a higher level? We do not practice qi here. You do not need to practice such low-level stuff, and we will push you beyond it, making your body reach a state free of any illness. In the meantime, we will install in your body a system of ready-made mechanisms necessary for laying a foundation at the low level. This way, you will practice cultivation at a very high level.

According to the conventions of cultivation practice, there are three levels if qi is included. In genuine cultivation practice, however, there are altogether two major levels (excluding practicing qi). One is *Shi-Jian-Fa*[6] cultivation practice, while the other is *Chu-Shi-Jian-Fa*[7] cultivation practice. The cultivation practices of Shi-Jian-Fa and Chu-Shi-Jian-Fa are different from

[5] *qi* (chee)—In Chinese culture, it is believed to be "vital energy"; but compared to gong, it is a lower form of energy.

[6] *Shi-Jian-Fa* (shr-jyen-fah)—"In-Triple-World-Fa"; Buddhism holds that one must go through samsara if one has not reached beyond the Triple-World-Fa or the Three Realms.

[7] *Chu-Shi-Jian-Fa*—"Beyond-Triple-World-Fa."

the "beyond-world" and the "in-world" in temples, which are theoretical terms. Ours is the genuine transformation of the human body through cultivation practice at two major levels. Because in the course of Shi-Jian-Fa cultivation practice one's body will be constantly purified, it will be completely replaced by the high-energy matter when one reaches the highest form of Shi-Jian-Fa. The cultivation practice in Chu-Shi-Jian-Fa is basically cultivation of a Buddha-body. That body is made of the high-energy matter, and all supernormal powers will be redeveloped. These are the two major levels to which we refer.

We believe in predestined relationship. I can do such a thing for everyone sitting here. Right now we have only more than two thousand people. I can also do it for several thousand or more people, even over ten thousand people. That is to say, you do not need to practice at a low level. Upon purifying your bodies and moving you up, I will install a complete cultivation practice system in your body. Right away you will practice cultivation at high levels. It will be done, however, only for practitioners who come to genuinely practice cultivation; your simply sitting here does not mean that you are a practitioner. These things will be provided as long as you fundamentally change your thinking, and it is not limited to just these. Later on you will understand what I have given everyone. We do not talk about healing illness here, either. Rather, we talk about holistically adjusting practitioners' bodies to enable you to practice *gong*.[8] With an ill body you cannot develop gong at all. Therefore, you should not come to me for curing illnesses, nor will I do such a thing. The primary purpose of my coming to the public is to bring people to higher levels, genuinely bringing people to higher levels.

---

[8] *gong* (gong)—1. cultivation energy; 2. practice that cultivates such energy.

7

Different Levels Have Different Fa

In the past, many qigong masters said that qigong has a so-called beginning level, intermediate level, and advanced level. That was all qi and only something at the level of practicing qi, but it was even classified as beginning-level, intermediate-level, and advanced-level qigong. With regard to genuine high-level things, the minds of the majority of our qigong practitioners were blank, as they simply did not know them at all. From now on, all of what we address will be the Fa at higher levels. In addition, I will restore the reputation of cultivation practice. In my lectures I will talk about some unhealthy phenomena in the community of cultivators. I will also address how we should treat and look at such phenomena. Moreover, teaching gong and Fa at higher levels involves many aspects and quite important issues, some of which are even very serious; I would like to point these out as well. Some interference in our ordinary human society, especially in the community of cultivators, comes from other dimensions. I would also like to make this public. At the same time, I will resolve these problems for practitioners. If these problems go unresolved, you will be unable to practice cultivation. To fundamentally resolve these issues, we must treat everyone as genuine practitioners. Of course, it is not easy to change your thinking right away; you will transform your thinking gradually during the lectures to come. I also hope that everyone will pay attention while listening. The way I teach gong is unlike how others do. Some people teach it just by talking briefly about the theories of their gong. Next, they connect their messages with you and teach a set of exercises, and that is all. People are already accustomed to this way of teaching gong.

Genuinely teaching gong requires teaching the Fa or the Tao. In ten lectures I will make known all of the high-level principles so that you can practice cultivation. Otherwise, you cannot practice cultivation at all. All of what others have taught are things at the level of healing and fitness. If you want to practice cultivation toward higher levels, you will not succeed in cultivation without the guidance of the high-level Fa. It resembles attending school: If you go to college with elementary school textbooks, you will still be an elementary school pupil. Some people think that they have learned many practices, such as this practice or that practice, and they have a pile of graduation certificates, but their gong still has not made any progress. They think that those are the true essence of qigong and what qigong is all about. No, they are only a skin-deep part of qigong and something at the lowest level. Qigong is not confined to these things, as it is cultivation practice as well as something very broad and profound. In addition, different Fa exist at different levels. Thus, it is different from those practices of qi that we know at present; it will be the same no matter how much more you learn. For instance, although you have studied British elementary school textbooks, American elementary school textbooks, Japanese elementary school textbooks, and Chinese elementary school textbooks, you remain an elementary school pupil. The more low-level qigong lessons you have taken and the more from them you have absorbed, the more harm you will incur—your body is already messed up.

I must emphasize yet another issue: Our cultivation practice requires teaching both gong and Fa. Some monks in temples, especially those of Zen Buddhism, may have different opinions. As soon as they learn about the teaching of Fa, they will be unwilling to hear it. Why is it? Zen Buddhism believes that Fa should not be taught, that Fa is not Fa if it is taught, and that there is no teachable Fa; one can only understand something via heart and soul. As a result, to this day Zen Buddhism has not been able to teach any Fa. Patriarch Boddhidarma of Zen Buddhism taught such things based upon a statement made by Sakyamuni[9] who said: "No Dharma[10] is definitive." He founded Zen Buddhism based on this statement by Sakyamuni. We consider this cultivation way to be "digging into a bull's horn."[11] Why is it said to dig into a bull's horn? When Boddhidarma began to dig into it, he felt that it was quite spacious. When Patriarch II dug into it, he felt that it was not very spacious. It was still passable by the time of Patriarch III, but for Patriarch IV it was already quite narrow. There was almost no room to move further for Patriarch V. By the time of Huineng, Patriarch VI, it had reached a dead end and could move no further. If today you visit a Zen Buddhist to study Dharma, you should not ask any questions. If you ask a question, he or she will turn around and whack your head with a stick, which is called a "stick warning." It means that you should not inquire, and you should become enlightened on your own. You would say, "I came to study because I don't know anything. What should I become enlightened about? Why do you hit me with a stick?!" This indicates that Zen Buddhism has reached the dead end of the bull's horn, and there is no longer anything to teach. Even Boddhidarma stated that his teaching could be passed down to only six generations, after which it would no longer serve any use. Several hundred years have passed. Yet, there are people today who still hold firmly to the doctrines of

---

[9] Sakyamuni—the historical Buddha, Guatama Siddhartha.

[10] Dharma—Buddha Sakyamuni's teachings.

[11] "digging into a bull's horn"—a Chinese expression for going down a dead end.

Zen Buddhism. What's the actual meaning of Sakyamuni's pronouncement, "No Dharma is definitive"? Sakyamuni's level was Tathagata.[12] Many monks later on were not enlightened at Sakyamuni's level, to the thinking in his realm of thought, to the real meaning of his professed Dharma, or to the actual meaning of what he said. Therefore, people later on interpreted it this way or that way with very confusing interpretations. They thought that "No Dharma is definitive" meant that one should not teach it, and it would not be Dharma if taught. Actually, that is not what it means. When Sakyamuni became enlightened under a Bodhi tree, he did not reach the Tathagata level right away. He was also constantly improving himself during the forty-nine years of his Dharma teaching. Whenever he upgraded himself to a higher level, he looked back and realized that the Dharma he just taught was all wrong. When he made progress again, he discovered that the Dharma he just taught was wrong again. After he made further progress, he realized again that the Dharma he just taught was wrong. He constantly made such progress during his entire forty-nine years. Whenever he reached a higher level, he would discover that the Dharma he taught in the past was at a very low level in its understanding. He also discovered that the Dharma at each level is always the manifestation of the Dharma at that level, that there is Dharma at every level, and that none of them is the absolute truth of the universe. The Dharma at higher levels is closer to the characteristic of the universe than that of lower levels. Therefore, he stated: "No Dharma is definitive."

In the end, Sakyamuni also proclaimed, "I haven't taught any Dharma in my lifetime." Zen Buddhism again misunderstood this as meaning there was no Dharma to be taught. By his later

[12] Tathagata— enlightened being with Fruit Status in the Buddha School who is above the levels of Bodhisattva and Arhat.

years, Sakyamuni had already reached the Tathagata level. Why did he say that he had not taught any Dharma? What issue did he actually raise? He was stating, "Even at my level of Tathagata, I haven't seen the ultimate truth of the universe nor what the ultimate Dharma is." Thus, he asked people later on not to take his words as the absolute or the unchangeable truth. Otherwise, it would later limit people at or below the Tathagata level, and they would be unable to make breakthroughs toward higher levels. Later, people could not understand the actual meaning of this sentence and thought that if taught, Dharma is not Dharma— they have understood it this way. In fact, Sakyamuni was saying that there are different Dharma at different levels, and that the Dharma at each level is not the absolute truth of the universe. Yet the Dharma at a given level assumes a guiding role at that level. Actually, he was telling such a principle.

In the past, many people, especially those from Zen Buddhism, held such prejudice and an extremely warped view. How do you practice and cultivate yourself without being taught and guided? There are many Buddhist stories in Buddhism. Some people may have read about a person who went to heaven. Upon arriving in heaven, he discovered that every word in the Diamond Sutra[13] up there was different from that down here, and the meaning was entirely different. How could this Diamond Sutra be different from that in the ordinary human world? There are also people who claim: "The scripture in the Paradise of Ultimate Bliss is totally different from that down here, and it's not at all the same thing. Not only are the words different, but the implications and the meaning are all different, as they've changed." As a matter of fact, this is because the same Fa has

---

[13]Diamond Sutra—a Buddhist scripture.

different transformations and forms of manifestation at different levels, and it can play different guiding roles for practitioners at different levels.

It is known that in Buddhism there is a booklet called A Tour to the Paradise of Ultimate Bliss. It states that while a monk was sitting in meditation, his *yuanshen*[14] went to the Paradise of Ultimate Bliss and saw its scenery. He spent one day there; when he returned to the human world, six years had passed. Did he see it? He did, but what he saw was not its true state. Why? It is because his level was not high enough, and what he was shown was only the manifestation of the Buddha Fa at his level. Because a paradise like that is a manifestation of the Fa's composition, he could not see its actual situation. This is what it means when I talk about "No Dharma is definitive."

Zhen-Shan-Ren is the Sole Criterion to Discern Good and Bad People

In Buddhism people have been discussing what the Buddha Fa is. There are also people who believe that the Dharma stated in Buddhism is the Buddha Fa in its entirety. Actually, it is not. The Dharma that Sakyamuni professed two thousand five hundred years ago was only for everyday people at a very low level; it was taught to those who just evolved from a primitive society and still possessed very simple minds. Today is the Dharma-ending Period[15] to which he referred. Now people can no longer

---

[14] *yuanshen* (yu-en-shun)—"essential soul."

[15] Dharma-ending Period—According to Buddha Sakyamuni, the Dharma-ending Period would begin five hundred years after he passed away, and his Dharma could no longer save people thereafter.

practice cultivation with that Dharma. In the Dharma-ending Period, even monks in temples have difficulty saving themselves, let alone offering salvation to others. The Dharma Sakyamuni taught at that time took that situation into consideration, and he did not articulate fully the Buddha Fa that he understood at his own level. It is also impossible to keep it unchanged forever.

As society develops, the human mind becomes more sophisticated, making it no longer easy for people to practice cultivation in this way. The Dharma in Buddhism cannot summarize the entire Buddha Fa, and it is only a tiny portion of the Buddha Fa. There are still many other great cultivation ways in the Buddha School that are being passed down among people. Throughout history they have been passed down to a single disciple. Different levels have different Fa, and different dimensions have different Fa, all of which are the various manifestations of the Buddha Fa in different dimensions and at different levels. Sakyamuni also mentioned that there were eighty-four thousand cultivation ways for cultivating Buddhahood. Buddhism, however, includes only over ten cultivation ways, such as Zen Buddhism, Pure Land, Tiantai, Huayan, and Tantrism; these cannot represent all of the Buddha Fa. Sakyamuni himself did not articulate all of his Dharma; he only taught the portion of it befitting people's ability of comprehension at that time.

What is the Buddha Fa, then? The most fundamental characteristic of this universe, Zhen-Shan-Ren, is the highest manifestation of the Buddha Fa. It is the most fundamental Buddha Fa. The Buddha Fa manifests different forms at different levels and assumes different guiding roles at different levels. The lower the level, the more complex. This characteristic, Zhen-Shan-Ren, is in the microscopic particles of air, rock, wood, soil, iron and steel, the human body, as well as in all matter. In ancient times it was said that the Five Elements[16] constitute all things and matter in the universe; they also carry this characteristic, Zhen-Shan-Ren. A practitioner can only understand the specific manifestation of the Buddha Fa at the level that his or her cultivation has reached, which is his or her cultivation Fruit Status[17] and level. Broadly speaking, the Fa is very immense. From the perspective of the very highest level, it is very simple, for the Fa resembles a pyramid in form. At the highest point, it can be summarized in three words: Zhen, Shan, Ren. It is extremely complex when manifesting at different levels. Take a human being as an example. The Tao School considers the human body a small universe. A person has a physical body, yet a person is not complete with only a physical body. One must also have human temperament, personality, character, and yuanshen in order to constitute a complete and independent person with individuality. The same is true with our universe, which has the Milky Way, other galaxies, as well as life and water. All things and matter in this universe are aspects of material existence. At the same time, however, it also possesses the characteristic Zhen-Shan-Ren. All microscopic particles of matter embody this characteristic—even the extremely microscopic particles have this property.

This characteristic, Zhen-Shan-Ren, is the criterion for measuring good and bad in the universe. What's good or bad? It is judged by this. The de[18] that we mentioned in the past is also the same. Certainly, the moral standard in today's society has

---

[16] Five Elements—metal, wood, water, fire, and earth.

[17] Fruit Status—one's level of attainment in the Buddha School, e.g. Arhat, Bodhisattva, Tathagata, etc.

[18] de (duh)—"virtue"; a white substance.

already changed and become distorted. Now, if someone learns from Lei Feng,[19] he or she might be branded mentally ill. But who in the 1950's or 1960's would say this person is mentally ill? The human moral standard is declining tremendously, and human moral values are deteriorating daily. People only pursue self-interest and will harm others for a tiny bit of personal gain. They compete and struggle against each other by resorting to all means. Think about it, everyone: Will this be allowed to continue? When someone is doing a wrong deed, he will not believe it if you point out to him that he is doing a wrong deed. That person indeed will not believe that he is doing something wrong. Some people evaluate themselves with the declined moral standard. Because the criteria for assessment have changed, they consider themselves better than others. No matter how the human moral standard changes, this characteristic of the universe remains unchanged, and it is the sole criterion that distinguishes good people from bad people. As a practitioner, one must then conduct oneself by following this characteristic of the universe rather than the standards of everyday people. If you want to return to the original, true self and move up in cultivation practice, you must conduct yourself according to this criterion. As a human being, you are a good person only if you can follow this universe's characteristic of Zhen-Shan-Ren. A person who deviates from this characteristic is truly a bad person. In the workplace or in society, some people may say that you are bad, yet you may not necessarily be bad. Some people may say that you are good, but you may not really be good. As a practitioner, if you assimilate yourself to this characteristic you are one that has attained the Tao—it's just such a simple principle.

In practicing Zhen-Shan-Ren, the Tao School emphasizes

---

[19] Lei Feng (lay fung)—a Chinese moral exemplar in the 1960's.

the cultivation of Zhen. Therefore, the Tao School believes in the cultivation of Zhen to nurture one's nature; one should tell the truth, do things truthfully, become a truthful person, return to the original, true self, and in the end, become a true person through cultivation. Nevertheless, it also includes Ren and Shan, but with an emphasis on the cultivation of Zhen. The Buddha School emphasizes cultivating Shan of Zhen-Shan-Ren. Because the cultivation of Shan can generate great, benevolent compassion, and when compassion develops one will find all beings suffering, the Buddha School thus develops an aspiration to offer salvation to all beings. It also has Zhen and Ren, but with an emphasis on the cultivation of Shan. Our Falun Dafa is based upon the highest standard of the universe, Zhen, Shan, and Ren, all of which we cultivate simultaneously. The gong that we cultivate is quite enormous.

Qigong is Prehistoric Culture

What is qigong? Many qigong masters speak about this. What I am saying is different from what they say. Many qigong masters talk about it at their levels, while I am talking about the understanding of qigong from a higher level. It is completely different from their understanding. Some qigong masters claim that qigong has a history of two thousand years in our country. There are also people who say that qigong has a history of three thousand years. Some people mention that qigong has a history of five thousand years, which approximates that of our Chinese civilization. Still others say that, based upon archaeological excavations, it has a history of seven thousand years, and thus far exceeds the history of our Chinese civilization. But no matter how they understand it, qigong would not exist much earlier than

17

the history of human civilization. According to Darwin's theory of evolution, humans evolved from aquatic-plants to aquatic-animals. Then, they moved to live on land and eventually trees. Again on land, they became apes, and in the end evolved into modern humans with culture and thought. Based on that calculation, it has not been over ten thousand years since the actual emergence of human civilization. Looking further back, there was not even notekeeping through tying knots. Those people were dressed in tree leaves and ate raw meat. Looking back still further, they were completely wild or primitive people. They might not have even known how to use fire.

Yet we have found a problem. A lot of cultural relics in many places of the world date back far beyond the history of our human civilization. These ancient remains have quite an advanced level of craftsmanship. In terms of artistic value, they are at quite an advanced level. Modern humankind is simply imitating the arts of ancient peoples, and their arts are of great artistic value. They are, however, relics from over 100 thousand years ago, several hundred thousand years ago, several million years, or even over 100 million years ago. Think about it, everyone: Aren't they making a mockery of today's history? It is, in fact, no joke, for humankind has always been improving and re-discovering itself. This is how society develops. The initial understanding may not be absolutely correct.

Many people may have heard of "prehistoric culture," also known as "prehistoric civilization." We will talk about prehistoric civilization. On this earth, there are continents of Asia, Europe, South America, North America, Oceania, Africa, and Antarctica. Geologists call these the continental plates. From the formation of the continental plates to this day, several tens of millions of years have passed. Namely, many continents have emerged from the ocean floor, and many continents have also sunk to the sea bottom. It has been over tens of millions of years since they stabilized at the present state. Under the water of many oceans, however, some tall and large ancient architecture has been discovered. These buildings were crafted very beautifully and are not the cultural heritage of our modern humankind. Then they must have been built before sinking to the ocean floor. Who created these civilizations tens of million of years ago? At that time, our human race was not even apes. How could we create something of such great wisdom? Archaeologists around the world have discovered an organism called trilobite that existed between 600 and 260 million years ago. This kind of organisms disappeared 260 million years ago. An American scientist has discovered a trilobite fossil with a human footprint on it; the footprint was clearly printed on the fossil by a person in shoes. Isn't this mocking historians? According to Darwin's theory of evolution, how could there be human beings 260 million years ago?

In the museum of the National University of Peru, there is a rock engraved with a human figure. Upon investigation, it was determined that this human figure was engraved thirty thousand years ago. This human figure, however, is dressed in clothes, hat, and shoes, with a telescope in hand, and he is observing the celestial body. How could people weave cloth and wear clothes thirty thousand years ago? More inconceivably, he was observing the celestial body with a telescope and had a certain amount of astronomical knowledge. We always think that it was Galileo, a European, who invented the telescope, giving it a history of only over three hundred years. Yet who invented the telescope thirty thousand years ago? There are still many unsolved puzzles. For instance, there are frescoes engraved in many caves of France, South Africa, and the Alps that appear realistic and lifelike. The figures therein engraved look remarkably exquisite and are colored with a mineral paint. These people, however, all don contemporary clothes that look something like Western suits, and they wear tight pants. Some people hold something like smoking pipes, while others carry walking sticks and wear hats. How could the apes of several hundred thousand years ago reach such an advanced artistic level?

To give another example of a more remote age, the Gabon Republic in Africa has uranium ore. This country is relatively underdeveloped. It cannot make uranium on its own and exports the ore to developed countries. In 1972, a French manufacturer imported its uranium ore. After lab tests, the uranium ore was found to have been extracted and utilized. They found this quite unusual and sent out scientists to study it. Scientists from many other countries all went there to investigate. In the end, this uranium mine was verified as a large-scale nuclear reactor with a very rational layout. Even our modern people cannot possibly create this, so when was it built then? It was constructed 2 billion years ago and was in operation for 500 thousand years. Those are simply astronomical figures, and they cannot be explained at all with Darwin's theory of evolution. There are many such examples. What today's scientific and technological community has discovered is sufficient to change our present textbooks. Once humankind's conventional mentalities form a systematic way of working and thinking, new ideas are very difficult to accept. When the truth emerges, people do not dare to accept it and instinctively reject it. Due to the influence of traditional conventions, no one today has systematically compiled such findings. Thus, human concepts always lag behind developments. Once you speak of these things, there will be people who call them superstitious and reject them—despite their already having been discovered. They are just not yet publicized widely.

Many bold scientists abroad have already publicly recognized this as prehistoric culture and a civilization prior to this of our humankind. In other words, there existed more than one period of civilization before our civilization. Through unearthed relics, we have found products that are not of only one period of civilization. It is thus believed that after each of the many times when human civilizations were annihilated, only a small number of people survived and they lived a primitive life. Then, they gradually multiplied in number to become the new human race, beginning a new civilization. Later, they were again exterminated and would then once again produce a new human race. It just goes through such different periodical changes. Physicists hold that the motion of matter follows certain laws. The changes of our entire universe also follow laws.

It is impossible that our planet Earth, in this immense universe and the Milky Way, has been orbiting very smoothly at all times. It might have bumped into a certain planet or run into other problems, leading to great disasters. From the perspective of our supernormal capabilities, it was just arranged that way. I made a careful investigation once and found that humankind has undergone complete annihilation eighty-one times. With a little remaining from the previous civilization, only a small number of people would survive and enter the next period, again living a primitive life. As the human population increased, civilization would emerge again in the end. Humanity has experienced such periodical changes eighty-one times, and yet I have not traced them to the end. Chinese people talk about cosmic timing, favorable earth conditions, and human harmony. Different cosmic changes and different cosmic timings can bring about different conditions in ordinary human society. According to physics, the motion of matter follows certain laws—the same is true with the motion of the universe.

The above reference to prehistoric culture primarily tells you that qigong was not invented by this humankind of ours, either. It was inherited through a quite remote age and it was also a type of prehistoric culture. From Buddhist scriptures we can also find some related statements. Sakyamuni once said that he succeeded in cultivation practice many hundred millions of *jie*[20] ago. How many years are there in one jie? One jie is a number for hundreds of millions of years. Such a huge number is simply inconceivable. If true, doesn't this agree with human history and the changes of the entire earth? In addition, Sakyamuni also mentioned that there were seven primitive Buddhas before him, that he had masters, etc., all of whom succeeded in cultivation practices many hundred million jie ago. If all this is true, are there such cultivation ways among those true orthodox practices and genuine teachings taught in our society today? If you ask me, it is certainly so, but they are seldom seen. Nowadays, sham qigong, phony qigong, and those people with *futi*[21] have all made up something at will to deceive people, and their number exceeds that of genuine qigong practices by many times. Discerning the genuine and the sham is difficult. A genuine qigong practice is not easy to distinguish, nor is it easy to find.

In fact, not only is qigong passed down from a distant age,

---

[20] *jie* (jyeh)—a number for hundreds of millions of years.
[21] *futi* (foo-tee)—spirit or animal that possesses a human body; spirit or animal possession.

Taiji,[22] Hetu, Luoshu, Zhouyi, Bagua,[23] etc., are all prehistoric leftovers. Thus, if we study and understand them from the perspective of everyday people today, we will not be able to comprehend them by any means. From an everyday person's level, perspective, and frame of mind, one cannot understand real things.

Qigong is Cultivation Practice

Since qigong has such a long history, what's it for? Let me tell everyone that since we are of a great cultivation way in the Buddha School, we of course cultivate Buddhahood. In the Tao School, one of course cultivates the Tao to attain the Tao. Let me tell everyone that "Buddha" is not a superstition. It is a word from Sanskrit, an ancient Indian language. When it was introduced to China, it was called "Fo Tuo." There were also people who translated it as "Fu Tu." As the word was passed around, our Chinese people left out one character and called it "Fo." What does it mean in Chinese? It means "an enlightened person," one who has become enlightened through cultivation practice. What's superstitious in this?

Think about it, everyone: One can develop supernormal capabilities through cultivation practice. In the world today, six supernormal capabilities are recognized, yet they are not limited to these alone. I would say that over ten thousand genuine supernormal capabilities exist. As a person sits there, without moving his hands or feet, he is able to do what others cannot do even with their hands and feet, and he can see the actual truth of

[22] Taiji (tie-jee)—the symbol of the Tao School.
[23] Hetu (huh-too), Luoshu (luoa-shew), Zhouyi (jo-ee), Bagua (bah-gwa)—as prehistoric diagrams, they disclose the changes of the course of nature.

23

each dimension in the universe. This person can see the truth of the universe and things that an everyday person cannot. Isn't he a person who has attained the Tao through practicing cultivation? Isn't he a great enlightened person? How can he be considered the same as an everyday person? Isn't he an enlightened person through cultivation practice? Isn't it correct to call him an enlightened person? In ancient Indian language he is called a Buddha. Actually, that is it. This is what qigong is for.

Speaking of qigong, some people might say, "Without an illness, who would practice qigong?" This implies that qigong is meant for healing illness. That is a very, very shallow understanding. This is not your fault because many qigong masters indeed do things such as healing illnesses and maintaining fitness. They all talk about healing and fitness. Nobody teaches anything toward higher levels. This does not mean that their practices are not good. Their mission is to teach things at the level of healing and fitness, and to publicize qigong. There are many people who would like to practice cultivation toward higher levels. They have such thoughts and wishes, but they have not obtained cultivation methods and great difficulties result; many problems also occur. Of course, genuinely teaching a practice at higher levels involves very profound issues. Therefore, we have been responsible to people and society, and the overall outcome of teaching the practice has been good. Some of the things are indeed quite profound and, when discussed, may sound like superstition. Nevertheless, we will try our best to explain them with modern science.

Once we talk about certain issues, some people will call them superstitions. Why is that? Such a person's criterion is that he will consider what science has not recognized, what he has not yet experienced, or what he thinks cannot possibly exist, all to be superstitious and idealistic—this is his mentality. Is this mentality correct? Should what science has not recognized or what is beyond its development be labeled as superstitious and idealistic? Then, isn't this person himself being superstitious and idealistic? With this mentality, how can science develop and make progress? Neither will human society be able to move forward. Everything that our scientific and technological community has invented was unknown to people in the past. If such things were all regarded as superstitions, there would, of course, have been no need for development. Qigong is not something idealistic. There are many people who do not understand qigong and, thus, always consider qigong idealistic. At present, with scientific apparatus we have found in a qigong master's body infrasonic waves, supersonic waves, electromagnetic waves, infrared, ultraviolet, gamma rays, neutrons, atoms, trace metal elements, etc. Aren't these something of material existence? They are also of matter. Isn't everything made of matter? Aren't other time-spaces also made of matter? How can qigong be labeled "superstitious?" Since it is used for cultivation of Buddhahood, it is bound to involve many profound issues, and we will address them all.

Since qigong serves such a purpose, why do we call it qigong? It is, as a matter of fact, not called "qigong." What's it called? It is called "cultivation practice," and it is just cultivation practice. Of course it has other specific names, but generically speaking it is called cultivation practice. Then, why is it called qigong? It is known that qigong has been promoted in society for over twenty years. It first appeared in the middle of the "Great Cultural Revolution."[24] Later on it reached its peak of popularity.

---

[24] "Great Cultural Revolution"—a communist political movement that denounced traditional values and culture (1966-1976).

Think about it, everyone: The leftist ideology was quite prevailing at that time. We will not mention what names qigong had in prehistoric civilizations. During its development, this human civilization underwent a feudalistic period. Therefore, it usually has names with feudalistic ingredients. Those practices related to religions usually have names with heavy religious overtones. For instance, the so-called "The Great Cultivation Way of Tao," "The Dhyana of Vajra," "The Way of Arhat,"[25] "The Great Cultivation Way of Buddha Dharma," "Nine-fold Internal Alchemy," etc., are all such things. If these names were used during the "Great Cultural Revolution," wouldn't you be criticized? Though those qigong masters' wish to promote qigong was good and they intended to help the general public heal illnesses, maintain fitness, and improve their physical conditions—how great that would be—it would not be allowed. People simply did not dare to use names this way. Therefore, in order to promote qigong, many qigong masters took out two words from the texts of <u>Dan Jing</u> and <u>Tao Tsang</u>,[26] and named it "qigong". Some people even concentrate their research in qigong terminology. There is nothing there to study. In the past, it was just called cultivation practice. "Qigong" is only a newly-crafted term that complies with modern people's mindset.

Why Doesn't Your Gong Increase with Your Practice?

Why doesn't your gong increase with your practice? Many people think this way: "I haven't received genuine teaching. If a master

---

[25] Arhat—enlightened being with Fruit Status in the Buddha School and one who is beyond the "Three Realms."

[26] <u>Dan Jing</u> (dahn jing), <u>Tao Tsang</u> (daow zang)—classic Chinese texts of cultivation practice.

teaches me some special skills and a few advanced techniques, my gong will increase." Nowadays, ninety-five percent of people think this way, and I find it quite ridiculous. Why is it ridiculous? It is because qigong is not a technique of everyday people. It is something completely supernormal. Accordingly, the principles of higher levels should be applied to examine it. Let me tell everyone that the fundamental reason for gong not developing is two words: cultivation and practice. People only pay attention to "practice" and ignore "cultivation." If you search externally for something, you will not obtain it by any means. With an everyday person's body, an everyday person's hands, and an everyday person's mind, do you think that you can transform high-energy matter into gong or increase gong? How can it be so easy! In my view, it is a joke. That is the same as pursuing something externally and seeking something externally. You will never find it.

It is not like a skill of everyday people that you can acquire by paying some money or learning some techniques. It is not like that, as it is something beyond the level of everyday people. You will thus be expected to follow supernormal principles. What's required of you, then? You must cultivate your inner self and not pursue things externally. So many people are seeking things externally. They pursue one thing today and another tomorrow. In addition, they are obsessively attached to seeking supernormal capabilities and carry all kinds of intentions. There are people who even want to become qigong masters and make a fortune by healing illnesses! To truly practice cultivation, you must cultivate your mind. This is called xinxing cultivation. For example, in a conflict between one another, you should care less about various personal feelings and desires. While competing for personal gain, you want to improve your gong—how can that be possible? Aren't you the same as an everyday person? How can your gong increase?

Therefore, only by emphasizing xinxing cultivation can your gong increase and your level be upgraded.

What is xinxing? It includes de (a type of matter), tolerance, enlightenment quality, sacrifice, giving up ordinary people's different desires and attachments, being able to suffer hardships, and so on. It encompasses things from many aspects. Every aspect of xinxing must be upgraded for you to make real progress. This is a crucial factor in improving *gongli*.[27]

Some people may think: "The xinxing issue you mentioned is something ideological and a matter of one's realm of thoughts. It has nothing to do with the gong we practice." Why isn't it the same issue? Throughout history, the issue of whether matter is over mind or vice versa has always been discussed and debated in the community of philosophers. In fact, let me tell everyone that matter and mind are one thing. In scientific research of the human body, today's scientists hold that a thought generated by the human brain is a substance. If it is something of material existence, isn't it something of the human mind as well? Aren't they the same thing? Just like the universe that I have described, it does not only have its material existence, but also, at the same time, it has its characteristic. An everyday person cannot detect the existence of this characteristic, Zhen-Shan-Ren, in the universe, because everyday people are all on the same level. When you rise above the level of everyday people, you will be able to detect it. How do you detect it? All matter in the universe, including all substances that permeate the universe, are living beings with thinking minds, and all of them are forms of existence of the universe's Fa at different levels. They do not let you ascend. Though you want to ascend, you cannot. They just do not let you

---

[27] *gongli* (gong-lee)—"energy potency."

move up. Why don't they let you move up? It is because your xinxing has not improved. There are different criteria for every level. If you want to reach a higher level, you must abandon your ill thoughts and clean out your filthy things in order to assimilate to the requirements of the standard at that level. Only by doing so can you ascend.

Once you upgrade your xinxing, your body will undergo a great change. Upon xinxing improvement, the matter in your body is guaranteed to transform. What kind of changes will take place? You will give up those bad things that you are attached to. For example, if a bottle filled with dirty things is sealed tightly and thrown into water, it will sink all the way to the bottom. You pour out some of its dirty contents. The more you empty the bottle, the higher it will float in the water. If it is emptied entirely, it will float on the surface completely. In the course of our cultivation practice, you must clean out various bad things in your body so that you can move up. This characteristic of the universe exactly plays this role. If you do not cultivate your xinxing or upgrade your moral standard, or if your ill thoughts and bad substances have not been removed, it will not let you ascend. How can you say that they aren't the same thing? Let me tell a joke. If a person, with all kinds of human sentiment and desire among everyday people, is allowed to ascend and become a Buddha, think about it, is this possible? He may have an evil thought upon finding a Bodhisattva[28] so beautiful. This person may start a conflict with a Buddha because his jealousy has not been eliminated. How can these things be allowed to take place? What should be done about it, then? You must eliminate all ill thoughts among everyday people—only then can you move up.

[28] Bodhisattva—enlightened being with Fruit Status in the Buddha School, and one who is higher than an Arhat and lower than a Tathagata.

In other words, you should pay attention to xinxing cultivation and practice cultivation according to the characteristic of the universe, Zhen-Shan-Ren. You must completely dispose of the desires of ordinary people, immoral thoughts, and the intention of wrongdoing. With every bit of improvement in your state of mind, some bad things will be eliminated from your body. In the meantime, you should also suffer a little bit and endure some hardships to reduce your karma. You can then move up a little bit; that is, the characteristic of the universe will not restrict you as much. Cultivation depends on one's own efforts, while the transformation of gong is done by one's master. The master gives you the gong that develops your cultivation energy, and this gong will function. It can transform the substance of de outside of your body into gong. As you constantly upgrade yourself and move up in cultivation practice, your *gongzhu*[29] will also continually make breakthroughs toward higher levels. As a practitioner, you must cultivate and temper yourself in the environment of everyday people and gradually abolish attachments and various desires. Oftentimes, what our humankind considers good is usually bad from the perspective of higher levels. Thus, what people consider good for a person is to fulfill more self-interest among everyday people, thereby living a better life. To the great enlightened beings, this person is worse off. What's so bad about this? The more one gains, the more one infringes upon others. One will get things one does not deserve. This person will be attached to fame and profit, thus losing de. If you want to increase gong without emphasizing xinxing cultivation, your gong will not increase at all.

The community of cultivators holds that one's yuanshen does

---

[29] *gongzhu* (gong-jew)—energy pole that grows above a practitioner's head.

not become extinct. In the past, people might call it superstitious to discuss human yuanshen. It is known that research on the human body in physics has found molecules, protons, electrons, going further down to quarks, neutrinos, etc. At that point, a microscope can no longer detect them. Yet, they are far from the origin of life and from the origin of matter. Everyone knows that it requires a considerable amount of energy collision and a great amount of heat to enable fusion or nuclear fission to occur. How can the nuclei in one's body easily become extinct as one dies? Therefore, we have found that when a person is dead, only the largest molecular elements in this dimension of ours have sloughed off, while the bodies in other dimensions are not degenerated. Think about it, everyone: What does a human body look like under a microscope? The entire human body is in motion. While you sit there still, the whole body is nevertheless in motion. Cell molecules are in motion, and the whole body is loose as if composed of sand. A human body looks just like that under a microscope, and this is quite different from what is seen with our flesh eyes. This is because this pair of human eyes create a false impression for you and prevent you from seeing these things. When one's *tianmu*[30] is open, it can see things by magnifying them; it is actually a human instinctual capability that is now called a supernormal capability. If you want to develop supernormal capabilities, you must return to your original, true self and go back through cultivation.

Let us talk about de. What specific connection does it have? We will analyze it in detail. As human beings, we have a body in each of numerous dimensions. When we examine the human body now, the largest elements are cells, and they comprise the human flesh body. If you can enter the space between cells and molecules

---

[30] *tianmu* (t'yen-moo)—"heavenly eye," also known as the "third eye."

or the spaces among molecules, you will experience being in another dimension. What does that body's form of existence resemble? Of course, you cannot use the concepts of this dimension to understand it, and your body must meet the requirement of that dimension's form of existence. The body in another dimension can become big or small to begin with. At that time, you will find it also a boundless dimension. This refers to a simple form of other dimensions that exist simultaneously in the same place. Everyone has a specified body in each of many other dimensions. In a specified dimension there is a field that surrounds the human body. What kind of field is it? This field is the de that we have mentioned. De is a white substance and not, as we believed in the past, something spiritual or ideological—it absolutely has a kind of material existence. Thus, in the past, elders talked about accumulating or losing de, and they spoke very sensibly. This de forms a field that surrounds one's body. In the past, the Tao School held that a master selects a disciple instead of a disciple choosing a master. What does it mean? A master would examine whether this disciple's body carried a great amount of de. If this disciple had a lot of de, it would be easy for him to practice cultivation. Otherwise, he would not be able to make it easily, and he would have much difficulty developing gong toward higher levels.

At the same time, there exists a black kind of substance that we call "karma" and Buddhism calls "sinful karma." These black and white substances exist simultaneously. What kind of relationship do these two substances have? We obtain that de through suffering, enduring setbacks, and doing good deeds; the black substance is accrued by committing bad deeds and doing wrong things or bullying people. Nowadays, some people not only are bent solely on profit, but also commit all kinds of vices.

They will do all kinds of evil things for money, and they will also commit murder, pay someone to kill, practice homosexuality, and abuse drugs. They do all kinds of things. One loses de when one commits wrongdoings. How does a person lose de? When a person swears at another, he thinks that he has gained the upper hand and feels good. There is a principle in this universe called "no loss, no gain." To gain, one has to lose. If you do not want to lose, you will be forced to lose. Who plays such a role? It is precisely the characteristic of the universe that assumes this role. Thus, it is impossible if you only wish to gain things. What will happen then? While swearing at or bullying another person, he is tossing de at this other person. Since the other person is the party that feels wronged and has lost something and suffered, she is compensated accordingly. While he is here swearing, with this swearing, a piece of de from his own dimensional field leaves and goes to her. The more he swears at her, the more de he gives her. The same is true with beating up or bullying others. As one hits or kicks another person, one will give one's de away according to how badly one beats up the other person. An everyday person cannot see this principle at this level. Feeling humiliated, she cannot put up with it and thinks, "Since you hit me, I have to return the same." "Wham," she gives that person a punch back and returns de to him. Neither have gained or lost anything. She may think, "You have hit me once, and I should hit you twice. Otherwise, I won't feel avenged." She will hit him again, and another piece of her de is given away to him.

Why is this de valued so much? What kind of relationship is there in the transformation of de? Religions state: "With de, one will gain something in the next lifetime if not in this life." What will one gain? With a lot of de, one may become a high-ranking official or make a big fortune. One can obtain whatever one wants, and this is exchanged with such de. Religions also mention that if one does not have any de, both one's body and soul will become extinct. One's yuanshen will be exterminated, and upon death one will be completely dead with nothing left. In our community of cultivators, however, we hold that de can be directly transformed into gong.

We will address how de is transformed into gong. The community of cultivators has a saying: "Cultivation depends on one's own efforts, while the transformation of gong is done by one's master." Yet, some people talk about "setting up a bodily crucible and furnace to make *dan*[31] using gathered medicinal herbs"[32] and mind activities, and they consider these very important. Let me tell you that they are not at all important, and it is an attachment if you think too much about them. Aren't you attached to a pursuit if you think too much about it? Cultivation depends on one's own efforts, while the transformation of gong is done by one's master. It is good enough if you have this wish. It is the master who actually does this, as you are simply unable to do it. With an ordinary person's body like yours, how can you transform it into a higher life's body made of high-energy matter? It is absolutely impossible and sounds like a joke. A human body's transformation process in other dimensions is quite intricate and complex. You cannot do such things at all.

What does the master give you? He gives you the gong that develops cultivation energy. Since de exists outside one's body, one's real gong is generated from de. Both the height of one's

---

[31] *dan* (dahn)—energy cluster in a cultivator's body, collected from other dimensions.

[32] "setting up a bodily crucible and furnace to make dan using gathered medicinal herbs"—Taoist metaphor for internal alchemy.

level and the strength of one's gongli are generated from de. The master transforms your de into gong that grows upward in a spiral form. The gong that truly determines one's level grows outside one's body, and it grows in a spiral form, eventually forming a gongzhu after it grows above one's head. With just one glance at the height of this person's gongzhu, one can discern the level of his gong. This is one's level and Fruit Status as mentioned in Buddhism. While sitting in meditation, some people's yuanshen can leave their bodies and reach a certain level. Even if it tries, his yuanshen cannot ascend any further, and it does not dare to move up. Since it moves up by sitting on his gongzhu, it can only reach that level. Because his gongzhu is just that high, it cannot move up any further. This is the issue of Fruit Status mentioned in Buddhism.

There is also a yardstick that measures xinxing level. The yardstick and gongzhu do not exist in the same dimension, but they exist simultaneously. Your xinxing cultivation has already made progress if, for instance, when someone swears at you among everyday people, you do not say a word and feel very calm; or when someone throws a fist at you, you do not say a word and let it go with a smile. Your xinxing level is already very high. So as a practitioner, what should you obtain? Aren't you going to obtain gong? When your xinxing is upgraded, your gong will increase. One's gong level is as high as one's xinxing level, and this is an absolute truth. In the past, whether people practiced qigong in parks or at home, they did it with much effort and dedication, and they practiced quite well. Once they stepped out the door, they would act differently and go their own way, competing and fighting with others for fame and profit among everyday people. How could they increase cultivation energy? It could not increase at all, and for the same reason neither would their illnesses be healed. Why can't some people cure their illnesses after a long period of practice? Qigong is cultivation practice and something supernormal, as opposed to everyday people's physical exercises. One must focus on xinxing in order to cure illness or increase cultivation energy.

Some people believe in setting up a bodily crucible and furnace to make dan from the gathered medicinal herbs, and they think that this dan is cultivation energy. It is not. This dan only accumulates a portion of energy, and it does not include all energy. What kind of matter is dan? It is known that we also have some other things for cultivating life, and that our bodies will develop supernormal capabilities and many other abilities; the majority are locked up and not allowed to be applied. There are many supernormal capabilities—up to ten thousand. As soon as one is developed, it is locked up. Why aren't they allowed to manifest? The purpose is to not let you apply them casually in ordinary human society to do things. You are not allowed to casually disturb ordinary human society, nor are you allowed to casually display your abilities in ordinary human society. This is because doing so could disturb the state of ordinary human society. Many people practice cultivation by way of enlightening. If you demonstrate all your abilities to them, they will see that everything is real and all will come to practice cultivation. People who have committed unpardonable evils will also come to practice cultivation, and this is not permitted. You are not allowed to show off this way. Also, you may easily commit wrongdoings since you cannot see the predestined relationship and the true nature of things. You think that you are doing a good deed, but it may be a wrong deed. Therefore, you are not allowed to apply them, because once you commit wrongdoings, your level will be lowered and your cultivation will be in vain. As a result, many supernormal capabilities are locked up. What will happen? By the time one becomes *kaigong*[33] and enlightened, this dan will be a bomb that explodes and opens up all supernormal capabilities, all locks in the body, and hundreds of energy passes. "Bang," everything will be shaken open. This is what the dan is used for. After a monk is cremated at death, sarira[34] remain. Some people claim that those are bones and teeth. How come everyday people do not have them? Those are just the exploded dan, and its energy has been released. It contains in itself a lot of substances from other dimensions. After all, it is also something of material existence, but it is of little use. People now take it as something very precious. It contains energy, and is lustrous, as well as very hard. It is just such a thing.

There is still another reason for failing to increase cultivation energy. Namely, without knowing the Fa of higher levels, one cannot move up in cultivation practice. What does it mean? As I just mentioned, some people have practiced many qigong exercises. Let me tell you that no matter how many more you study, it is still useless. You remain only an elementary school pupil—an elementary school pupil in cultivation practice. They are all principles at a low level. Such low-level principles cannot play any role in guiding your cultivation practice toward higher levels. If you study elementary school textbooks in college, you will remain an elementary school pupil. No matter how many you study, it will be useless. Instead, you will be worse off. Different levels have different Fa, and Fa assumes different guiding roles at different levels. Thus, low-level principles cannot

---

[33] *kaigong* (kye-gong)—the final release of cultivation energy; full enlightenment.

[34] sarira—relics of a monk after cremation.

guide your cultivation practice toward higher levels. What we will talk about later are all principles for cultivation practice at higher levels. I am incorporating things from different levels in the teaching. They will thus always play a guiding role in your future cultivation practice. I have several books, audiotapes, and videotapes. You will find that after watching and listening to them once, they will still guide you as you watch and listen again after a while. You are also constantly improving yourselves, and they continually guide you—this is the Fa. The above are the two reasons for not being able to increase cultivation energy. Without knowing the Fa at higher levels, one cannot practice cultivation. Without cultivating one's inner self and one's xinxing, one cannot increase cultivation energy. These are the two reasons.

Characteristics of Falun Dafa

Our Falun Dafa is one of the eighty-four thousand cultivation ways in the Buddha School. During the historical period of this human civilization, it has never been made public. In a prehistoric period, however, it was once widely used to provide salvation to humankind. In this final period of Last Havoc,[35] I am making it public again. Therefore, it is extremely precious. I have talked about the form of directly transforming de into cultivation energy. Cultivation energy is not, in fact, obtained through practice. It is acquired through cultivation. Many people attempt to increase their cultivation energy and only pay attention to how to practice, without caring for how to do cultivation. Actually, cultivation

---

[35] Last Havoc—The community of cutivators holds that the universe has three phases of evolution (The Beginning Havoc, The Middle Havoc, The Last Havoc), and that now is the final period of The Last Havoc.

energy is completely acquired through xinxing cultivation. Why, then, do we also teach the exercises here? First, let me talk about why a monk does not practice any exercises. He basically just sits in trance, chants the scriptures, cultivates xinxing, and his cultivation energy then increases. He increases the cultivation energy that upgrades his level. Since Sakyamuni taught people to give up everything in the world, including their bodies, physical exercises become therefore unnecessary. The Tao School does not offer salvation to all beings. What it faces are not all kinds of people with different mentalities and levels, some of whom are more selfish and others less selfish. It selects its disciples. If three disciples are selected, only one of them receives the real teaching. It has to make sure that this disciple is very virtuous, very good, and will not go awry. It thus emphasizes teaching technical things to cultivate life and to cultivate something like supernatural powers or skills, etc. This requires some physical exercises.

Falun Dafa is also a cultivation practice of mind and body, and it requires exercises. On the one hand, the exercises are used to strengthen supernormal capabilities. What is "strengthening?" It is the reinforcement of your supernormal capabilities by your powerful energy potency, thus making them progressively stronger. On the other hand, many living beings need to be developed in your body. In high-level cultivation practice, the Tao School requires the birth of *yuanying*,[36] while the Buddha School requires the Vajra's indestructible body. Furthermore, many supernatural abilities must be developed. These things need to be developed through the physical exercises, and they are what our exercises cultivate. A complete cultivation practice of mind and body requires both cultivation and practice. I think that

---

[36] *yuanying* (yu-en-ying)—Taoist term for "the immortal infant."

everyone now understands how cultivation energy comes into being. The gong that really determines your level of achievement is not at all developed through practice, but via cultivation. By upgrading your xinxing and assimilating to the characteristic of the universe in your cultivation among everyday people, the characteristic of the universe will no longer restrict you; you are then allowed to move up. Your de will then begin transforming into cultivation energy. As your xinxing standard improves, so grows your cultivation energy. It is just such a relationship.

Ours is a genuine cultivation practice of both mind and body. The cultivation energy that we cultivate is stored in every cell of the body, and the gong of high-energy matter is even stored in the original miniscule particles of matter at an extremely microscopic level. As your energy potency becomes greater, the density and power of cultivation energy will also increase. Such high-energy matter has intelligence. Because it is stored in each cell of the human body all the way to the origin of life, it will gradually become the same form as the cells in your body, assuming the same molecular combinations and form of nuclei. Its essence has changed, however, for this body is no longer composed of original flesh cells. Won't you be beyond the Five Elements? Of course, your cultivation practice is not over yet, and you still need to practice cultivation among everyday people. Therefore, on the surface you still appear to be an ordinary person. The only difference is that you look younger than those of your age. Certainly, the bad things in your body, including illnesses, must be removed first, but we do not treat diseases here. We are purifying your body, and the term is not "healing diseases," either. We just call it "purifying the body," and we clean out the bodies of true practitioners. Some people come here just to have illnesses healed. As to seriously ill patients, we do not let them attend the classes since they cannot give up the attachment to having illnesses cured or the idea of being ill. If one has a serious illness and feels very uncomfortable, can one let go of it? This person is unable to practice cultivation. We have stressed from time to time that we do not admit patients with serious illnesses. This is cultivation practice here, which is too far from what they think about. They can find other qigong masters to do those things. Of course, many practitioners have illnesses. Because you are true practitioners, we will take care of these things for you.

After a period of cultivation practice, our Falun Dafa practitioners look quite different in appearance. Their skin becomes delicate and reddish-white. For the elderly, wrinkles become fewer or even extremely few, which is a common phenomenon. I am not talking here about something inconceivable, as many of our veteran practitioners sitting here know this situation. In addition, elderly women will regain their menstrual period since a cultivation practice of mind and body requires menses to cultivate the body. One's period will come, but the menstrual flow will not be much. At present, that little bit will suffice. This is also a common phenomenon. Otherwise, how can they cultivate their bodies without it? The same is true for men: The elderly and the young will all feel that the entire body is light. As for true practitioners, they will experience this transformation.

This practice of ours cultivates something very immense, as opposed to the many practices that imitate animals in their exercises. This practice cultivates something simply quite enormous. All of the principles that Sakyamuni and Lao Zi[37] discussed in their time were confined to principles within our

---

[37] Lao Zi (laow-dzz)—founder of the Tao School.

Milky Way. What does our Falun Dafa cultivate? Our cultivation practice is based upon the principles of the universe's evolution, and it is guided by the standard of the universe's highest characteristic, Zhen-Shan-Ren. We cultivate something so enormous that it equates to cultivating the universe.

Our Falun Dafa has another extremely unique, most distinctive feature that is unlike any other practice. At present, all qigong practices popular in society take the path of cultivating dan or practicing dan. In qigong practices that cultivate dan, it is very difficult for one to achieve kaigong and enlightenment while among ordinary people. Our Falun Dafa does not cultivate dan. Our practice cultivates a Falun in the lower abdomen. I personally install it for practitioners in the class. While I am teaching Falun Dafa, we install it for everyone in succession. Some people can feel it while others cannot; the majority of people can feel it. This is because people have different physical conditions. We cultivate Falun instead of dan. Falun is a miniature of the universe that possesses all of the universe's capabilities, and it can operate and rotate automatically. It will forever rotate in your lower abdominal area. Once it is installed in your body, year-in and year-out it will not stop and will forever rotate like this. While rotating clockwise, it can automatically absorb energy from the universe. Additionally, it can itself transform energy to supply the energy required for transforming every part of your body. Also, it emits energy while rotating counter-clockwise, releasing undesirable elements that will disperse around your body. When it emits energy, the energy can be released to quite a distance, and then it will bring in new energy again. The emitted energy can benefit the people around you. The Buddha School teaches self-salvation and salvation of all sentient beings. One does not only cultivate oneself, but also offers salvation to all sentient beings. Others can benefit as well, and you can unintentionally rectify other people's bodies, heal their illnesses, and so on. Of course, the energy is not lost. When Falun rotates clockwise, it can collect the energy back since it rotates continuously.

Some people may wonder, "Why does this Falun rotate continuously?" There are also people who ask me, "Why can it rotate? What's the reason?" It is easy to understand that dan can form when energy accumulates, but it is inconceivable that Falun rotates. Let me give you an example. The universe is in motion, and all of the universe's Milky Ways and galaxies are also in motion. The nine planets orbit the sun, and Earth also rotates by itself. Think about it, everyone: Who's pushing them? Who has given them the force? You cannot understand it with an ordinary person's mentality, as it is just this rotating mechanism. The same is also true with our Falun, for it just rotates. By increasing the exercise time, it has solved for everyday persons the problem of practicing cultivation amidst normal living conditions. How is it increased? Since it rotates continuously, it constantly absorbs and transforms energy from the universe. When you go to work, it is cultivating you. Of course, in addition to Falun, we will also install in your body many energy systems and mechanisms that will, together with Falun, rotate and transform you automatically. Therefore, this gong transforms people all automatically. Thus, it becomes that "the gong cultivates practitioners," which is also called "the Fa cultivates practitioners." The gong cultivates you when you are not practicing, just as it also cultivates you when you are practicing. While having a meal, sleeping, or working, you are always being transformed by the gong. What are you exercising for? You exercise to strengthen the Falun and reinforce all of these energy mechanisms and systems that I have provided. When one practices cultivation at higher levels, it should be completely in the state of *wuwei*,[38] and the exercise movements also follow the mechanisms. There is not any guidance of mind, nor should one use any breathing methods, etc.

We practice without any concern for time or location. Some people have asked, "What's the best time to practice? Midnight, dawn, or noontime?" We do not have any requirement for the exercise time. When you do not practice at midnight, the gong cultivates you. When you do not practice at dawn, the gong also cultivates you. When you are asleep, the gong cultivates you as well. When you are walking, the gong still cultivates you. The gong also cultivates you when you are at work. Doesn't it greatly reduce your practice time? Many of you have the heart to truly attain the Tao, which, of course, is the purpose of cultivation practice. The ultimate goal of cultivation practice is to attain the Tao and complete cultivation. Yet, some people have limited time left in their lives. Their years for living are numbered and may not be enough for cultivation. Our Falun Dafa can solve this problem and shorten the course of practice. Meanwhile, it is also a cultivation practice of mind and body. When you continually practice cultivation, you will constantly prolong your life. With consistent practice, your life will be constantly prolonged. Those elderly people with good in-born quality will have sufficient time for practice. There is a criterion, however, that the life prolonged beyond your predestined time to live is completely reserved for your practice. If your mind goes wrong a little bit, your life will be in danger because your lifetime should have long been over. You will have such a restriction until you reach cultivation beyond Shi-Jian-Fa. After that, one will be in another state.

---

[38] *wuwei* (woo-way)—"non-action"; "without intention."

We do not require facing certain directions for practice or require certain ways to end the practice. Because Falun rotates constantly, it cannot be stopped. If there is a phone call or someone knocks at the door, you may go ahead and take care of it right away without having to finish the practice. When you stop to do something, Falun will at once rotate clockwise and take back the emitted energy from around your body. For those who intentionally hold qi and pour it into their heads, it will still be lost, no matter how you hold it. Falun is something with intelligence, and knows itself to do these things. We do not require directions, either, because the whole universe is in motion. The Milky Way is in motion, and the nine planets are orbiting the sun. Earth is also self-rotating. We practice according to this great principle of the universe. Where is east, south, west, or north? There is none. Practicing in any direction is practicing to all directions, and practicing in any direction is the same as practicing to the east, south, west, and north simultaneously. Our Falun Dafa will protect practitioners from deviating. How does it protect you? If you are a true practitioner, our Falun will safeguard you. I am rooted in the universe. If anyone can harm you, he or she would be able to harm me. Put simply, that person would be able to harm this universe. What I have said may sound quite inconceivable. You will understand it later as you study further. There are also other things that are too profound for me to make known. We will systematically expound the Fa of higher levels, from the simple to the profound. It will not work if your own xinxing is not righteous. If you pursue something, you may get into trouble. I have found that many veteran practitioners' Falun have become deformed. Why? You have intermingled other things with your practice, and you have accepted other people's things. Why didn't Falun protect you, then? If it is given to you, it is yours, and it is dictated by your mind. It is a principle of this universe that nobody should interfere with what you pursue. If you do not want to practice cultivation, no one can force you—that would be the same as doing a wrong deed. Who can force you to change your heart? You must discipline yourself on your own. Taking the best of every school is accepting things from everyone. If you practice one qigong practice today and another tomorrow to cure your illness, is your illness cured? No. You can only postpone it. Practicing cultivation at higher levels requires one to focus on one school and stay with it. If you follow a practice, you must give your heart to it until completely enlightened in that school. Only then can you practice cultivation in another school, and that will be a different system. Because a system of genuine teachings is passed down from a very remote age, it will have gone through quite a complex process of transformation. Some people go by how they feel in practicing something. What does your feeling account for? It is nothing. The actual transformation process takes place in other dimensions and is extremely complex and intricate. There cannot be one bit of error. It is just like a precision instrument that will be out of order as soon as you add a foreign part to it. Your body in each dimension is changing; this is extraordinarily subtle and cannot go wrong for even a bit. I have already told you that cultivation depends on one's own efforts, while transformation of gong is done by one's master. If you casually take other people's things and add them to your practice, the foreign messages will interfere with the things in this school of practice, and you will go awry. In addition, this will be reflected in ordinary human society and bring about the problems of ordinary people. This is caused by your pursuit, and others cannot intervene. It is an issue of your enlightenment quality. Concurrently, what you add will mess up your gong, and you can no longer practice cultivation. This problem will take place. I am not saying that everyone has to study Falun Dafa. If you do not study Falun Dafa and have received true teachings from other qigong practices, I will approve of it as well. Let me tell you, however, that to truly practice cultivation toward higher levels, one must be single-minded with one practice. There is one thing that I must also point out: At present, no other person is truly teaching people toward higher levels like me. In the future you will realize what I have done for you. Thus, I hope that you do not have very poor enlightenment quality. A lot of people want to practice cultivation toward higher levels. This is now provided right before you, and still you may not be aware of it. You have been everywhere looking for a teacher and spent a fortune, yet you have found nothing. Today, it is offered to you at your doorstep, and maybe you have not realized it! This is an issue of whether you can become enlightened to it and whether you can be saved.

LECTURE TWO

The Issue of Tianmu

Many qigong masters have already spoken of tianmu. The Fa, however, has different manifestations at different levels. A practitioner whose cultivation has reached a particular level can only see manifestations at that level. He is unable to see the truth beyond that level, nor will he believe it. Therefore, he only regards what he sees at his level as correct. Before his cultivation reaches a higher level, he thinks that those things do not exist and are not believable; this is determined by his level, and his mind is unable to elevate. In other words, on the issue of tianmu, some people talk about it one way while others talk about it another way. As a result, they have confused it, and in the end nobody can explain it clearly. Tianmu, in fact, is something that cannot be explained clearly at the low level. In the past, the structure of tianmu belonged to the secret of secrets, and everyday people were forbidden from knowing it. Therefore, throughout history nobody has talked about it. But here we do not address it based on theories from the past. We use modern science and the simplest modern language to explain it, and we are addressing its fundamental issues.

The tianmu that we refer to is, in fact, located slightly above and between one's eyebrows, and it is connected to the pineal body. This is the main channel. The human body has many additional eyes. The Tao School says that each aperture is an eye. The Tao School calls an acupuncture point in the body an

48

"aperture" while Chinese medicine calls it an acupuncture point. The Buddha School holds that each sweat pore is an eye. Therefore, some people can read with the ears, and some can look with the hands or from the back of the head; still others can look with the feet or stomach. It is all possible.

Speaking of tianmu, we will first talk about this pair of human flesh eyes. Nowadays, some people think that this pair of eyes can see any matter or object in this world. Therefore, some people have developed the stubborn notion that only what one can see through the eyes is real and concrete. They do not believe what they cannot see. In the past, such people were considered to have poor enlightenment quality, though some people could not explain clearly why these people's enlightenment quality was poor. No seeing, no believing. That may sound quite reasonable. Yet from the perspective of a slightly higher level, it is not reasonable. Every time-space is made of matter. Of course, different time-spaces have different physical structures and various manifesting forms of different lives.

Let me give you an example. In Buddhism, it is said that every phenomenon in human society is illusory and unreal. How are they illusions? Real and concrete physical objects are placed right here, so who would claim that they are false? A physical object's form of existence appears like this, but the way it actually manifests is not. Our eyes, nonetheless, have the capability to stabilize physical objects in our physical dimension to the state that we can see now. The objects are not actually in this state, and they are not in this state even in our dimension. For instance, what does a person look like under a microscope? The whole body is made of loose, tiny molecules, just like grains of sand that are in motion. Electrons orbit nuclei, and the whole body is squirming and moving. The surface of the body is neither smooth nor regular. Any matter in the universe, such as steel, iron, and rock are the same, and inside, all of their molecular elements are in motion. You cannot see their entire form, and they are actually not stable. This table is also squirming, yet your eyes cannot see the truth. This pair of eyes can give one a false impression like that.

It is not that we cannot see things at the microscopic level, or that people do not have this capability. People are born with this capability, and they can see things at a certain microscopic level. Precisely because in this physical dimension we have this pair of eyes, people receive a false impression and are prohibited from seeing things. Thus, in the past it was said that if people did not believe what they could not see, such people would be regarded by the community of cultivators as having poor enlightenment quality, as being deluded by the false impressions of everyday people, and as being lost among everyday people. This is a statement historically made by religions. Actually, we have also found it quite reasonable.

This pair of eyes can stabilize things in this physical dimension of ours to such a state. Besides that, they do not have any other significant capability. When one looks at something, the image does not form directly in one's eyes. The eyes are like the lens of a camera, acting only as a tool. When viewing at a distance, the lens extends; our eyes also assume this function. When looking in the dark, the pupils enlarge. When a camera takes a picture in the dark, its aperture also enlarges. Otherwise, the entire picture is dark with insufficient light exposure. When one walks into a very bright outdoor place, one's pupils contract instantly. One's eyes would otherwise be dazzled by the light, and one would be incapable of seeing things clearly. A camera works by the same principle, and the aperture also needs to contract. It can only capture the image of an object, and it is just a tool. When we actually see things, a person, or see an object's form of existence, the images are formed in the brain. Namely, what we see through the eyes is sent to the pineal body in the rear of the brain via the optic nerve, and it is then reflected as images in that area. This is to say that the actual reflected images are seen in the pineal body of the brain. Modern medicine also recognizes this.

The opening of tianmu that we address avoids using the human optic nerve and opens a passageway between one's eyebrows so that the pineal body can directly see the outside. This is called the opening of tianmu. Some people may ponder: "This isn't realistic. After all, this pair of eyes can still serve as a tool, and they can capture images of objects, something impossible without the eyes." Modern medical dissection has already discovered that the front section of the pineal body is equipped with the complete structure of a human eye. Because it grows inside one's skull, it is thus said to be a vestigial eye. Whether it is a vestigial eye or not, our community of cultivators has reservations. Yet modern medicine has, after all, already recognized that there is an eye in the middle of the human brain. The passageway that we open targets exactly that location, and this happens to agree completely with the understanding of modern medicine. This eye does not create false images like our pair of flesh eyes, as it sees both the nature of matter and the essence of matter. Therefore, a person with high-level tianmu can see beyond our dimension into other time-spaces, and he can see scenes that ordinary people cannot see. A person with a low-level tianmu may have the penetrative vision to see things through

51

a wall and look through a human body. It has precisely this supernormal capability.

The Buddha School talks about five levels of eyesight: Flesh Eyesight, Celestial Eyesight, Wisdom Eyesight, Fa Eyesight, and Buddha Eyesight. These are the five major levels of tianmu, and each is subdivided into upper, middle and lower levels. The Tao School talks about nine times nine or eighty-one levels of Fa Eyesight. We are opening tianmu for everyone here, but we do not open it at or below Celestial Eyesight. Why? Though you sit here and have begun to practice cultivation, you are, after all, just beginning from the level of an everyday person with many everyday people's attachments still not abandoned. If your tianmu is opened below Celestial Eyesight, you will have what everyday people regard as supernormal capabilities, as you can see things through a wall and see through a human body. If we provided this supernormal capability widely and if everyone's tianmu were opened to this level, it would severely disturb ordinary human society and disrupt the state of ordinary human society: state secrets would be jeopardized; it would be the same whether people wore clothes or not, and you could see people in a house from outside; while strolling on the street, you could pick up all top prizes of the lottery if you saw them. That would not be permitted! Think about it, everyone: Would that still be a human society if everyone's tianmu were opened to Celestial Eyesight? Severely disturbing the state of human society is absolutely prohibited. If I indeed opened your tianmu to that level, you might become a qigong master right away. Some people dreamed before about becoming qigong masters. If their tianmu were opened all of a sudden, they would be able to treat patients. Wouldn't I be taking you down an evil path in that case?

52

Then, at what level do I open your tianmu? I will open your tianmu directly at the level of Wisdom Eyesight. If it were opened at a higher level, your xinxing would not be adequate. If it were opened at a lower level, it would severely disturb the state of ordinary human society. With Wisdom Eyesight, you do not have the ability to see things through a wall or see through a human body, but you can see the scenes existing in other dimensions. What benefits does this have? It can enhance your confidence in the practice. When you indeed see something that everyday people cannot see, you will think that it certainly exists. No matter whether you can see something clearly at present, your tianmu will be opened at this level, and this is good for your practice. A true Dafa practitioner can obtain the same result by reading this book, provided that he is strict with himself in improving xinxing.

What determines one's tianmu level? It is not that once your tianmu is opened, you are able to see everything—it is not so. There is still a classification of levels. So, what determines the levels? There are three factors. The first is that one's tianmu must have a field going from the inside to the outside, and we call this the essence of qi. What use does it have? It is like a television screen: Without phosphor, after a television is turned on, it is still just a light bulb. It will only have light, but no images. It is because of phosphor that images are displayed. Of course, this example is not quite fitting because we see things directly while a television set displays images through a screen. That is roughly the idea. This bit of the essence of qi is extremely precious, and it is made of a finer substance that is refined from de. Normally, each person's essence of qi is different. Perhaps two out of ten thousand people are at the same level.

Tianmu level is the direct manifestation of our universe's

Fa. It is something supernatural and closely related to one's xinxing. If a person's xinxing level is low, his level is low. Because of low-level xinxing, much of this person's essence of qi is lost. If a person's xinxing level is high, and in ordinary human society he has from childhood to adulthood cared little for fame, profit, interpersonal conflicts, personal gain, and various human sentiments and desires, his essence of qi may be preserved relatively better. Therefore, after his tianmu is opened, he can see things more clearly. A child under six can see things very clearly once his tianmu is opened. It is also easy to open his tianmu. If I say a word, it will open.

Because of contamination from the powerful current or big dye vat of ordinary human society, the things that people consider correct are, actually, often wrong. Doesn't everyone want to live a good life? Desiring a good life may infringe upon others' interests, whet one's selfish desires, take away others' benefits, or lead to bullying and harming others. One will compete and fight for personal gain among everyday people. Isn't this going against the characteristic of the universe? Thus, what people consider correct might not necessarily be correct. In educating a child, an adult often teaches him, "You should learn to be smart," so that in the future he will get a foothold in ordinary human society. From the perspective of our universe, "to be smart" is already wrong, for we require following the course of nature and caring little for personal gain. Being so smart, he intends to pursue self-interest. "Whoever bullies you, go to his teacher and find his parents." "Pick up money if you see it on the ground." The child is taught this way. From childhood to adulthood, as he receives more things, he will gradually become increasingly selfish in ordinary human society. He will take advantage of others and lose de.

This substance, de, does not vanish after one loses it. It is transferred to another person. Yet, this essence of qi can disappear. If one is very wily from childhood to adulthood with a strong desire for self-interest and solely seeks profit, this person's tianmu will, after opening, normally not work or see things clearly. This does not mean, however, that it will never be functional from that point on. Why? Because in the course of cultivation practice we try to return to our original, true selves, and through persistent practice we will be able to constantly compensate for it and recover it. Therefore, one must pay attention to xinxing. We stress holistic improvement and holistic upgrade. If xinxing is upgraded, everything else will follow up. If xinxing is not upgraded, that bit of essence of qi will not be recovered, either. This is the principle.

The second factor is that when a person practices qigong on his own, his tianmu can also open if his inborn quality is good. Oftentimes, some people become frightened at the moment when their tianmu opens. Why are they frightened? It is because people usually practice qigong at midnight, when the night is dark and quiet. As a person practices, he may suddenly see a large eye before his eyes, scaring him abruptly. This scare is unusually great, and he will not dare to practice qigong after that. How frightening! A blinking eye that is so big is looking at you, and it is vividly clear. Consequently, some people call it a demon's eye, while others call it a Buddha's eye, and so on. In fact, it is your own eye. Of course, cultivation depends on one's own efforts, while transforming gong is done by one's master. The whole process of transforming cultivation energy is very complex, and occurs in other dimensions. The body does not only change in just another one dimension, but in all different dimensions. Can you do that by yourself? You cannot. These things are arranged by the master and performed by the master. Therefore, it is said that cultivation depends on one's own efforts, while transforming gong is done by one's master. You can only have such a wish and think about it like that, but it is the master who actually does these things.

Some people open their tianmu through their own practice. We refer to that eye of yours, but you are incapable of developing it by yourself. Some people have masters who, upon finding out that their tianmu are open, will transform one for them. It is called the real eye. Of course, some people do not have a master, but there may be a master who passes by. The Buddha School states: "Buddhas are omnipresent." They are so numerous that they are everywhere. Some people also say: "There are spiritual beings three feet above one's head," meaning that they are simply countless. If a passing-by master sees that you have practiced very well with tianmu opened and that you need an eye, he or she will transform one for you, which can also count as a result of your own cultivation. In offering salvation to people, there is no condition or consideration for cost, reward, or fame. They are thus far more noble than the heroes of everyday people. They do it completely out of their benevolent compassion.

After one's tianmu is opened, a situation will occur: one's eyes will be severely dazzled by light and feel irritated. It is actually not irritating your eyes. Instead, it is your pineal body that is irritated, though you feel as if your eyes are irritated. That is because you have not yet acquired this eye. After you are supplied with this eye, your flesh eyes are no longer irritated. A number of our practitioners will be able to feel or see this eye. Because it embodies the same nature as the universe, it is very

56

innocent and also curious. It looks in to examine whether your tianmu is open and if it can see things. It looks inside at you as well. At this point your tianmu is open. While it looks at you, you will be scared upon suddenly seeing it. In fact, this is your own eye. From now on, when you look at things, you will see things through this eye. Even if your tianmu is open, you will be completely unable to see things without this eye.

The third factor is the differences that are manifested in different dimensions after one makes breakthroughs in levels. This is the issue that truly determines one's level. In addition to the main channel for seeing things, people also have many sub-channels. The Buddha School holds that each sweat pore is an eye, while the Tao School claims that every aperture of the body is an eye. That is, all acupuncture points are eyes. Of course, what they discuss is still one form of the Fa's transformations in the body; one can see things from any part of the body.

The level that we refer to is different from that. In addition to the main channel, there are also several major sub-channels in several places, i.e., above the two eyebrows, above and below the eyelids, and at the *shangen* point.[1] They determine the issue of making breakthroughs in levels. Of course, for an average practitioner, if he can see things with these several places, he has already reached a very high level. Some people can also see things with their flesh eyes. They, too, have succeeded in cultivating these eyes that are also equipped with different forms of supernormal capabilities. If this eye is not used well, however, one will always look at one object without seeing the other. That will not work, either. Thus, some people often see one side with

---

[1] *shangen* (shahn-ghun) point— acupuncture point located between one's eyebrows.

one eye and the other side with the other eye. Yet, there is no sub-channel below this eye (the right eye) because it is related directly to the Fa. People tend to use the right eye to commit wrongdoings; so no sub-channel exists below the right eye. These refer to several major sub-channels that are developed in Shi-Jian-Fa cultivation.

After reaching an extremely high level and beyond Shi-Jian-Fa cultivation, an eye that resembles a compound eye will form. Specifically, in the upper face a large eye will appear with numerous tiny eyes within it. Some great enlightened people at very high levels have cultivated so many eyes that they are all over their faces. All eyes see things through this large eye, and they can see whatever they want. With one glance, they are able to see all levels. Today, zoologists and entomologists conduct research on flies. A fly's eye is very big; through microscopy, it is known to have numerous tiny eyes inside it, and this is called a compound eye. After practitioners reach an extremely high level, this situation may occur. One has to be many times higher than the Tathagata level to make this possible. Yet, an ordinary person cannot see it. People at the average level also cannot see its existence, and because it exists in another dimension they can only see that he or she is like a normal person. This explains the breakthroughs in levels. That is to say, it is an issue of whether one can reach different dimensions.

I have basically outlined the structure of tianmu for everyone. We open your tianmu with an external force, so it is relatively faster and easier. When I was talking about tianmu, each of you could feel that your forehead was tight; the muscles felt like they were piling up together and drilling inward. It was so, wasn't it? It was like this. As long as you truly put your mind to studying

Falun Dafa here, everyone will feel it; the external force comes very strongly when drilling inward. I have released the specialized energy that opens tianmu. Meanwhile, I have also sent out Falun to repair your tianmu. While I was talking about tianmu, I was opening tianmu for everyone, provided they practice cultivation in Falun Dafa. However, not everyone can necessarily see things clearly, nor can everyone necessarily see things with it. That has something to do directly with you, yourself. Never mind, as it does not matter if you cannot see things with it. Take your time to cultivate it. As you constantly upgrade your level, you will gradually be able to see things, and your clouded vision will become increasingly clear. As long as you practice cultivation and make up your mind to practice cultivation, you will recover all of what you have lost.

It is relatively difficult to open tianmu by yourself. Let me talk about several forms of opening tianmu on one's own. For instance, when looking at your forehead and tianmu during the sitting meditation, some of you sense that it is dark inside the forehead, and that there is nothing there. As time passes, one will find that it gradually turns white in the forehead. After a period of cultivation practice, one will discover that it gradually begins to be bright inside the forehead, and then it turns red. At this time, it will blossom like the flowers seen on television or in a movie in which the flowers blossom in a second. Such scenes will appear. The red color will start out flat, and then it will suddenly stand out in the middle and turn constantly. If you want to turn it on your own completely to the end, even eight or ten years may not be long enough since the entire tianmu is blocked.

Some people's tianmu are not blocked, and they are equipped with a passageway. But, it does not have any energy there, because they do not practice qigong. Thus, when they practice qigong, a ball of black matter will suddenly appear before their eyes. After they practice for some time, it will gradually turn white and then become bright. In the end, it will glow brighter and brighter, and the eyes will feel somewhat dazzled. Some people, therefore, say, "I saw the sun," or " I saw the moon." In fact, they saw neither the sun nor the moon. What did they see, then? It was their passageway. Some people make rapid breakthroughs in their levels. Upon having the eye installed, they can see things right away. For others, it is quite difficult. When they practice qigong, they will feel as if running to the outside along this passageway, which is like a tunnel or a well. Even in their sleep, they feel as if running to the outside. Some may feel as if riding a horse; some may feel as if flying; some feel as if running; and some feel as if rushing forth in a car. Because it is very difficult to open tianmu on one's own, they always feel that they cannot dash to the end. The Tao School regards the human body as a small universe. If it is a small universe, think about it, it is more than 108 thousand *li*[2] from the forehead to the pineal body. Thus, one always feels as if rushing to the outside and unable to reach the end.

It is quite reasonable that the Tao School regards the human body as a small universe. It does not mean that its composition and structure are similar to those of the universe, nor does it refer to the existing form of the body in our physical dimension. We ask, "According to the understanding of modern science, what, at a more microscopic level, is the state of the physical body that is made of cells?" There are different molecular compositions. Smaller than molecules are atoms, protons, nuclei, electrons, and

---

[2] *li* (lee)—a Chinese unit for distance (=0.5 km). In Chinese, "108 thousand li" is a common expression to describe a very far distance.

quarks. The most microscopic particles now studied are neutrinos. Then, what is the most microscopic particle? It is indeed too difficult to study. In his later years, Sakyamuni made this statement: "It's so immense that it has no exterior, and so tiny that it has no interior." What does it mean? At the level of Tathagata, the universe is so immense that its boundary is imperceptible, yet so tiny that nor are its most microscopic particles of matter perceptible. Consequently, he stated: "It's so immense that it has no exterior, and so tiny that it has no interior."

Sakyamuni also spoke of the theory of three thousand worlds. He stated that, in our universe and our Milky Way, there are three thousand planets with living beings that have physical bodies like our human race. He also stated that there were three thousand such worlds in a grain of sand. A grain of sand is thus just like a universe, with people having wisdom like ours, planets, mountains, and rivers. It sounds quite inconceivable! If so, think about it, everyone: Is there sand in those three thousand worlds? And are there another three thousand worlds in that grain of sand? Then, is there sand in those three thousand worlds? Then, are there still three thousand worlds in that grain of sand? Accordingly, at the level of Tathagata, one is unable to see its end.

The same is true with human molecular cells. People ask how big the universe is. Let me tell you that this universe also has its boundary. Even at the level of Tathagata, however, one will regard it as boundless and infinitely immense. Yet, the human body's inside is as big as this universe, from molecules to microscopic particles at the microscopic level. This may sound very inconceivable. When a human being or a life is created, his unique life elements and essential quality are already composed at the extremely microscopic level. Thus, in studying this subject, our modern science lags far behind. In comparison with those lives of higher wisdom on the planets throughout the entire universe, our human race's scientific level is quite low. We cannot even reach other dimensions that exist simultaneously in the same place, while flying saucers from other planets can travel directly in other dimensions. The concept of that time-space is completely different. Thus, they can come and go at will and at a speed so fast that the human mind cannot accept it.

In talking about tianmu, I brought up the issue of when you feel as though dashing to the outside along a passageway, you feel that it is boundless and endless. Some people may see another situation where they do not feel as though rushing along a channel, but dashing forward along a boundless and endless road. While dashing to the outside, there are mountains, rivers, and cities on both sides. That may sound even more inconceivable. I recall that a qigong master made such a statement: "There is a city in each sweat pore of the human body, and trains as well as cars run in it." Upon hearing this, others are astonished and find it inconceivable. You know that the microscopic particles of matter include molecules, atoms, and protons. When investigating further, if you can see the plane of each level instead of a point, and see the plane of molecules, the plane of atoms, the plane of protons, and that of nuclei, you will see the forms of existence in different dimensions. All matter, including the human body, exists simultaneously in connection with dimensional levels of the cosmic space. When our modern physics studies the microscopic particles of matter, it only studies a microscopic particle through splitting it and fission. It will study its elements after nuclear fission. If there were such an instrument through which we could expand and see the level at which all atomic elements or molecular elements could manifest in their entirety, or if this scene were observed, you would reach beyond this dimension and see the real scenes existing in other dimensions. The human body corresponds to external dimensions, and they all have such forms of existence.

There are still some other different situations as one opens tianmu on one's own. We have mainly talked about some very common phenomena. Some people also find that their tianmu rotates. Those who practice in the Tao School often see something rotating inside their tianmu. After the Taiji plate cracks open with a snap, one will see images; however, it is not that there is a Taiji in your head. It was the master who installed a set of things for you at the very beginning, one of which is the Taiji. He sealed your tianmu. By the time your tianmu is opened, it will crack open. The master intentionally arranged it that way, and it was not something originally from your head.

Still, some people seek to open tianmu. The more they practice for this, the more unlikely it is to open. What's the reason? They have no idea themselves. It is mainly because tianmu cannot be pursued; with more desired, less is obtained. When a person wants it desperately, not only will it not open, but instead something neither black nor white will emit from his tianmu. It will cover up his tianmu. As time passes, it will form a very large field. The more it flows forth, the more it accumulates. The more unlikely it is for tianmu to open, the more he will pursue it, and the more this substance will come out. As a result, it will cover his whole body to such an extent that it becomes very thick with a very large field. Even if this person's tianmu is indeed opened, he still cannot see anything because it is sealed by his own attachment. Only if he no longer thinks about it in the future and completely gives up this attachment, will it gradually disappear. It will, however, take a very painful and long period of cultivation practice to remove it. This is very unnecessary. Some people do not know it. Though the master tells them not to go after it or pursue it, they do not believe it. They keep pursuing it, and in the end, the results turn out just the opposite.

The Supernormal Capability of Clairvoyance

One supernormal capability directly related to tianmu is called clairvoyance. Some people claim: "While sitting here I can see scenes in Beijing and in America, as well as on the other side of the earth." Some people cannot comprehend it, nor can this be explained scientifically. How is it possible? Some people explain it this way or that way, and cannot explain it sensibly. They wonder how people can become so capable. It is not like that. A practitioner at the level of Shi-Jian-Fa cultivation does not have this capability. What he sees, including clairvoyance and many supernormal capabilities, all function within a specific dimension. At most, they are not beyond this physical dimension where our human race exists. They are typically not even beyond the person's own dimensional field.

Within a specific dimension, the human body has a field which is different from the field of de. They are not in the same dimension, but are the same size. This field corresponds to the universe. Whatever exists in the universe out there is correspondingly reflected here. Everything can be reflected. It is a kind of image, but it is not real. For instance, there exist on this earth America and Washington, D.C. Within a person's field, America and Washington, D.C. are reflected, but they are reflected images. Reflected images are nonetheless a form of matter's existence, and they are the result of a corresponding reflection that changes according to changes over there. Thus, the supernormal capability of clairvoyance that some people refer to is to look at things within one's own dimensional field. When a person practices cultivation beyond Shi-Jian-Fa, he will no longer look at things this way. He will look at things directly, and that is called the divine power of Buddha Fa. It is something with mighty power.

In Shi-Jian-Fa cultivation, what is the supernormal capability of clairvoyance all about? I am going to explain it for everyone. Within this field, there is a mirror in one's forehead. A non-practitioner's mirror faces toward himself, but a practitioner's mirror turns over. When a person's supernormal capability of clairvoyance is about to emerge, it will rotate back and forth. It is known that a movie film shows twenty-four frames per second in order to make pictures with continuous motion. If less than twenty-four frames are shown per second, the images will skip and jump. The mirror's rotating speed is faster than twenty-four frames per second, and it reflects what it receives and turns over to let you see. Upon turning over again, the images will then be erased. It reflects and turns, and then it erases the images. The rotation continues incessantly. Thus, what you see is in motion. It lets you see what is reflected within your own dimensional field, and it corresponds to what is in the large universe.

Then, how can one see what's behind one's body? With such a small mirror, how can it reflect everything around one's body? You know that when one's tianmu is opened beyond Celestial Eyesight and is about to attain Wisdom Eyesight, it is close to reaching beyond our dimension. At this point when the breakthrough is imminent, tianmu will experience a change. When it looks at physical objects, they will all have vanished. People and walls will all have vanished—everything vanishes. There will no longer be any material existence. That is, upon taking a closer look, you will find that in this particular dimension people no longer exist; there is only a mirror standing within the scope of your dimensional field. Yet, this mirror in your dimensional field is as big as the entire field of your dimensional field. Thus, when it rotates back and forth, it reflects everything everywhere. Within your dimensional field, it can show you everything, provided it corresponds to what is from the universe. This is what we call the supernormal capability of clairvoyance.

When those who study the science of the human body test this supernormal capability, they can usually discredit it easily. The reason for the rejection is as follows. For instance, when a person is asked about someone's relative in Beijing, "What's the relative doing at home?" after the relative's name and general information are provided, the person can see her. He will describe what the building looks like, how to enter the door, and how the room is furnished upon entering the room. What he said is all correct. What is the relative doing? He says that the relative is writing something. In order to verify it, they will call up the relative and ask, "What are you doing right now?" "I'm having a meal." Won't that disagree with what he saw? In the past, this was the reason for not recognizing this supernormal capability. The environment that he saw, however, was not wrong at all. Because our space and time, which we call "time-space," has a time difference from the time-space of the dimension where the supernormal capability exists, the concepts of time are different on the two sides. She was writing something before, and now she is having a meal; there is such a time difference. As a result, if those who study the human body draw deductive hypotheses and conduct research based upon conventional theories and modern science, even after another ten thousand years their efforts will still be fruitless, for these are something beyond ordinary people in the first place. Accordingly, humankind needs to change its mentality and should no longer understand these things this way.

The Supernormal Capability of Suming Tong[3]

Another supernormal capability directly related to tianmu is called suming tong. Today, six types of supernormal capabilities are publicly recognized in the world, including tianmu, clairvoyance, and suming tong. What is suming tong? It is that someone is able to tell another person's future and past. With a strong capability, one is able to tell the rise and fall of a society. With a greater capability, one can see the law of all cosmic changes. This is the supernormal capability of suming tong. Because matter is in motion and follows a certain law, in a special dimension, all matter has its form of existence in many other dimensions. For instance, when a person's body moves, the cells in the body will also move, and at the microscopic level all elements, such as all molecules, protons, electrons, and the most microscopic particles, will also move. Yet they have their own independent forms of existence, and the forms of the body in other dimensions will also undergo a change.

Haven't we addressed that matter does not become extinct? Within a specific dimension, what a person has done or what a person does with a wave of his hand is all material existence, and anything he does will leave an image and message. In another

---

[3] Suming Tong (sue-ming tong)—precognition and retrocognition.

dimension it does not become extinct and will stay there forever. A person with supernormal capabilities will know what happens by looking at the existing images in the past. After you have the supernormal capability of suming tong in the future, the form of my lecture today will still exist when you take a look at it. It already exists there simultaneously. Within a special dimension that does not have the concept of time, when a person is born, his or her entire lifetime already exists there simultaneously. For some people, even more than one lifetime exists there.

Some people may wonder, "Is it that our individual efforts for changing ourselves become unnecessary?" They cannot accept it. In fact, individual efforts can change minor things in one's life. Some minor things can be altered slightly through individual efforts, but it is precisely because of your efforts for change that you may obtain karma. Otherwise, the issue of committing karma will not exist, nor will there be the issue of doing good deeds or wrong deeds. When one insists upon doing things this way, one will take advantage of others and do wrong deeds. Accordingly, that is why cultivation practice requires time and time again that one should follow the course of nature since you will harm others with your efforts. If your life does not have something to begin with and you obtain what should belong to another person in society, you will owe that person a debt.

As for major events, an everyday person cannot change them at all. There is but one way to do so. It is if this person does only bad deeds, and nothing but bad deeds, he can change his life. What he faces, however, is complete destruction. From a high level, we find that when a person is dead, his yuanshen does not become extinct. Why doesn't yuanshen become extinct? In fact, we have seen that after a person is dead, his corpse in the mortuary is nothing but a body of human cells in our dimension. In this dimension, different cell tissues of the internal organs and all cells in the entire human body slough off, while in other dimensions the bodies made of particles more microscopic than molecules, atoms, protons, etc., are not at all dead. They exist in other dimensions and still live in the microscopic dimensions. What someone who does all kinds of evil deeds faces is the total disintegration of all of his cells, which Buddhism calls the extinction of body and soul.

There is another way to change one's life, and this is the only way: It is that this person takes the path of cultivation practice from now on. Why can one's life be changed if one takes the path of cultivation practice? Who can easily change such a thing? Once this person thinks about taking the path of cultivation practice and once this thought occurs, it shines like gold, shaking the world in ten directions. In its view of the universe, the Buddha School has the theory of the ten-directional world. In the eyes of a higher being, a person's life is not meant for just being human. This being thinks that one's life is born in the space of the universe and embodies the same quality as the universe; life is benevolent and made of the matter Zhen-Shan-Ren. Yet a life also establishes social relations. During social interactions in the community, some lives become corrupt and thus fall to a lower level. When they cannot stay at that level and again become worse, they will fall to an even lower level. They keep falling and falling until, in the end, they reach this level of everyday people.

At this level, these people should be destroyed and eliminated. Yet, out of their great, benevolent compassion, those great enlightened people specially created a space just as this of our human society. In this dimension of space, one is given this additional human flesh body and this extra pair of eyes that can only see things in this physical dimension. That is, one gets lost in delusion and is not allowed to see the truth of the universe, something which can be seen in all other dimensions. In this delusion and under such conditions, one is given this kind of opportunity. Because one is deluded, it is also most painful. With this body, one is made to suffer. If a person wants to return from this dimension to his origin, the Tao School says that he must practice cultivation to return to his original, true self. If he has the heart for cultivation practice, it is his Buddha-nature that has emerged. This heart is considered most precious, and people will help him. Under such difficult circumstances, this person is still not lost and wants to come back. As a result, people will help him and unconditionally give him a hand—they will help him with anything. Why can we do such a thing for a practitioner but not for an ordinary person? This is the reason.

As for an everyday person who wants to cure illness, we cannot help him with anything at all. An everyday person is just an everyday person. An everyday person should conform to the state of ordinary human society. Many people say that Buddha offers salvation to all beings and the Buddha School teaches salvation of all beings. Let me tell you that you may examine all of the Buddhist scriptures, and none of them says that treating diseases for everyday people is offering salvation to all beings. It is those sham qigong masters of recent years who have botched up this issue. Those genuine qigong masters, the ones who paved the road, did not tell you to treat diseases for others at all. They only taught you to practice, heal illness, and keep fit on your own. You are an everyday person. How can you cure diseases after studying it for two days? Isn't that deceiving others? Doesn't it encourage your attachment? That's pursuing fame, self-interest, and something supernatural to show off among everyday people! It is absolutely prohibited. Therefore, the more some people pursue something, the less they will obtain. You are not allowed to do that, nor are you allowed to disturb the state of ordinary human society so casually.

There is such a principle in this universe that when you want to return to your original, true self, others will help you. They think that a human life should return to where he comes from instead of staying among everyday people. If a person were allowed to have no illness and live comfortably, he would not even be interested in becoming an immortal—even if he were asked. How wonderful it would be if one could suffer no illness or hardship and have whatever one wants! It would really be a world of immortals. But you dropped to this level because you became corrupt, so you will not be comfortable. Man can easily commit wrongdoings in delusion, and Buddhism calls this karmic retribution. Therefore, when some people have some tribulations or misfortune, they are repaying their karma in accordance with the retribution of their karma. Buddhism also holds that Buddhas are everywhere. If a Buddha waved his hand once, all of humankind's diseases could be wiped out; this is absolutely achievable. With so many Buddhas around, why hasn't anyone done this? It is because a person committed wrongdoings in the past that he suffers these hardships. If you have cured his illness, that is the same as violating the principle of the universe, for one can then do wrong deeds and owe someone something without having to pay for it. This is not allowed. Thus, everyone preserves the state of ordinary human society, and no one wants to disturb it. Cultivation practice is the only way to find yourself comfortably free of illness and to accomplish the goal of being truly free! Only by having people practice the orthodox Fa can there be true salvation of all beings.

Why can many qigong masters cure diseases? Why do they talk about healing illness? Some people may have considered these questions. The majority of these qigong masters are not from orthodox practices. It is permitted when, during the course of his cultivation, a real qigong master who finds all living beings suffering helps someone out of his compassion and sympathy. He cannot cure diseases, however, and he can only temporarily repress or postpone them. You do not have them now, but you will get them later, as he delays your illness to sometime later. He will transfer them elsewhere or to the bodies of your relatives. He is unable to truly eliminate the karma for you completely. He is not allowed to casually do that for an everyday person, but only for practitioners. This is the principle.

In the Buddha School, "salvation of all beings" implies bringing you out of everyday people's most agonizing state to higher levels. You will no longer suffer, and will be set free— that is what it implies. Didn't Sakyamuni talk about the other side of nirvana? That is the actual meaning of salvation of all beings. If you live comfortably among everyday people, with a lot of money, and if your bed is padded with money and you have no suffering, you would not be interested if you were asked to become an immortal. As a practitioner, your course of life can be altered. Only through cultivation practice can your life be altered.

The way the supernormal capability of suming tong works is similar to having a small television screen in one's forehead. Some people have it on the forehead; some people have it close to the forehead. Some have it inside the forehead. Some people can see things with their eyes closed. If the capability is strong, one can see things with eyes open. Others, however, cannot see them, as they are something within the scope of one's dimensional field. In other words, after this supernormal capability develops, there must be another one that serves as a carrier to reflect the scenes from other dimensions. Consequently, it can be seen by this tianmu. One can see very accurately a person's future and past. No matter how well the fortune-telling works, it cannot tell the minor events and their details. This person, however, is able to see things very clearly, including the time of year. The details of changes are all visible since what one sees is the actual reflection of people and things from different dimensions.

As long as you all practice Falun Dafa, everyone's tianmu will be opened. But the supernormal capabilities we address later are not provided. With the constant upgrading of your level, the capability of suming tong will naturally emerge. This scenario will occur in your future cultivation practice, and you will know what is going on when this capability develops. Therefore, we have taught these principles of the Fa.

Transcending the Five Elements and the Three Realms

What is "transcending the Five Elements and the Three Realms?" This is a very delicate issue to raise. Before, many qigong masters spoke of this issue, and they were choked by questions from those who did not believe in qigong, "Which one of you that practices qigong has transcended the Five Elements and isn't within the Three Realms?" Some people are not qigong masters, and they label themselves as qigong masters. If they are not clear about it, they should be quiet. However, they still dare to talk about it, and other people then make them speechless. This has brought much damage to the community of cultivators, causing great chaos. Some people use the opportunity to attack qigong. Transcending the Five Elements and the Three Realms is a saying in the community of cultivators. It is rooted in religion and comes from religion. Therefore, we cannot address this issue without considering its historical background and the circumstances at that time.

What is transcending the Five Elements? Both ancient Chinese physics and modern physics consider the Chinese theory of Five Elements correct. It is true that the Five Elements of metal, wood, water, fire, and earth constitute everything in our universe. Thus, we talk about the theory of Five Elements. If a person is said to have transcended the Five Elements, in modern language it means that he has reached beyond this physical world of ours. It sounds quite inconceivable. Think about this issue, everyone: A qigong master has gong. I have participated in an experiment, and many other qigong masters have also undergone this experiment to measure their energy. The material elements in cultivation energy can be detected by many present-day apparatus. That is to say, as long as there is such an apparatus, the elements emitted by a qigong master and the existence of his gong can be detected. Modern apparatus can detect infrared rays, ultraviolet rays, ultrasonic waves, infrasonic waves, electricity, magnetic force, gamma rays, atoms, and neutrons. A qigong master possesses all of these substances, and there are some other substances emitted by qigong masters that are undetectable because no such apparatus exists. As long as there is such an apparatus, everything is detectable. The substances emitted by qigong masters are found to be extremely abundant.

Under the special effect of a magnetic field, a qigong master can emit a powerful and very beautiful aura. The greater one's energy potency, the larger the generated energy field. An everyday person also has an aura, but it is very tiny and weak. In the research of high-energy physics, people believe that energy is made of particles such as neutrons and atoms. Many qigong masters, including the well-known ones, have undergone testing. I have also been tested, and the detected radiation of the generated gamma rays and thermal neutrons was eighty to one hundred seventy times more than normal matter. At this point, the testing apparatus' indicator reached the limit, as its needle stopped at the maximum point. In the end, the apparatus could not tell how much more energy I had. It is simply inconceivable that a person has such powerful neutrons! How can one generate such powerful neutrons? This also verifies that we qigong masters do have gong and energy. This has been validated by the scientific and technological community.

To transcend the Five Elements, a cultivation practice of both mind and body is required. If a practice is not one of mind and body and only improves gong for a person's level without cultivating the body, it is not concerned with this issue and does not require transcending the Five Elements. A cultivation practice of mind and body stores energy in all cells of the body. The average practitioners or those who just begin to develop gong generate very coarse grains of energy with gaps and low density. Thus, it has little power. When one's level becomes higher, it is completely possible that the density of one's energy will be one hundred times, one thousand times, or 100 million times higher than that of ordinary water molecules. The higher one's level, the denser, finer-grained, and more powerful one's energy. Under this circumstance, the energy is stored in each cell of the body. Such energy is not only stored in each cell of the body in this physical dimension, but it also fills up the molecules, atoms, protons, and electrons of all bodies in other dimensions, until it reaches the extremely microscopic cells. As time passes, one's whole body will be filled with such high-energy matter.

This high-energy matter has intelligence, and it is very capable. Once it increases and becomes denser, it will fill up all cells in the human body and repress human flesh cells—the most incompetent cells. Once the cells are repressed, they will no longer undergo metabolism. In the end, the human flesh cells will be completely replaced. Of course, it is easy for me to say. Coming to this point in cultivation will be a gradual and slow process. When your cultivation reaches this point, high-energy matter will replace all cells in your body. Think about it: Is your body still made of the Five Elements? Is it still matter from this dimension of ours? It is already made of the high-energy matter collected from other dimensions. The element de is also matter that exists in another dimension. It is not restricted by this time field in our dimension.

Modern science holds that time has a field. If something is not within the scope of a time-field, it is not restricted by that time. In other dimensions, the concepts of time-space are different from ours here. How can the time here regulate matter from other dimensions? It does not whatsoever. Think about it, everyone: Won't you have transcended the Five Elements by then? Will your body still be that of an everyday person? It will not be so at all, but ordinary people cannot tell the difference. Though one's body is transformed to this extent, it is not the end of cultivation practice. One needs to continue making breakthroughs toward higher levels in cultivation. Thus, one must still practice cultivation among everyday people; it will not work if people cannot see this person.

What will happen later? Although in the course of cultivation all of this person's cells at the molecular level are replaced by the high-energy matter, atoms have their order of combinations, and the molecular combinations and atomic configurations will not change. The molecular combinations for cells are in such a state that they feel soft when you touch them. The molecular combinations for bones have a high density and bones feel hard. The density for blood molecules is very low, so it is fluid. An everyday person cannot discern the changes in you from the appearance, as your cells' molecules still retain their original structure and combination; their structure does not change. Yet the energy inside has changed. Thus, from this point on this person will not age naturally, and his cells will not die. Accordingly, he will stay young continuously. In the course of cultivation practice, one will look young and, in the end, stay that way.

Of course, one's bones may still fracture when a car hits one's body. One will still bleed if cut by a knife, for one's molecular combinations have not changed. It is only that the cells will not naturally die out or become naturally aged. There is no metabolism. This is what we call "transcending the Five Elements." What superstition is this? It can even be explained in scientific principles. Some people are unable to explain it, so they make careless remarks. Others will thus say that they promote superstition. Since this statement comes from religion, it is not a term crafted by our modern qigong.

What is "transcending the Three Realms?" I mentioned the other day that the key to increasing gong lies in our cultivating xinxing and becoming assimilated to the characteristic of the universe. The characteristic of the universe will then not constrain you. Once you upgrade xinxing, the element de will transform into gong that constantly grows upward to a high level, thus forming a gongzhu. Whatever the height of this gongzhu, that is the height of your energy level. There is this saying: "The great Fa is boundless." Cultivating it depends entirely on your heart. As to how high your cultivation level can reach, it all depends on your endurance and your ability to bear hardships. If you use up your own white substance, your black substance can be transformed into the white substance by undergoing suffering. If it is still not enough, you may bear the sins of your friends or relatives who do not practice cultivation, and you can still increase gong. This requires that someone has reached an extremely high level in cultivation practice; an ordinary practitioner should not think of bearing sins for relatives. With that large amount of karma, an average person could not succeed in cultivation. I am explaining here principles at different levels.

The Three Realms that religions mention refer to the nine levels of heaven or the thirty-three levels of heaven—namely, heaven, Earth, and the underworld, including all beings within the Three Realms. They hold that all beings within the thirty-three levels of heaven go through the reincarnation cycle of samsara. "Samsara" means that one is a human being in this life, and one may become an animal in the next life. It is said in Buddhism: "One should make good use of the limited time in this life. If you don't practice cultivation now, when will you?" This is because animals are prohibited from practicing cultivation, nor are they allowed to listen to the Fa. Even if they practice cultivation, they will not achieve the Right Fruit[4] in cultivation. If their gong level becomes high, heaven will kill them. You might

---

[4] Right Fruit—attainment of Fruit Status in the Buddha School.

not get a human body in several hundred years; perhaps, you obtain it in one thousand years. Once you get a human body, you do not even know how to treasure it. If you reincarnate into a piece of rock, you will be unable to come out in ten thousand years. If that piece of rock is not smashed or weathered away, you will never be able to emerge. Attaining a human body is so difficult! If a person can truly obtain Dafa, this person is simply most fortunate. A human body is hard to acquire—that is what it means.

In cultivation practice we are concerned with the issue of levels, and this depends entirely on one's own cultivation practice. If you want to transcend the Three Realms and if your gongzhu is cultivated to a very high level, aren't you beyond the Three Realms? When someone's yuanshen leaves the body during the sitting meditation, it can reach a very high level right away. One practitioner wrote in his experience report, "Teacher,[5] I've reached many levels of heaven and seen some scenes." I told him to climb up further. He said, "I can't do it. I don't dare to climb any further, and I'm unable to climb any further." Why? It is because his gongzhu was only that high, and he had reached there by sitting atop his gongzhu. That is the Fruit Status in cultivation which Buddhism mentions, and his cultivation had reached that status. To a practitioner, however, it is still not the pinnacle of one's Fruit Status. One is still constantly moving up and constantly upgrading oneself. If your gongzhu reaches beyond the boundary of the Three Realms, aren't you beyond the Three Realms? We have investigated and found that the Three Realms mentioned in religions are only within the scope of our nine major planets.[6]

---

[5] Teacher—(also called Master) respectful way to address a teacher in China.

[6] the nine major planets in this solar system.

Some people speak of ten major planets. I would say that it is not true at all. I have found that some of those qigong masters in the past had very high gongzhu that reached beyond the Milky Way; they passed far beyond the Three Realms. Just now I spoke about transcending the Three Realms. It is actually an issue of levels.

The Issue of Pursuit

Many people come to our cultivation site with the attachment of pursuit. Some people want to attain supernormal capabilities; some want to listen to some theories; some want diseases cured; some also intend to procure Falun. There are all kinds of mentalities. Still, others say: "Someone in my family isn't here to attend the lecture. I'll pay some tuition, and please give him a Falun." It has taken us many generations, an extremely long period of time, and a frightening number of years to form this Falun. How could you buy a Falun with a few dozen *yuan*?[7] Why can we give it to all of you unconditionally? It is because you want to be practitioners. No sum of money can buy this heart. Only when your Buddha-nature emerges can we do it this way.

You are clinging to the attachment of pursuit. Do you come here just for this? My *fashen*[8] in another dimension knows everything on your mind. Because the concepts of the two time-spaces differ, in another dimension the formation of your thoughts is seen as an extremely slow process. It will know everything even before you think of it. Therefore, you should abandon all of your incorrect thoughts. The Buddha School believes in

---

[7] *yuan* (yu-en)—a unit of Chinese currency (approx. = USD$0.12).

[8] *fashen* (fah-shun)—"law body"; a body made of gong and Fa.

predestined relationship. Everyone comes here because of a predestined relationship. If you obtain it, perhaps you are supposed to have it. You should therefore treasure it and not be attached to any pursuit.

In religious cultivation practice of the past, the Buddha School required emptiness. One should not think about anything and enter the door of emptiness. The Tao School taught nothingness, as there is nothing. One should not want anything, nor should one pursue anything. A practitioner speaks of having the heart for practicing gong, but not attaining it intentionally. In cultivation and practice one should be in a state free of intention. As long as you focus on cultivating your xinxing, you will make breakthroughs in your level and certainly get things you deserve. If you cannot give something up, isn't it an attachment? All at once we have here taught such high-level Fa, and the requirement for your xinxing is, of course, also of a high standard. Therefore, one should not come to learn the Fa with the attachment of pursuit.

To be responsible to everyone, we lead you to the right path, and we must explain this Fa to you thoroughly. When someone pursues tianmu, it will be blocked by itself and be sealed off. In addition, I am telling everyone that all supernormal capabilities one develops in Shi-Jian-Fa cultivation practice are original, inborn capabilities of this flesh body. Nowadays we call them supernatural capabilities. They can only work in this dimension of ours and subdue everyday people. What do you go after these petty tricks for? You pursue this or that, but after going beyond Shi-Jian-Fa they do not work in other dimensions. By the time of Chu-Shi-Jian-Fa cultivation, all of these supernormal capabilities must be discarded and compressed into a very deep dimension for preservation. In the future, they will serve you as a record of

81

your cultivation practice, and they can only assume this little use.

After reaching Chu-Shi-Jian-Fa, one must start cultivation all over again. One's body is one that has transcended the Five Elements, as I just mentioned. It is a Buddha-body. Shouldn't that kind of body be called a Buddha-body? This Buddha-body must all over again practice cultivation from the start and also re-develop supernormal capabilities. Instead of being called "supernormal capabilities," they are now called "the divine powers of the Buddha Fa." They are boundlessly powerful and can act on different dimensions, being something really effective. What's the use of your pursuing supernormal capabilities? As for all those who go after supernormal capabilities, aren't you planning to use them and show them off among everyday people? Otherwise, why would you want them? They are invisible and intangible. Even for the purpose of decoration, one wants to find something that looks good. It is guaranteed that subconsciously you have the intention of using them. They cannot be pursued as ordinary human skills. They are something completely supernatural, and you are prohibited from showing them off among everyday people. Showing off itself is a very strong attachment and a very bad attachment that a practitioner must relinquish. If you want to make money and a fortune with them, or if you wish to achieve your personal goals among everyday people with them, these are prohibited. That is trying to use high-level things to disturb and undermine ordinary human society. That thought is even worse. Therefore, they are denied casual application.

Normally, supernormal capabilities are more likely to develop for two groups of people: children and the elderly. In particular, elderly women usually maintain good xinxing without many attachments among everyday people. After their supernormal capabilities develop, they can easily control themselves without the desire to show them off. Why is it difficult for young people to develop supernormal capabilities? In particular, a young man still wants to strive to accomplish some objectives in ordinary human society! Once he has supernormal capabilities, he will use them to achieve his goals. Using them as a means to realize his goals is absolutely forbidden, so he does not develop supernormal capabilities.

The issue of cultivation practice is not child's play, nor is it a technique of everyday people—it is a very serious matter. Whether you want to practice cultivation or are able to practice cultivation depends completely upon how your xinxing is upgraded. It would be terrible if someone could really attain supernormal capabilities through pursuing them. You would find that he does not care about cultivation or think about this issue at all. Because his xinxing is at the everyday people's level and his supernormal capabilities come through pursuit, he might commit every sort of wrongdoing. There is a lot of money in the bank, and he would remove some of it. There are many lottery ticket sales on the street, and he would get the first prize. Why haven't these things happened? Some qigong masters say: "Without being virtuous, one can easily do bad things after developing supernormal capabilities." I say this is a wrong statement—it is not the case at all. If you do not value virtues or do not cultivate your xinxing, you simply will not develop any supernormal capabilities. With good xinxing, some people develop supernormal capabilities at their levels. Later, they cannot handle themselves well and do things that they should not. This situation also exists. Once one does something bad, however, one's supernormal capabilities will be weakened or lost. Once they are gone, they are lost forever. Furthermore, the worst thing is that they make one develop attachments.

One qigong master claims that if a person studies his practice for three or five days, this person will be able to cure diseases. That is like an advertisement, and he should be called a qigong merchant. Think about it, everyone: Being an everyday person, how can you cure another person's illness by just emitting some of your qi? An everyday person's body also has qi inside, just as you do. You have just started the practice, and it is merely that your *laogong* point[9] is opened, so you can absorb and release qi. When you heal other people's illnesses, they also have qi in their bodies. Perhaps their qi will heal your diseases! How can one's qi dominate that of another person? Qi cannot heal illness at all. In addition, when you treat a patient, you and your patient form a field through which the patient's pathogenic qi will all come to your body. You have as much of it as your patient does, though it is rooted in the patient's body. Too much pathogenic qi can cause you to become ill as well. Once you think that you can cure diseases, you will begin the practice of seeing patients. You will not turn down requests and will develop an attachment. How delightful it is being able to heal others' diseases! Why can they be healed? Haven't you thought about it? Sham qigong masters all have futi on their bodies. In order to make you believe them, they give you some of their message which will be used up after you have healed three, five, eight, or ten patients. It consumes energy, and afterwards this bit of energy will no longer exist. You do not have your own gong, so where can you possibly get it? As qigong masters, we have practiced cultivation for several

---

[9] *laogong* (laow-gong) point—acupuncture point at the center of the palm.

dozen years. It was very hard to practice cultivation in the past. Practicing cultivation is very difficult if one takes a deviant path or a small road instead of following an orthodox way.

Although you may find that some grand qigong masters are well known, they have practiced cultivation for decades to develop that bit of gong. You have never practiced cultivation. How can you have gong after attending a qigong class? How is that possible? You will develop an attachment afterwards. Once an attachment develops, you will become anxious if you cannot cure an illness. In order to save one's reputation, what is on one's mind while treating illness? "Please let me have this illness so that the patient can be healed." That is not out of compassion, as one's attachments to fame and self-interest have not been given up at all. This person is unable to develop this compassion one bit. He is afraid of losing his reputation. He would rather have this illness himself in order to keep his reputation. What a strong attachment to fame! Once this wish is made, well, that illness will be transferred to his body at once—it will really happen. He will go home with the illness while the patient is healed. After seeing the patient, he will suffer at home. He thinks that he has cured an illness. When others call him a qigong master, he will become delighted and very pleased. Isn't that an attachment? When he cannot cure an illness, he drops his head and feels fizzled out. Isn't it caused by his attachment to fame and personal gain? In addition, all of the pathogenic qi from his patients will come to his body. Though those sham qigong masters have taught him how to remove it from his body, I am telling you that he cannot remove it at all, not even a bit, because he himself does not have the ability to distinguish bad qi from good qi. As time passes, his body will be all dark inside, and that is karma.

When you really want to practice cultivation, it is going to be quite an ordeal. What will you do about it? How much must you suffer to transform the karma into the white substance? It is very difficult. In particular, the better one's inborn quality, the easier to encounter this issue. Some people always seek to treat illness. If you have a pursuit, an animal will see it and come to possess you. This is futi. Don't you want to treat illness? It will help you do this. But, it does not help you treat illness without a reason. No loss, no gain. It is very dangerous, and you will end up inviting it. How can you continue your cultivation practice? It will all be over.

Some people with good inborn quality exchange their inborn quality with others for karma. That person is ill and has a lot of karma. If you heal a patient who has a serious illness, after the treatment you will feel very uncomfortable at home. In the past, many people felt this way after seeing a patient: The patient is recovering, but you are very ill at home. As time passes, more karma transfers to you; you give others de for karma. No loss, no gain. Though what you get is illness, karma must be paid for with de. This universe has this principle that no one will stop you as long as this is what you want, nor will anyone say that you are good. The universe has a specific rule, namely, whoever has more karma is a bad person. You are giving away your inborn quality to another person for karma. With more karma, how could you practice cultivation? Your inborn quality will be totally ruined by that person. Isn't that scary? That person's illness is gone; he feels comfortable now, but you are suffering at home. If you heal a couple of cancer patients, you will have to take their places. Isn't this dangerous? That is just the way it is, and many people do not know the truth.

Do not be taken in by how reputable some sham qigong masters are. A well-known person does not necessarily know things well. What do everyday people know? Once things are hyped up, they accept them. Though you find them doing those things now, they are not only harming others, but also themselves. In one or two years you will see what happens to them. Cultivation practice cannot be undermined in this way. Cultivation practice can treat illness, but it is not to be used for the purpose of healing illness. It is something supernormal instead of an everyday person's technique. Your casually ruining it is absolutely forbidden. Nowadays some sham qigong masters have made things chaotic, and use qigong as a means of securing fame or fortune. They are cults expanding their evil influence, and they outnumber those genuine qigong masters many times. Everyday people all say things and do things this way, and you just believe them? You may think qigong is just like that, but it is not. What I am saying is the genuine principle.

When different social interactions unfold among everyday people, one will commit wrongdoings for personal gain and owe others. One must undergo suffering to repay debts. Suppose that you treat an illness at will. How can you be allowed to really cure an illness? Buddhas are everywhere. With so many of them, why don't they do such a thing? How wonderful it would be if a Buddha made all of humankind comfortable! Why doesn't he? One must repay one's own karma, and no one dares to violate this principle. During the course of cultivation practice, a practitioner may occasionally help another person out of compassion; however, that will only postpone the illness. If you do not suffer now, you will suffer later. Also, one might transform it so that you will lose money or have a tribulation instead of becoming ill. It might be like this. Truly eliminating a person's karma all at once can only be done for practitioners, and not for everyday people. I am not teaching the principles of my practice alone here. I am addressing the principles of the entire universe, and I am discussing the actual facts in the community of cultivators.

Here, we do not teach you to treat illness. We are leading you to the Great Way, the orthodox way, and we are uplifting you. Thus, in my lectures I will always say that practitioners of Falun Dafa are not allowed to treat illness. If you treat illness, you are not a practitioner of Falun Dafa. Because we are leading you to the righteous way, during Shi-Jian-Fa cultivation practice your body will be purified constantly until it is completely transformed by high-energy matter. How can you practice cultivation if you still collect those dark things in your body? Those things are karma! You will be unable to practice cultivation at all. With too much karma, you will be unable to bear it. If you suffer too much, you will be unable to practice cultivation. This is the reason. I have made public this Dafa, and you may still not know what I have taught. Since this Dafa can be made public, there are ways to protect it. If you treat illness for others, my fashen will take back everything given to your body for cultivation. We cannot allow you to casually ruin something so precious over fame and self-interest. If you do not follow the requirements of the Fa, you are not a practitioner of Falun Dafa. Because you want to be an everyday person, your body will be reset to the level of everyday people and the bad things will be returned to you.

After the lecture yesterday, many of you felt that your entire body was light. Nonetheless, the very few people with serious illnesses went ahead and began to feel uncomfortable yesterday.

After I removed the bad things from your body yesterday, most of you felt that your whole body was light and very comfortable. Nevertheless, our universe has this principle of "no loss, no gain." We cannot remove everything for you. It is absolutely prohibited for you to not endure some suffering. That is, we have removed the fundamental causes of your illnesses and your poor health. But, you still have a field of illness. A person whose tianmu opens at a very low level can see in your body clusters of black qi and turbid pathogenic qi, which is also a condensed cluster of black qi in high density. Once it diffuses, it will spread all over your body.

From today on, some people will feel chilly all over their bodies as though they suffer a heavy cold, and their bones may ache as well. Most of you will feel uncomfortable somewhere. Your legs may ache and your head may feel dizzy. The ill part of your body, which you thought was healed before through qigong exercises or by a qigong master, will again have illness. This is because that qigong master did not cure the illness for you—he only postponed it. It was still there and would recur later if not at that time. We must dig it out and eliminate it completely from its root. With this, you may feel that your illnesses have recurred. This is to remove your karma fundamentally. Thus, you will have reactions. Some people may have physical reactions somewhere. Some may feel uncomfortable in one way or another as different kinds of discomfort will manifest. These are all normal. I am telling everyone that no matter how uncomfortable you are, you must continue to attend this class. Once you walk into the classroom, all of your symptoms will vanish and there will not be any danger. There is one point to make to everyone: No matter how much you suffer from the "illness," I hope that you will continue to come, because it is difficult to obtain the Fa. When you feel very uncomfortable, it indicates that things will turn around after reaching the extreme point. Your whole body will be purified and it must be completely purified. The cause of your illness has been removed, and what remains is only this bit of black qi that will come out on its own to let you suffer some and have some pain. It is forbidden for you not to suffer even a little bit.

In ordinary human society, you compete with others for fame and personal gain. You cannot sleep or eat well, and your body is in very bad shape. When your body is seen from another dimension, the bones are all black. With this body, it is impossible for you to not have any reaction when it is purified all at once. Thus, you will have reactions. Some people will throw up and have loose bowels. Many practitioners from different places have raised this issue previously in their experience reports, "Teacher, after attending your class I was looking for a toilet all the way home." This is because all your internal organs must be purified. A few individuals may fall asleep and wake up as soon as I finish my lecture. Why is that? It is because their brains have illnesses that need to be treated. One will be unable to stand it if one's brain is worked on. Therefore, one must be put into a state of anesthesia or become unconscious. Nevertheless, some people do not have a problem hearing me. Though they may sleep soundly, they heard everything without missing a single word. They will become energetic afterwards, and will not feel sleepy even if they go two days without sleep. There are different syndromes which all need adjustment. Your entire body will be purified.

If you are a true practitioner of Falun Dafa, and when you can give up your attachments, each of you will have reactions from this point on. Those who cannot give up their attachments may claim that they have released them, but in fact they have not given them up. It is thus very difficult to achieve. There are also people who later understand the content of my lectures. They begin to let go of their attachments and their bodies are purified. While others' bodies all feel light, these people just begin to heal their illnesses and feel uncomfortable. In every class there are such people who lag behind with poorer enlightenment quality. Therefore, it is all normal no matter what you encounter. This situation always occurred when I held classes in other places. Some people were in great discomfort and would not move in their seats, waiting for me to step down from the podium to treat them. I would not do it. If you cannot even pass this test, how can you still practice cultivation in the future when you encounter many big tribulations? Can't you overcome such a petty tribulation? Everyone can make it. Therefore, nobody should come to me for healing illness, nor will I treat illness. Once you bring up the word "illness," I am unwilling to listen.

Human beings are very difficult to save. There are always about five or ten percent of the people in each class who cannot keep up with the others. It is impossible for everyone to attain the Tao. Even for those who can continue their cultivation practice, it remains to be seen whether you can succeed and if you are determined to practice cultivation. It is impossible for everyone to become a Buddha. True Dafa practitioners will undergo the same experiences by reading this book, and they will be able to obtain whatever they deserve all the same.

LECTURE THREE

I Treat All Practitioners as My Disciples

Does everyone know what I'm doing? I treat all practitioners, including those who are able to truly practice cultivation through self-study, as my disciples. In teaching gong at the high level, it will not work if I do not treat you this way. Otherwise, it is the same as being irresponsible and causing trouble. We have given you so many things and let you know so many principles that should not be known by everyday people. Besides providing you with many other things, I have taught you this Dafa. Among some other issues involved, your body has been purified. Accordingly, it is simply unacceptable for me to not treat you as disciples. Casually disclosing so many heavenly secrets to everyday people is not allowed. But, there is one point to be made. Now, times have changed. We do not practice the ritual of kowtowing or bowing. That kind of formality serves little use, and it performs like a religion. We do not practice it. What's the use of your kowtowing and worshipping Teacher if once you step out this door, you still continue to conduct yourself as usual and do whatever you want, competing and fighting for your fame and self-interest among everyday people? You may also damage the reputation of Falun Dafa under my banner!

True cultivation practice depends fully upon your heart. As long as you practice cultivation and are sure-footed as well as determined in practicing cultivation, we shall treat you as disciples. It is unfeasible for me not to treat you this way. Yet, there are some people who might not truly regard themselves as practitioners and not continue cultivation practice. For some people it is impossible. But many people will truly go on practicing cultivation. As long as you keep it up, we shall treat you as disciples.

Can you be considered a Falun Dafa disciple if you just practice these few sets of exercises everyday? Not necessarily. This is because true cultivation practice must follow the requirements of the xinxing standard that we have established, and you have to truly upgrade your xinxing—then, it is true cultivation practice. If you only practice the exercises without improving xinxing and without the powerful energy that strengthens everything, it cannot be called cultivation practice; nor can we treat you as Falun Dafa disciples. If you go on like that without following the requirements of our Falun Dafa and behave yourself as usual among everyday people without upgrading your xinxing, you may still run into some other troubles though you practice the exercises. You may even claim that it is the practice of Falun Dafa that makes you go astray. This is all possible. Therefore, you must truly follow our xinxing requirements—only then are you a genuine practitioner. I have made it clear to everyone. Accordingly, please do not come to me for the formality of worshipping the master. As long as you truly practice cultivation, I shall treat you this way. My fashen are so many that they are innumerable. Besides these practitioners, no matter how many more people there are, I am still able to take care of them.

The Buddha School Qigong and Buddhism

The Buddha School qigong is not the Buddhist religion. I must make this point clear to everyone. In fact, the Tao School qigong is not the Taoist religion, either. Some of you are always confused by these things. Some people are monks from temples, and some are lay Buddhists. They think that they know a little more about Buddhist religion, so they enthusiastically promote Buddhism among our practitioners. Let me tell you that you should not do such a thing because it is something from a different cultivation school. Religion has religious forms. Here we are teaching the cultivation part of our school. Except for those monks and nuns who are Falun Dafa disciples, everyone else should not observe religious forms. Therefore, our school is not Buddhism in the Dharma-ending Period.

The Dharma in Buddhism is only a tiny part of the Buddha Fa. There are still many kinds of great high-level Fa. Different levels also have different Fa. Sakyamuni said that there were eighty-four thousand cultivation ways. The Buddhist religion includes only a few cultivation ways. It only has Tiantai, Huayan, Zen Buddhism, Pure Land, Tantrism, etc. They do not even account for a small number! Therefore, Buddhism cannot represent the entire Buddha Fa, and it is only a tiny part of the Buddha Fa. Our Falun Dafa is also one of the eighty-four thousand cultivation ways in the Buddha School, and it has nothing to do with the original Buddhism or Buddhism in the Dharma-ending Period; nor is it related to modern religions.

Buddhism was founded by Sakyamuni in ancient India twenty-five hundred years ago. When Sakyamuni became kaigong and enlightened, he recalled what he had cultivated previously and made it public to save people. No matter how many thousands of volumes of scriptures have come out of that school, it actually consists of only three words. The characteristics of this school are: "precept, samadhi,[1] wisdom." Precepts are for giving up all everyday people's desires and forcing you to abandon the pursuit of self-interest, cutting off everything that is secular, and so on. In this way, one's mind will be empty without thought of anything, and it can become tranquil. They complement each other. Upon being able to achieve tranquility, one can sit in meditation for actual cultivation and rely on trance to make progress in cultivation. This is the part of genuine cultivation practice in that school. It does not care for exercises, nor does it change one's *benti*.[2] A person only cultivates that gong which determines the height of his level. Therefore, he only cultivates his xinxing. He does not cultivate his body, so he does not care for the transformation of gong. Meanwhile, through meditation he strengthens his ability for staying in trance, and sits in meditation to suffer and eliminate karma. "Wisdom" refers to that one becomes enlightened with great wisdom, and one can see the truth of the universe as well as the truth of different dimensions in the universe. All the divine powers emerge. The awakening to wisdom and enlightenment is also called kaigong.

When Sakyamuni founded this cultivation way, there were eight religions prevailing in India at the same time. There was a deeply-rooted religion called Brahmanism. Throughout his lifetime, Sakyamuni battled ideologically with other religions. Because what Sakyamuni taught was an orthodox Fa, the Buddhist Dharma that he taught became more and more popular in the course of teaching while other religions increasingly weakened. Even the deeply-rooted Brahmanism was on the brink of

---

[1] Samadhi—in Buddhism, "meditation in trance."

[2] *benti* (bun-tee)—one's physical body and the bodies in other dimensions.

extinction. After Sakyamuni's nirvana,[3] however, other religions, especially Brahmanism, regained popularity. Yet, what situation emerged in Buddhism? Some monks became kaigong and enlightened at different levels, but their levels of enlightenment were quite low. Sakyamuni reached the level of Tathagata, but a lot of monks did not reach this level.

The Buddha Fa has different manifestations at different levels. However, the higher the level, the closer it is to the truth. The lower the level, the further away from the truth. Those monks became kaigong and enlightened at low levels. To interpret what Sakyamuni said, they used the manifestation of the universe that they saw at their levels and the situations and principles that they understood. That is, some monks interpreted Sakyamuni's Dharma one way or another. Instead of using Sakyamuni's original words, some monks also preached what they understood as Sakyamuni's words; this made the Buddhist Dharma distorted beyond recognition, and it was no longer the Dharma taught by Sakyamuni. In the end, this caused the Buddhist Dharma to disappear in India. This is a serious lesson in history. So later on, India no longer had Buddhism. Prior to its disappearance, Buddhism went through many reforms. It eventually incorporated something from Brahmanism and became the present-day Indian religion called Hinduism. It no longer worships any Buddha. It worships something else, and does not believe in Sakyamuni. This is the situation.

During its development, Buddhism underwent several relatively major reforms. One took place shortly after Sakyamuni

---

[3] nirvana—(from Sanskrit) departing the human world without this physical body, the method of completing cultivation in Buddha Sakyamuni's School.

passed away. Some people founded Mahayana[4] based on the high-level principles Sakyamuni taught. They believed that the Dharma Sakyamuni taught publicly was intended for everyday people's self-salvation and the attainment of Arhatship. That Dharma did not offer salvation to all beings and was therefore called Hinayana.[5] Monks in Southeast Asia continue to follow the original cultivation way of Sakyamuni's time. In China, we call it the "Small Vehicle" Buddhism. Of course, they do not think so themselves. They believe that they have inherited Sakyamuni's original tradition. It is indeed so, as they have basically inherited the cultivation way of Sakyamuni's time.

After this reformed Mahayana was introduced to China, it took root in our country and became the present-day Buddhism taught in China. Actually, it has assumed a completely different look from Buddhism in Sakyamuni's time. Everything has changed, from the attire to the entire enlightening state and the entire course of cultivation practice. In original Buddhism, only Sakyamuni was worshipped as its founder. Now, however, Buddhism has many Buddhas and great Bodhisattvas. In addition, faith is now dedicated to many Buddhas. Many Tathagatas are worshipped, and Buddhism has become a religion that worships many Buddhas, including Buddha Amitabha, Medicine Buddha, the Great Sun Tathagata, etc. There are many great Bodhisattvas as well. In this way, all of Buddhism has become totally different from what Sakyamuni founded in his time.

During this time period, another reform took place when Bodhisattva Nagarjuna taught a secret cultivation practice. It came from India and was introduced to China through Afghanistan and,

---

[4] Mahayana—"the Great Vehicle Buddhism."
[5] Hinayana—"the Small Vehicle Buddhism."

later, Xinjiang.[6] It happened in the Tang Dynasty,[7] so it was called Tang Tantrism. Due to the influence of Confucianism, China's moral values were different from those of other nationalities in general. This secret practice contained double cultivation of a man and a woman, and society could not accept it at that time. It was therefore wiped out when Buddhism was suppressed during Huichang's time in the Tang Dynasty, and so Tang Tantrism disappeared from China. Now, there is an Eastern Tantrism in Japan that came from China at that time; however, it did not undergo *guanding*.[8] According to Tantrism, if one studies Tantrism without guanding, one is considered to be doing the same as stealing the Dharma, and one cannot be recognized as having been taught in person. Another cultivation way, introduced to Tibet from India and Nepal, was called "Tibetan Tantrism," and it has been passed down to this day. Basically, this is the situation in Buddhism. I have just summarized very briefly the course of its development and evolution. Over the course of Buddhism's entire development, some practices surfaced such as Zen Buddhism founded by Boddhidarma, Pure Land Buddhism, and Huayan Buddhism. They were all founded upon some understanding of what Sakyamuni said at that time. All of these belong to the reformed Buddhism. There are over ten such cultivation ways in Buddhism, and all have assumed the form of religion. Therefore, they all belong to Buddhism.

As for the religions founded in this century, or not just this century but also the many new religions founded in different parts

---

[6] Xinjiang (sheen-jyang)—a province in Northwestern China.

[7] Tang (tahng) Dynasty—one of the most prosperous periods in Chinese history (618 A.D.-907 A.D.).

[8] *guanding* (gwan-ding)—pouring energy into the top of one's head; initiation ritual.

of the world in last several centuries, most of these are sham. To save human beings, the great enlightened people all have their own paradises. These Tathagata Buddhas such as Sakyamuni, Buddha Amitabha, and the Great Sun Tathagata each have their own paradises for saving people. In our Milky Way, there are over one hundred such paradises. Our Falun Dafa also has a Falun Paradise.

In terms of salvation, where can those sham practices take their followers? They cannot save people, as what they preach is not Fa. Of course, some people, when they first founded religions, did not intend to become the demons who undermine orthodox religions. They became kaigong and enlightened at different levels. They saw some principles, but they were far from the enlightened beings who can save people. They were at very low levels, and they discovered some principles. They realized that some things among everyday people were wrong, and they would also tell people how to do good deeds. At the beginning, they were not against other religions. People worshipped them in the end, believing what they said to be sensible; in turn, people trusted them more and more. As a result, people worshipped them instead of religions. Upon developing an attachment to fame and self-interest, they would ask the public to honor them with some titles. After that, they would found new religions. I am telling you that all of these are evil religions. Even if they do not harm people, they are still evil practices because they have interfered with people's faith in orthodox religions. Orthodox religions can save people, but they cannot. As time passes, they do bad deeds on the sly. Recently, many of these things have also been introduced to China. The so-called Guanyin sect[9] is one of them. Therefore, be

_____
[9] Guanyin (gwan-yeen) sect—a cult named after Bodhisattva Avalokitesvara, the "Goddess of Mercy."

on your guard. It is said that there are over two thousand practices in a certain East Asian country. All kinds of beliefs exist in Southeast Asian countries and in other Western countries. One country openly has a devil-worshipping practice. All of these things are demons that have come forth in the Dharma-ending Period. The Dharma-ending Period does not only pertain to Buddhism, but also the corruption of many dimensions beneath a very high-level dimension. "Dharma-ending" does not only refer to that in Buddhism; it also means that in human society there are no spiritual obligations to maintain morality.

Practicing Only One Cultivation Way

We teach that a person must practice only one cultivation way. No matter how you practice cultivation, you should not mess up your cultivation by adding other things. Some lay Buddhists practice both Buddhism and our Falun Dafa. I am telling you that in the end you will not obtain anything because no one will give you anything. Because we are all of the Buddha School, there is a xinxing issue and, at the same time, an issue of specializing in only one practice. You only have one body. Which school's cultivation energy will your body develop? How can it be transformed? Where do you want to go? You will go wherever your cultivation way takes you. If you follow Pure Land Buddhism in cultivation, you are going to Buddha Amitabha's Paradise of Ultimate Bliss. If you follow Medicine Buddha in cultivation, you are going to the Glazed Paradise. This is what is said in religion, and it is called "no second cultivation way."

The practice that we address here truly refers to the entire process of energy transformation, and this follows one's own

100

school of cultivation practice. Where, then, would you say you want to go? If you step on two boats at the same time, you cannot attain anything. Not only qigong practice cannot be mixed with Buddhist practices in temples, but even things from among cultivation practices, qigong practices, or religions cannot be incorporated. In cultivation, even within the same religion, several denominations cannot be intermingled. One must choose only one cultivation way. If you cultivate Pure Land Buddhism, you should cultivate only Pure Land Buddhism. If you cultivate Tantrism, you should only cultivate Tantrism. If you cultivate Zen Buddhism, you should only cultivate Zen Buddhism. If you step on two boats at the same time and cultivate both this and that, you cannot attain anything. That is to say, even in Buddhism you are required to not practice another system, and you are not permitted to mix cultivation practices. A Buddhist is also practicing gong and cultivation. His or her process of transforming gong follows the process of cultivation practice and transformation in that cultivation way. There is also in other dimensions a process of evolving gong, and this is an extremely complex and intricate process that cannot be mixed casually with other things in cultivation.

Upon learning that we practice qigong from the Buddha School, some lay Buddhists take our practitioners to temples for conversion. Let me tell each of you sitting here that no one should do such a thing. You are undermining both our Dafa and the ordinances in Buddhism. At the same time, you are interfering with practitioners, rendering them unable to attain anything. This is not allowed. Cultivation practice is a serious matter. One must be single-minded in one practice. Though this portion that we teach among everyday people is not religion, its goal in cultivation practice is the same. Both try to achieve kaigong, enlightenment, and completion in cultivation.

Sakyamuni stated that by the Dharma-ending time monks in temples would have a difficult time saving themselves, let alone those lay Buddhists who are being looked after by no one. Though you have a "master," that so-called master is also a practitioner. If the master does not truly practice cultivation, it is useless. Without cultivating the heart, no one can make it. Conversion is a formality of everyday people. Are you a member of the Buddha School after conversion? Will Buddha then take care of you? There is no such thing. Even if you kowtow everyday until your head bleeds, or even if you burn bundles of incense, it is still useless. You must truly cultivate your heart to make it work. By the Dharma-ending time, the universe has gone through very big changes. Even religion's places of worship are no longer good. Those with supernormal capabilities (including monks) have also discovered this situation. At present, I am the only person in the world teaching orthodox Fa in public. I have done something unprecedented. I have furthermore opened this door so widely in the Dharma-ending time. In fact, this opportunity does not come along in one thousand years or ten thousand years. But, whether one can be saved—in other words, whether one can practice cultivation—still depends upon oneself. What I am telling you is a principle of the enormous universe.

I am not saying that you have to study my Falun Dafa. What I said is a principle. If you want to practice cultivation, you must practice only one cultivation way. Otherwise, you cannot practice cultivation at all. Of course, if you do not want to practice cultivation, we will leave you alone. This Fa is taught only to those genuine practitioners. Therefore, one must be single-minded in only one practice, and even ideas from other practices should not be intermingled. I do not teach mind activities here; there is no mind activity in our Falun Dafa. Thus, no one should add to it any thought. Be sure to keep this in mind: There is virtually no mind activity. The Buddha School requires emptiness, and the Tao School teaches nothingness.

On one occasion I had my mind connected with four or five great enlightened people and great Taos from extremely high levels. Speaking of high levels, their levels were so high that everyday people would find it simply inconceivable. They wanted to know what was on my mind. I have practiced cultivation for so many years. It is absolutely impossible for other people to read my mind, and other people's supernormal capabilities cannot reach me at all. Nobody is able to understand me or know what is on my mind. They wished to know what I was thinking. With my consent, therefore, they linked my mind with theirs for a period of time. After the connection, it was a little unbearable for me because no matter how high or how low my level is, I am among everyday people and still doing something purposeful—that is, saving people—and my heart is devoted to saving people. But how peaceful were their minds? Their minds were tranquil to the point of being scary. It is possible for one person to reach this tranquility. But with four or five people sitting over there with tranquility like that, it resembles a pond of still water with nothing in it. I tried in vain to experience them. For those several days, I really felt mentally very uncomfortable and experienced a unique feeling. It was something beyond the imagination and awareness of everyday people. It was completely free of attachment and empty.

There is no mind activity whatsoever for cultivation at very high levels. This is because while you were at the foundation building level of everyday people, that foundational system was already laid. After reaching high-level cultivation, our cultivation system in particular works automatically, and cultivation practice is completely automatic. As long as you upgrade your xinxing, your gong grows. You do not even have to do any exercises. Our exercises are for reinforcing the automatic mechanism. Why does one sit still in meditation? One is completely in a state of wuwei. You may find that the Tao School teaches this exercise or that exercise, the so-called mind activities, or the guidance by the mind. Let me tell you that as soon as the Tao School reaches beyond the level of qi, it will have nothing and use neither this nor that mind activity. Therefore, some people who have practiced other qigong can never give up breathing methods, mind activities, and so on. I am teaching them something from college, and they always ask me about an elementary school pupil's things, such as how to guide and use mind activities. They are already accustomed to that approach. They think that qigong is like that when, in fact, it is not.

Supernormal Capabilities and Energy Potency

Many of you are not clear about the terminology in qigong, and some people are also routinely confused by it. They take supernormal capabilities as energy potency, or vice versa. The gong that we attain through cultivating xinxing and assimilating to the characteristic of the universe evolves from our de. It determines the height of one's level, the strength of one's energy potency, and the Fruit Status of one's cultivation. This is the most crucial gong. During the course of cultivation, what situations will emerge for a person? One can develop some unusual and supernatural capabilities that, in short, we call supernormal capabilities. The gong that improves one's level is, as I just mentioned, called energy potency. The higher one's level, the greater one's energy potency and the more powerful one's supernormal capabilities.

Supernormal capabilities are only by-products of one's cultivation process; they do not represent the level or the height of one's level, nor the power of one's energy potency. Some people develop more of them while others develop fewer. Furthermore, supernormal capabilities are not something that can be pursued as the main objective of cultivation. Only when one is determined to truly practice cultivation can one develop them; however, they cannot be treated as the main objective of cultivation. What do you cultivate them for? Do you want to use them among everyday people? You are absolutely prohibited from using them at will among everyday people. Thus, the more you pursue them, the less you get. It is because you are pursuing something. Pursuit itself is an attachment. In cultivation practice, attachments are what need to be eliminated.

Many people have, without supernormal capabilities, reached a very high realm of cultivation. The master has locked those up in case they cannot handle themselves well and will commit wrongdoings. Therefore, they are not allowed to use their supernatural capabilities. There are quite a lot of people like that. Supernormal capabilities are directed by one's mind. One might not be able to control oneself during sleep. With a single dream one might turn the heaven and the earth upside down by the next morning, and that is not allowed. Because cultivation practice takes place among everyday people, those with great supernormal capabilities are usually not allowed to use them. Most of them are locked up, but it is not absolute. There are many people who

105

practice cultivation very well and can conduct themselves well. They are allowed to have some supernormal capabilities. Regarding these people, even if you ask them to casually show off their supernormal capabilities, they absolutely will not do it; they are able to control themselves.

Reverse Cultivation and Energy Borrowing

Some people have never practiced qigong, or they may have learned a few things in a qigong class. But those are for healing illnesses and keeping fit, and they are not cultivation practice. In other words, these people have never received genuine teaching, yet they suddenly get gong overnight. We shall talk about where this kind of gong comes from. There are several types.

One belongs to reverse cultivation. What is reverse cultivation? Some people are relatively old and want to practice cultivation. It is too late for them to practice cultivation from scratch. When qigong was at its peak of popularity, they also wanted to practice cultivation. They knew that qigong practice could do good things for other people, and that they could also upgrade themselves at the same time. They had this wish and wanted to improve and practice cultivation. However, when qigong was popular a few years ago, those qigong masters were all promoting qigong, and nobody actually taught things at the high level. Even to this day, when it comes to truly teaching qigong publicly at the high level, I am the only person doing so. There is no second person doing this. All of the people in reverse cultivation were over fifty and at a relatively old age. They had very good in-born quality and carried in their bodies very good things. Almost all of them were good enough to be disciples or successors of those masters. Yet, these people were quite elderly. If they wanted to practice cultivation, it would be easier said than done. Where could they find a master? But as soon as they wanted to practice cultivation and with this thought in their hearts, it would shine like gold and shake the world of ten directions. People often speak of the Buddha-nature, and this would be the Buddha-nature that had emerged.

From the high-level perspective, one's life is not meant to be a human being. Because one's life is created in the space of the universe, it is assimilated to Zhen-Shan-Ren, the characteristic of the universe. Its nature is kind and benevolent. Nonetheless, after the number of lives increases, a social relationship forms. As a result, some people become selfish or bad and cannot stay at very high levels. They must drop to a lower level where they again become bad, and they have to drop further down to the next level. This goes on until in the end they drop to this ordinary human level. Upon dropping to this level, they should be completely destroyed. Out of benevolence and compassion, however, those great enlightened people decided to give humankind another opportunity in the most painful environment; they thus created such a dimension.

In other dimensions, people do not have bodies like this. They can levitate and become large or small. But in this dimension people are provided with this kind of body, our flesh bodies. With this body, one cannot put up with it if the body is cold, hot, tired, or hungry. In any case, it is suffering. When you are ill, you suffer. One has to go through birth, old age, illness, and death so that one can repay karmic debts through suffering. You are given another opportunity to see whether you can return to the origin. Therefore, human beings have dropped into a maze. After you come down here, this pair of eyes are created for you so that you cannot see other dimensions and the truth of matter. If you can return to the origin, the bitterest suffering is also most precious. In order to return to one's origin by practicing cultivation in the maze and through awakening to things, there are numerous tribulations; one can thus make it quickly. If you become worse your life will be eliminated. Therefore, in the eyes of other lives, one's life is not for being human. It is meant to return to one's original, true self. An everyday person cannot realize this. An everyday person is just an ordinary person in ordinary human society, a person who thinks about how to advance himself and live well. The better he lives, the more selfish he becomes; the more he wants to possess, the further away he moves from the characteristic of the universe. He then heads for destruction.

Seen from a high level, while you may think you are advancing forward, you are actually moving backward. Humankind thinks that it is developing science and making progress; it is, in fact, only following the law of the universe. Zhang Guolao, one of the Eight Deities,[10] rode backward on his donkey. Few people know why he rode backward on his donkey. He discovered that going forward is moving backward, so he rode the donkey the other way around. Therefore, once people want to practice cultivation, the great enlightened people will value this heart very much and will extend help unconditionally. It is just like the practitioners sitting here today. If you want to practice cultivation, I can help you unconditionally. Yet, it cannot be done if you want to cure illnesses and go after either this or that as an ordinary person, and I will be unable to help you. Why is that? It is because you want to be an everyday person, and everyday people should go through birth, old age, illness, and

[10] the Eight Deities—well-known Taos in Chinese history.

108

death—it should be like that. Everything has its karmic relationship that cannot be interfered with. Your life initially did not include cultivation practice, but now you want to practice cultivation. Accordingly, your future life must be rearranged, and so it is permitted to adjust your body for you.

Once a person wants to practice cultivation and this wish is developed, the great enlightened people will see it and consider it very precious. But how can they help him? Where in the world can he find a master? In addition, he is over fifty years old. The great enlightened people cannot teach this person. It is because if they were to manifest themselves and teach him Fa as well as exercises, it would be disclosing heavenly secrets; they would have to drop down themselves. People drop into the maze because they have committed wrongdoings, and so they must practice cultivation by becoming enlightened in the maze. Therefore, the great enlightened people cannot teach him. If a Buddha shows up in real life before people's eyes and teaches them both Fa and the exercises, even those with unforgivable sins will come to learn. Everyone will believe it. Then, what's there for people to be enlightened to? There will not be an issue of enlightenment. Because people have dropped into the maze on their own, they should be eliminated. You are given another opportunity to return from the maze to your origin. If you are able to return to the origin, you will make it. If you cannot make it, you will continue the cycle of samsara or be eliminated.

One makes one's own path. What happens if a person wants to practice cultivation? They have figured out a way. Qigong was very popular at that time, and that was also a change in the cosmic climate. In order to cooperate with this cosmic climate, the enlightened people would supply gong to this person via a soft tube on the merit of her xinxing level. Like a water faucet, the energy would come if it was turned on. If the person wanted to release gong, the gong would come. She herself could not emit gong, as she did not possess gong of her own. It was just like that. This is called "reverse cultivation" and one completes one's cultivation from the high level backward to the low level.

We normally practice cultivation from the low level to the high level up until kaigong or completion of cultivation. This reverse cultivation was for those elderly people who did not have enough time to practice cultivation from the low level to the high level. Therefore, it would be quicker if they practiced from the high level to the low level. This was also a phenomenon created at that time. Such a person has to have very high-level xinxing, and she was given the energy on the merit of her xinxing level. What were the purposes? One was to cooperate with the cosmic climate at that time. When this person was doing a good deed, she could suffer tribulations at the same time. This is because amidst everyday people different ordinary human attachments could interfere with her. When she cured a patient's illness, the patient might not appreciate it. When she treated the patient, she might have removed a lot of bad things from this patient's body. Although she healed this patient to such an extent, there might not have been any obvious changes at that time. The patient, however, would not be happy in his mind. Instead of expressing gratitude, he might accuse her of cheating. With these problems, she was undergoing psychological tribulations in this environment. The purpose of giving her energy was to enable her to practice cultivation and upgrade herself. While doing good deeds, she could develop her own supernormal capabilities and build up her own cultivation energy; however, some people did not know this principle. Didn't I mention that no one could teach this person the Fa? If the person could understand it, she would get it. It is an issue of enlightening. If the person could not understand it, nothing could be done.

When some people received the energy, they would one night suddenly feel very warm during sleep and could hardly use their bedcovers. After they got up the next morning, they would get an electric shock wherever they put their hands. They knew that they had obtained energy. If someone had pain somewhere in the body, they could take care of the problem with their hands, and it worked quite well. From then on they knew that they had energy. They became qigong masters and hung up signs. They labeled themselves qigong masters and established their practices. At the beginning, this person was very good. When she cured illnesses for other people, they would give her money or some gifts—all of which she might turn down or refuse to accept. Yet, this person could not resist contamination from the big dye vat of everyday people. Because these reverse cultivation people had never gone through genuine xinxing cultivation, it was very difficult for them to conduct their xinxing well. Gradually, this person would accept small gifts. Later, she would also accept big gifts. In the end, she would even be offended when the gifts were few. Finally, she would say, "Why do you give me so many things? Give me money!" She would not be pleased if given too little money. Getting an earful of other people's flattery about how capable she was, she would also not respect qigong masters from orthodox schools. If someone said something bad about her, she would be upset. This person's attachments to fame and self-interest were all developed. She considered herself better than others and extraordinary. She mistakenly thought that she was given the energy to become a qigong master and make a big fortune, while in fact it was for her to practice cultivation. Once the attachments to fame and profit were developed, this person's xinxing level had actually dropped.

I have stated that one's gong level is as high as one's xinxing level. When one's xinxing level drops, one is also not supplied with so much energy because it must be given according to the xinxing level. The gong level is as high as the xinxing level. The more one is attached to fame and self-interest, the lower the level one will drop to among everyday people. One's energy will also consequently decrease. In the end, when one has completely dropped to the bottom, one will no longer be given the energy. This person will have no energy. A few years ago there were quite a few such people, and comparatively more were women over fifty years old. Though you might see an elderly woman practicing qigong, she had never received any real teaching. She might have learned in a qigong class a few movements for healing and fitness. One day, she suddenly had energy. Once her xinxing became poor or if her attachments to fame and self-interest were developed, her level would drop. She would end up being nobody now, and her energy disappeared as well. Nowadays, there are a lot of these reverse cultivation people whose levels have dropped. Only a few of them are still around. Why? She did not know that it was provided for her to practice cultivation, and she wrongly thought that it was for her to make a fortune, earn fame, and become a qigong master. Actually, it was for her to practice cultivation.

What is "energy borrowing?" It has no age limit, but there is one requirement: One must have very good xinxing. This person knows that qigong can enable one to practice cultivation, and he also wants to practice cultivation. He has the heart for cultivation practice, but where can he find a master? A few years ago, there were indeed true qigong masters teaching qigong. What they taught, however, was something completely for healing and fitness. Nobody taught high-level qigong, nor would they do this.

Speaking of energy borrowing, I will bring up another issue. In addition to *zhu yuanshen*[11] (*zhu yishi*),[12] one also has *fu yuanshen*[13] (*fu yishi*).[14] Some people have one, two, three, four, or five fu yuanshen. The gender of one's fu yuanshen may not be the same as that of the person. Some are male and some are female. They are all different. In fact, the gender of zhu yuanshen also is not necessarily the same as that of the physical body, because we have found that at present many men have female yuanshen, while many women have male yuanshen. This agrees exactly with the cosmic climate as the Tao School describes it, for the *yin* and the *yang*[15] are reversed, with yin in prosperity and yang in decline.

One's fu yuanshen normally comes from a higher level than one's zhu yuanshen. Especially for some people, their fu yuanshen comes from a very high level. Fu yuanshen is not futi, as it was born with you simultaneously from your mother's womb. It shares

[11] *zhu yuanshen* (jew yu-en-shun)—one's main soul; zhu yishi or main consciousness.

[12] *zhu yishi* (jew yee-shi)—one's main consciousness; zhu yuanshen or main soul.

[13] *fu yuanshen* (foo yu-en-shun)—one's secondary soul (s); fu yishi or secondary consciousness.

[14] *fu yishi* (foo yee-shi)—one's secondary consciousness; fu yuanshen or secondary soul(s).

[15] *yin* (yeen) and *yang* (yahng)—The Tao School believes that everything contains opposite forces of yin and yang which are mutually exclusive, yet interdependent, e.g. female (yin) vs. male (yang).

the same name as you, for it is part of your body. Normally, when people think about something or do something, it is up to zhu yuanshen to make the decision. Fu yuanshen mainly tries its best to prevent one's zhu yuanshen from committing wrongdoings. When zhu yuanshen is very stubborn, however, fu yuanshen is unable to give help. Fu yuanshen is not fooled by ordinary human society while zhu yuanshen is easily deceived.

Some fu yuanshen come from very high levels and are probably on the brink of achieving the Right Fruit in cultivation. Fu yuanshen wants to practice cultivation, but it cannot do anything about it if zhu yuanshen does not want to do it. When qigong was very popular, one day zhu yuanshen also wanted to practice qigong. The thought of cultivation toward the high level was of course very pure and simple; one did not have the desire for things such as fame and personal gain. Fu yuanshen, however, was delighted, "I want to practice cultivation, but I don't make decisions. Now you want to practice cultivation, and that's just what I want." Yet where could the person find a master? Fu yuanshen was quite able, and it would leave the body to find the great enlightened person that it knew in its previous life. Because some fu yuanshen came from very high levels, they could leave the body. After arriving up there, it expressed its wishes for cultivation and for borrowing gong. They found it very good, and would certainly extend help in its cultivation. Accordingly, fu yuanshen borrowed some gong. Normally, this gong is radiating energy delivered through a pipeline. Some borrowed energy also comes in forms, and it normally carries supernormal capabilities.

In this way, this person might at the same time have supernormal capabilities. The person was also as I just described, feeling very warm one night during sleep. When he woke up the

114

next morning he had energy. He got an electric shock wherever he put his hand. He was able to heal illnesses for others, and he also realized that he had obtained energy. Where did the energy come from? He was unclear about this. He had only a rough idea that it came from the space of the universe. But he did not know specifically how it came. Fu yuanshen would not tell him, because it was fu yuanshen who practiced cultivation. He only knew that he had obtained the energy.

There was usually no age limit for people who borrowed energy, and there were relatively more young people involved. Therefore, a few years ago there were also some people in their twenties, thirties, and forties who came to public. There were some elderly people as well. It was more difficult for a young person to conduct himself or herself well. Maybe you would have found this person usually very good, caring little for fame and self-interest, when he did not have many abilities in ordinary human society. Once he became well-known, fame and profit would easily interfere. He would think that he still had a long way to go in life, and he still wanted to make every effort to achieve some goals of ordinary people. So, once he developed supernormal capabilities and some abilities, they would be used as a means to pursue his personal goals in ordinary human society. They would then not work and were prohibited from being used this way. The more he used them, the less his energy. Finally, he would end up with nothing. There are even more people whose levels have dropped this way. I have found that now there is no one left.

The two cases I just addressed both involved energy that was obtained by people with relatively good xinxing. This energy was not developed through their own cultivation practice. It came from the great enlightened people, and thus the energy itself was good.

Futi

Many of you may have heard in the community of cultivators something about animal possessions by things such as foxes, weasels, ghosts, and snakes. What's it all about? Some people talk about developing supernormal capabilities through practicing qigong. In fact, supernormal capabilities are not developed; instead, they are human inborn capabilities. It is only that with the progress of human society, people focus more on the tangible things of our physical world, thus becoming more dependent upon our modern tools. Consequently, our human inborn capabilities are becoming more degenerated. In the end, they are made to disappear completely.

In order to have supernormal capabilities, one must develop them through cultivation practice and return to one's original, true self. But an animal does not have this sophisticated mind, so it connects with the characteristic of the universe via its primordial instinct. Some people claim that animals can practice cultivation, that foxes know how to cultivate dan, or that snakes know how to practice cultivation, and so on. It is not that those animals know how to practice cultivation. At the beginning, they also do not know at all what cultivation is. They just have that primordial instinct. Then, under special conditions and circumstances, it may have some effect over a period of time. They will be able to obtain energy and develop supernormal capabilities.

In this way, an animal will have some abilities. In the past, we would say that this animal had become very sagacious with some abilities. In the eyes of everyday people, animals are so formidable that they can easily manipulate people. Actually, I say that they are not formidable and are nothing before a true practitioner. Though you may find one that has practiced cultivation for nearly one thousand years, a tiny finger will be more than enough to crush it. We have said that animals have this primordial instinct, and they can have some abilities. However, there is a principle in our universe: Animals are not allowed to succeed in cultivation. Therefore, all of you can read in ancient books that once every several hundred years animals are killed in a big calamity or a small disaster. After a period of time, animals will develop energy and must be killed or struck by lightening, etc. They are forbidden from practicing cultivation because they do not have the human inborn nature; they cannot practice cultivation like human beings as they do not possess human qualities. If they succeed in cultivation, they are bound to be demons. They are thus not allowed to succeed in cultivation. Otherwise, they will be killed by heaven. They know it as well. But as I have said, human society is now in great decline and some people commit all kinds of sins. At this stage, isn't human society in danger?

Things are bound to turn about after reaching the limit! We have found that whenever human societies in prehistoric times experienced periodical destruction, it always took place when humankind was morally corrupt to the extreme. Now, the dimension inhabited by human beings as well as many other dimensions are all in a very dangerous situation. The same is true with other dimensions at this level; they also hurry to escape and want to move up to higher levels. They think that by climbing to higher levels they can escape. Yet, how can it be that easy? In order to practice cultivation, one must have a human body. Accordingly, that is one reason why some qigong practitioners have acquired futi.

Some people wonder, "Since there are so many great enlightened people or high-level masters, why don't they take care of this?" There is another principle in our universe: If you pursue or want something, others are not willing to interfere. Here, we teach everyone to follow the righteous way, and at the same time explain the Fa to you thoroughly to let you become enlightened on your own. It is your own business whether you want to learn it. The master takes you through the entrance, and it is up to you to practice cultivation. Nobody will force you or make you practice cultivation. It is your own business whether you practice cultivation. In other words, no one will interfere with it in terms of which path you take, what you want, or what you try to get. We can only advise people to be good.

Though you find that some people practice qigong, their energy is actually obtained by futi. How does one get futi? How many qigong practitioners throughout the country have futi behind their bodies? If I reveal the number, many people will be too scared to practice qigong. The number is frighteningly large! So, why is there this situation? These things are causing trouble for ordinary human society. Why is it becoming such a serious phenomenon? It is also induced by people themselves since humankind is being corrupted and demons are everywhere. In particular, all those sham qigong masters carry futi on their bodies, and this is what they transmit in their teaching. Throughout human history, animals have been forbidden to possess people. When they did, they were killed; whoever saw it would not allow it. In our society today, however, some people pray to them for help, want them, and worship them. Some people may think, "I wasn't asking for it specifically!" You did not ask for it, but you sought supernormal capabilities. Will a great enlightened person from an orthodox cultivation practice give them to you? Pursuit is an attachment of everyday people, and this attachment must be given up. So who gives them to you? Only demons from other dimensions and different animals can give them to you. Isn't it the same as your asking for futi? It will come, then.

How many people practice qigong with the right mind? Qigong practice requires one to value virtues, do good deeds, and be kind. One should conduct oneself this way in everything and under all circumstances. Whether practicing qigong in a park or at home, how many people think this way? No one knows what kind of qigong some people practice. While practicing and swaying the body, one mutters, "Oh, my daughter-in-law doesn't respect me. My mother-in-law is so terrible!" Some people even comment on everything—from their workplace to state affairs. There is nothing that they will not talk about, and they will be quite upset if something does not agree with their way of thinking. Would you call that qigong practice? Further yet, such a person practices a standing exercise there with legs shaking from fatigue. Yet his mind is not at rest: "Nowadays things are so expensive and prices are rising. The workplace can't pay my salary. Why can't I develop some supernormal capabilities from practicing qigong? If I develop supernormal capabilities, I, too, will become a qigong master and make a fortune. I could see patients and make money." Once he sees that other people have developed supernormal capabilities, he becomes even more anxious. He will go after supernormal capabilities, pursuing tianmu and the ability to heal illness. Think about it, everyone: How far this is from Zhen-Shan-Ren, the characteristic of our universe! It goes entirely the opposite way. To put it seriously, this person is practicing evil cultivation! However, he does it unknowingly. The more he thinks this way, the worse his mind becomes. This person has not obtained the Fa and does not know to value virtue. Then he thinks that he can develop energy simply by doing the exercises and that he can get whatever he wants through pursuit. That is what this person thinks.

It is precisely because of one's ill intentions that one brings to oneself bad things. An animal, however, can see it: "This person wants to make a fortune through qigong practice. The other person wants to be famous and get supernormal capabilities. My goodness, his body isn't bad and also carries very good things. But his mind is really bad, and he's pursuing supernormal capabilities! He may have a master, but even if he does have a master, I'm not afraid." The animal knows that a master from an orthodox cultivation practice will not give him supernormal capabilities upon seeing him pursuing them in such a way. The more he wants them, the less his master will give him, as it is exactly the attachment that is to be discarded. The more he thinks this way, the fewer supernormal capabilities he receives, and the less likely that he will be enlightened to it. The more he pursues them, the worse his mind becomes. In the end, after seeing that this person is hopeless, his master will leave him with a sigh and no longer take care of him. Some people do not have a master and are probably looked after by a passingby master, since there are a lot of great enlightened people in different dimensions. One great enlightened person may take a look at the person and follow him for a day. Then the enlightened person will leave him after finding out that he is not good enough. The next day another great enlightened person may come by, and will also leave him after discovering that he is no good.

The animal knows that whether or not he has a master or a passing-by master, his master will not give to him what he is pursuing. Because animals are unable to see the dimensions where the great enlightened people stay, they are not afraid, and they take advantage of a loophole. There is a principle in our universe that normally other people cannot interfere with whatever one pursues and wants for oneself. The animal has taken advantage of this loophole, "If he wants something, I'll supply him. It isn't wrong for me to help him, is it?" The animal will give it to him. Initially, the animal does not dare to possess him, and it will first give him some energy to try out. One day, the person suddenly finds himself with the energy that he has been seeking, and he can also heal illnesses. Upon seeing that it works, the animal will use it like a musical prelude, "Since he wants it, I'll attach to his body. That way I can give him more things and do it easily. Doesn't he want tianmu? Now I'll give him everything." It will then possess him.

While this person's pursuing mind thinks of these things, his tianmu opens and he can also give off energy with some petty supernormal capabilities. He gets very excited and thinks that he has finally got what he sought through practicing. Actually, he has achieved nothing through his practice. He thinks that he can see through the human body and detect where illness resides in one's body. In fact, his tianmu is not opened at all; it is that animal that controls his mind. That animal reflects what it sees with its eyes into his brain, so he thus thinks that his tianmu has opened. "Release the gong? Go ahead." When he holds out his hand to release energy, that animal also stretches out its paw from his back. As soon as he gives off the energy, the forked tongue from that snake's head will come out to lick the ill part or the swollen part of the patient. There are quite a few such cases, and these people all got futi through their own pursuits.

Because this person pursues something, going after fortune and fame, he has thus acquired supernormal capabilities. He can treat illnesses, and his tianmu can also see things. This makes him very happy. The animal sees it, "Don't you want to make a fortune? Great, I'll let you make money." It is very easy to manipulate an ordinary person's mind. The animal can make many people, quite a lot, come to him for treatment. My goodness, while he is treating an illness here, the animal makes newspaper reporters advertise him in newspapers over there. It manipulates everyday people to do these things. If a patient does not pay him enough money, it is not allowed; the animal will cause the patient to have a headache. Anyway, one must pay him a lot of money. He has achieved both fame and fortune, as money is made and fame is achieved. He has also become a qigong master. Normally, such a person does not value xinxing and dares to say anything. He will consider himself second only to heaven, daring to claim that he himself is the reincarnated Lady Queen Mother[16] or the Great Jade Emperor.[17] He will even dare to call himself a Buddha. Because he has not truly undergone xinxing cultivation, he pursues supernormal capabilities in his practice. Consequently, he brings futi to himself.

Some people may think, "What's wrong with that? It's good as long as there is money or a fortune to be made, and one can

---

[16] Lady Queen Mother—in Chinese mythology, the highest-level female deity within the Three Realms.

[17] Great Jade Emperor—in Chinese mythology, the deity that supervises the Three Realms.

also achieve fame." Many people think this way. Let me tell everyone that the animal actually has its own intention, and it would not give you anything without a reason. This universe has a principle: "no loss, no gain." What does it obtain? Didn't I just address this issue? It wants to acquire the essence in your body so as to cultivate a human form, and it collects the human essence from a person's body. A human body only has this one piece of essence. If one wants to practice cultivation, there is only this one piece. If you let the animal get it, you must forget about practicing cultivation. How will you practice cultivation? You will have nothing left and cannot practice cultivation at all. Some people may claim: "I don't want to practice cultivation, either, and I just want to make money. As long as I have money, it's fine. Who cares!" Let me tell you that you may want to make a fortune, but you will not think this way after I tell you the reason. Why? If it leaves your body early, your four limbs will feel very weak. Afterwards, you will be this way for the rest of your life because it has taken too much of your essence. If it leaves your body late, you will be a vegetable and lie in bed for the rest of your life with only one breath of air. Though you have money, are you able to spend it? Though you have fame, are you able to enjoy it? Isn't this frightening?

These cases are particularly notable among practitioners today, and they are quite numerous. An animal can not only possess a person, but also kill one's yuanshen and get into one's *niwan* palace[18] and stay there. Though the person looks like a human being, he is not. Even these things can take place nowadays. This is because human moral values have changed. When someone does something wrong, this person will not believe

---

[18] *niwan* (nee-wahn) palace—Taoist term for pineal body.

123

it if you tell him that he is committing a wrongdoing. He thinks that it is right and proper to make money, seek money, or make a fortune, and that it is correct. Therefore, he will harm and do damage to others. To make money, he will commit any sin and dare to do anything. Without losing something, the animal will not gain anything. How can it give you something for nothing? It wants to get things in your body. Of course, we have said that one gets into trouble because one's own values and mind are not correct or righteous.

We are teaching Falun Dafa. In practicing cultivation of our school, you will not have any problems as long as you can conduct your xinxing well, since one righteous mind can subdue one hundred evils. If you cannot maintain your xinxing well and go after this or that, you are bound to get yourself into trouble. Some people just cannot give up what they once practiced. We require people to practice only one cultivation way since one should be single-minded in true cultivation practice. Though some qigong masters have written books, I am telling you that those books contain all kinds of things and are the same as what they practice: they are snakes, foxes, and weasels. When you read those books, these things will come out from the words. I have said that the sham qigong masters outnumber the real ones by many times, and you are unable to distinguish them. Therefore, you must conduct yourselves well. I am not saying here that you must practice Falun Dafa; you may practice in any school you want. Yet there was a saying in the past: "One would rather not obtain the orthodox Fa in one thousand years than cultivate a wild fox practice for one day." Thus, one must conduct oneself well and truly practice cultivation in an orthodox Fa. Do not mix it with anything else in cultivation, not even with any mind intention. Some people's Falun are deformed. Why are they deformed? They

124

claim that they have not practiced other qigong. Whenever they are practicing, however, in their minds they add things from their previous practices. Aren't those things being brought into the practice? On the issue of futi, this is all we will address.

The Cosmic Language

What is "the cosmic language?" It refers to when a person can suddenly speak an unknown language. He mumbles something that he cannot understand, either. One with telepathic ability can catch its general idea but remains unable to tell specifically what this person is talking about. Also, some people can speak many different languages. Some even consider it quite remarkable and regard it as an ability or a supernormal capability. It is neither a supernormal capability nor a practitioner's ability; nor can it represent one's level. Then, what's it all about? It is that your mind is being controlled by a foreign spirit. Yet you may still find it quite good and you want it, as you are happy about it. The more you are pleased, the better it controls you. As a true practitioner, how can you let it control you? Furthermore, it comes from a very low level. As genuine practitioners, we thus should not invite these troubles.

Being the soul of all matter, human beings are most precious. How can you be controlled by these things? How sad that you would disown your own body! Some of these things are attached to human bodies. Some are not, but stay within a distance from people. But, they are manipulating and controlling you. When you want to talk, they will let you talk and mumble. The language can also be passed to another person if that person also wants to learn it. When that person is bold enough to try it, he or she can also speak it. In fact, those things also come in groups. If you want to speak it, one will come to you and let you utter it.

Why can this situation take place? As I have said, they want to upgrade their own levels. But, there are no hardships over there, so they cannot practice cultivation and improve themselves. They have come up with an idea. They want to help people by doing good deeds, but they do not know how. Yet they know that the energy they give off can repress a patient's illness and relieve a patient's suffering for the moment, though it cannot cure the illness. Accordingly, they know that this can be achieved by using a person's mouth to give off the energy. This is what happens. Some people call it a heavenly language, and there are others who call it the Buddha's language. That is slandering Buddha. I call it sheer nonsense!

It is known that a Buddha does not casually open his mouth to talk. Should he open his mouth and talk in our dimension, he could cause an earthquake for humankind. With such loud sound, how can it be allowed? Some people say, "My tianmu has seen a Buddha talking to me." He was not talking to you. Some people also saw my fashen doing the same thing. He was not talking to you, either. The message he gave was in stereo sound. When you heard it, it sounded as though he was talking. He usually talks in his dimension. After it is transmitted here, however, you cannot hear clearly what he says because the concepts of time and space are different between the two dimensions. One *shichen*[19] in our dimension is two hours. In that big dimension over there, one shichen of ours is one year, and ours is slower than the time over there.

---

[19] *shichen* (shr-chuhn)—a Chinese unit of time for two hours.

There was a saying in the past: "It's only one day in heaven, but one thousand years have passed on earth." This refers to unitary paradises which do not have the concepts of time and space. Namely, those are paradises where the great enlightened people stay, such as the Paradise of Ultimate Bliss, the Glazed Paradise, the Falun Paradise, and the Lotus Paradise. It refers to those places. In that big dimension, however, time is instead faster than ours. If you are able to receive it, you can hear someone talking. Some people have the ability of clairaudience and have their ears open. They are able to hear someone talking, but not clearly. Whatever you hear will resemble the chirping of a bird or the high-speed playing of a record player; one cannot tell what it is. Of course, some people can hear music and talking. But the time difference must be eliminated through a supernormal capability which serves as a carrier. Sound can then reach your ears, and so you can hear it clearly. It is just like that. Some people call it the Buddha's language, but it is not at all.

When two great enlightened people meet each other, they can understand everything with a smile. This is due to soundless telepathy, and what is received is in stereo sound. When they smile, their ideas are already communicated. This is not the only method they use, as they sometimes use another way. You know that in Tantrism, Tibetan lamas are very particular about using hand signs. But if you ask a lama what hand signs are, he will tell you that they are the supreme yoga. What, specifically, are they for? He does not know, either. Actually, they are the language of the great enlightened people. When there are many people, one uses big hand signs; they are very beautiful and made of various big hand signs. When there are only a few people, one uses small hand signs; they are also very beautiful and made of various small hand signs. They are very sophisticated and rich, because they

127

are a language. In the past, this was a heavenly secret, and now we have disclosed it. What is used in Tibet are only a few movements solely for the practice, and people have classified and systematized them. They only serve as a language in the practice and are just a few forms for the practice. The genuine hand signs are quite sophisticated.

What Has Teacher Given to Practitioners?

After seeing me, some people will hold my hand and not let it go. When others see these people shaking my hand, they will also shake my hand. I know what is on their mind. Some people are very happy to shake hands with Teacher. Some people want to get some messages and will not release my hand. We have told you that true cultivation practice is your own business. We are not here for healing and fitness, or to give you some messages and heal your illnesses; nor are we concerned with those things. Your illnesses will be cured directly by me. Those who practice at exercise sites will have my fashen to cure their illnesses. Those who study Dafa by reading the book on their own will also have my fashen to cure their illnesses. Do you think that you will increase gong by touching my hand? Isn't that a joke?

Gong depends upon cultivating one's own xinxing. If you are not truly practicing cultivation, gong does not grow; this is because there is a xinxing standard. While your gong grows, one at the high level can see that when your attachment, a substance, is removed, a yardstick grows above your head. In addition, this yardstick exists in the form of gongzhu. The yardstick is as high as your gongzhu. It represents the gong that you have cultivated. It also represents the height of your xinxing level. It will not work no matter how much of it other people add to you. Not even a tiny bit can be added, for it will not stay there and all of it will come off. I can make you immediately reach the state of "three flowers gathering above the head." Once you step out this door, however, the gong will come off because it is not yours, and it is not from your cultivation. Because your xinxing standard is not there yet, it cannot stay there. Whoever wishes to add it to you will be unable to do it, because it comes completely from one's own cultivation and from cultivating one's own mind. You can move up only by developing gong solidly, improving yourself constantly, and assimilating to the characteristic of the universe. Some people ask for my autograph, but I am not willing to give it. Some people brag that they have Teacher's autograph. They want to show it off or want Teacher's message to protect them. Isn't this another attachment? You must practice cultivation on your own. What messages are you talking about? Should you ask for this in high-level cultivation? What does that account for? That is only something for healing and fitness.

At a very microscopic level, the gong you develop, or every microscopic particle from that gong, looks exactly the same as you. After reaching beyond Shi-Jian-Fa, you will practice cultivation of a Buddha-body. That gong will assume the appearance of a Buddha. It is very beautiful, sitting on a lotus flower. Every microscopic particle is like that. An animal's gong, however, is something like small foxes or snakes. At a very microscopic level, their fine particles are all these things. There is also something called messages. Some people stir up tea and ask you to drink it since it is supposed to be gong. An everyday person only wants to temporarily relieve pains by postponing and repressing his illness. After all, an everyday person is an everyday person. We are not concerned with how he messes up

129

his body. You are practitioners. That is why I tell you these things. From now on, you should not do these things. Never ask for those things such as the so-called "messages," this or that. One qigong master claims, "I give you messages, and you can receive them in all parts of the country." What do you receive? I tell you that these things are not of much use. Supposing that they are good, they are still only for healing and fitness. As practitioners, however, our gong comes from our own cultivation. Messages from other people cannot upgrade one's level, but only treat illnesses for everyday people. One must maintain a righteous mind; no one can practice cultivation for another. Only when you truly practice cultivation on your own can you upgrade your level.

What have I given you, then? Everyone knows that many of our practitioners have never practiced qigong and their bodies carry illnesses. Although a lot of people have practiced qigong for many years, they still linger at the level of qi without having obtained any gong. Of course, some people have treated patients without knowing how they did it. When I spoke about the issue of futi, I already removed futi—no matter what they were—from the bodies of genuine Dafa practitioners, and I have removed all those things inside and outside their bodies. When those who truly practice cultivation on their own read this Dafa, I will clean out their bodies as well. In addition, your home environment must also be cleaned. As soon as possible, you should throw away the spirit tablet[20] for the fox or the weasel that you previously enshrined. They have all been disposed of and no longer exist. Because you want to practice cultivation, we can open for you the most convenient door, and these things can therefore be done

[20] spirit tablet—enshrined wooden tablet in the home for worshipping ancestors or other spirits at home.

for you. Yet, they are only done for true practitioners. Of course, some people do not want to practice cultivation and to this moment do not understand it. Accordingly, we cannot take care of them, either. We only take care of true practitioners.

There is another type of person. Someone was told in the past that he had futi. He felt that way as well. However, upon having it removed for him, his mind still worries about it. He always thinks that the condition still exists. He still thinks that it is there, and this is already an attachment called suspicion. As time passes, this person may bring it to himself again. One should give up this attachment, as this futi no longer exists. Some people were already cleared of these things in our previous classes. I have already done those things for them and removed all futi.

The Tao School requires laying a foundation in low-level practice. The heavenly circulation, *dantian*,[21] and some other things must also be developed. Here we shall provide you with Falun, *qiji*,[22] and all the mechanisms for cultivation practice and so on—more than ten thousand of them. They will all be given to you like seeds being planted in your body. After removing your illnesses, I will do everything that needs to be done and give you everything that should be given. Then, you will be able to truly continue your cultivation practice in our school until the end. Otherwise, without giving you anything, it is only for healing and fitness. Frankly, some people do not value xinxing, and they would be better off doing physical exercises.

If you are truly practicing cultivation, we must be responsible to you. Those self-taught practitioners will also obtain the same

---

[21] *dantian* (dahn-tyen)—"field of dan"; the lower abdominal area.

[22] *qiji* (chee-jee)—"energy mechanism."

things, but they must be genuine practitioners. We give all these things to true practitioners. I have said that I must truly treat you as my disciples. In addition, you must study the high-level Fa thoroughly and know how to practice cultivation. The five sets of exercises will be taught to you all at once, and you will learn them all. In the time to come, you will be able to reach a very high level—one which is so high that it is beyond your imagination. As long as you practice cultivation, it will not be a problem for you to achieve the Right Fruit in cultivation. In teaching this Fa, I have incorporated different levels. In your future cultivation practice at different level, you will always find it assuming a guiding role for you.

As a practitioner, your path of life will be changed from now on. My fashen will rearrange it for you. How is it rearranged? How many years does a person still have in life? One would not know it oneself. Some people may get a serious illness after a year or half a year, or they may be ill for several years. Some people may suffer cerebral thrombosis or other illnesses, and cannot move at all. How can you practice cultivation for the rest of your life? We must fix all of them for you and prevent these things from occurring. We, however, must make it clear ahead of time that we can only do these things for true practitioners. They are not allowed to be done casually for an everyday person. Otherwise, it is the same as doing a bad deed. For everyday people, things such as birth, old age, illness, and death all have karmic relationships, and they cannot be undermined at will.

We regard practitioners as the most precious people. Thus, we can only do things for practitioners. How do we do these? If a master has great virtues—that is, if a master possesses great energy potency—this master can eliminate your karma. If a master's energy level is high, he can eliminate a lot of your karma. If a master's energy level is low, he can only eliminate a little of your karma. Let us use an example. We shall put together your different karma in your future life, and eliminate part of it or half of it. The remaining half is still higher than a mountain, and you cannot overcome it. What should be done? When you achieve the Tao, many people in the future will benefit. This way, many people will bear a share for you. Of course, it is nothing to them. Through practice you will also develop many beings in your body. In addition to your zhu yuanshen and your fu yuanshen, many others of you will all take a share for you. There will be almost nothing left for you by the time you go through tribulations. Though there is almost nothing left, it is still quite a lot, and you are still unable to overcome it. Then, what happens? It will be divided into numerous portions for different phases of your cultivation practice. They will be used to upgrade your xinxing, transform your karma, and increase your gong.

Moreover, it is not an easy thing if one wants to practice cultivation. I have said that this is a very serious matter. It is something beyond ordinary people and more difficult than anything of ordinary people. Isn't it supernatural? Therefore, the requirement for you is higher than any matter of everyday people. As human beings, we have yuanshen, and yuanshen does not become extinct. If yuanshen does not become extinct, think about it, everyone: Didn't your yuanshen commit wrongdoings in the social interactions of your previous life? It is very likely. You might have done things such as killing lives, owing something to someone, bullying someone, or harming someone. If it is true, when you practice cultivation here, they can see you clearly over there. They do not care if you are healing illness and keeping fit, as they know that you are then only postponing the debt. If you do not repay it now, you will repay it later, and you will pay more for it in the future. So they do not care if you do not repay it at the moment.

When you say that you are going to practice cultivation, they will not let you do it, "You want to practice cultivation and leave. When you've developed gong, we won't be able to reach you or touch you." They will not let it happen, and they will try everything to stop you from practicing cultivation. Accordingly, all kinds of methods will be used to interfere with you. They will even come to really kill you. Of course, your head will not be chopped off here while doing the sitting meditation. That is impossible since it must comply with the state of ordinary human society. Perhaps, you will be hit by a car upon stepping out the door, or you might fall from a building or run into other dangers. These things might take place and will be quite perilous. Genuine cultivation practice is not as easy as you imagine. Do you think that if you want to practice cultivation you'll be able to make it? Once you want to truly practice cultivation, your life will be in danger right away and this issue will concern you immediately. Many qigong masters dare not teach students toward high levels. Why? They just cannot take care of this matter, and they cannot protect you.

In the past there were many people teaching the Tao. They could only teach one disciple, and about all they could do was to look after one disciple. However, as to doing it on such a large scale, an average person would not dare. But we have told you here that I can do it, because I have numerous fashen who possess my mighty divine powers. They can demonstrate great supernatural powers—very mighty powers of the Fa. In addition, what we do today is not as simple as what we see on the surface.

I was not hot-headed when I came to public. I can tell you that there are many great enlightened people watching this event. This is the last time we teach the orthodox Fa in the Dharma-ending Period. In doing so, we also do not allow it to go astray. If you truly follow the righteous way in cultivation practice, nobody will dare to do something to you at will. Besides, you have the protection of my fashen, and you will not be in any danger.

What is owed must be repaid. Therefore, some dangerous things may occur in the course of cultivation practice. When these things take place, however, you will not be scared, nor will real danger be allowed to happen to you. I can give you some examples. When I taught a class in Beijing, a practitioner crossed the street on her bike. At a turn of the street, a luxury car came and knocked down this practitioner, a woman over fifty years old. It collided with her at once and hit her very hard. With the sound of "bang," it hit her head, and her head hit the car roof squarely. At that point, this practitioner's feet were still on the bike pedals. Though her head was hit, she did not feel any pain. Not only did she not feel any pain, but her head did not bleed, either; nor did it swell. The driver was scared to death and jumped out of the car. He hastily asked her if she was injured and suggested that they go to the hospital. She replied that she was all right. Of course, this practitioner had a very high xinxing level and would not get the driver into trouble. She said that everything was fine, but the collision left a big dent on the car.

All things like that come to take away one's life. But one will not be endangered. The last time we held a class at Jilin University, a practitioner pushed his bike as he was going through the main entrance of Jilin University. As soon as he walked into the middle of the road, all of a sudden two cars sandwiched him.

The cars almost hit him, but he was not scared at all. Normally, we are not frightened at all upon running into these things. At that very second, the cars stopped and nothing happened.

There was such an instance in Beijing. It gets dark quite early in winter, and people go to bed early. The streets were very quiet without a soul. A practitioner was hurrying home on a bike with only a jeep running ahead of him. Suddenly, that jeep put on its brakes. He was not aware of it and continued to ride his bike forward with his head down. But that jeep suddenly backed up, and it moved back at a very high speed. If the two forces had met, it would have taken away his life. Just before they were to collide, a force suddenly pulled his bike back more than half a meter, and the jeep stopped at the wheel of his bike all at once. Perhaps, the jeep driver discovered that someone was behind him. This practitioner was also not scared at that moment. All of those who have encountered these situations were not scared, although they might have been afterwards. The first thing on his mind was, "Wow! Who pulled me back? I have to thank him." When he turned around and was about to express his gratitude, he found the street very quiet with no one around. He understood at once, "It was Teacher who protected me!"

Another case took place in Changchun.[23] A building was under construction near a practitioner's home. Nowadays, buildings are built very high, and the scaffolding is made of iron poles that are two inches in diameter and four meters long. After this practitioner walked a short distance from home, an iron pole fell vertically from the high-rise building all the way to his head. The people on the street were all astonished. He said, "Who patted me?" He thought that someone had patted his head. At that very

---

[23] Changchun (chahng-choon)—capital city of Jilin Province.

136

moment, he turned his head and saw a big Falun rotating above his head. That iron pole had slid down along his head and stuck into the ground without falling down. If it had indeed stuck into a person's body—think about it, everyone—it would have penetrated the body as if stringing sugar-coated hawthorn fruits, as it was so heavy. It was very dangerous!

There are so many of these cases that they cannot be numbered. Yet, no danger has occurred. Not everyone will encounter these kinds of things, but some individuals will run into them. Whether you come across them or not, I can assure you that you will not be in any danger—I can guarantee this. Some practitioners do not follow the xinxing requirements, as they only practice the exercises without cultivating their xinxing. They cannot be regarded as practitioners.

Speaking of what Teacher has given, these are what I have given you. My fashen will protect you until you are able to protect yourself. At that time, you will practice cultivation beyond Shi-Jian-Fa, and you will have already achieved the Tao. But you must treat yourself as a true practitioner, and then you can make it. There was a person who was walking on the street with my book in his hand, yelling, "I have Teacher Li's protection, so I'm not afraid of being hit by a car." That was undermining Dafa. This type of person will not be protected. Actually, a true practitioner will not do such thing.

Energy Field

While we practice, there is a field around us. What field is it? Some people call it a qi field, a magnetic field, or an electric

137

field. In fact, it is incorrect no matter what field you call it since the matter contained in this field is extremely rich. Almost all the matter that constitutes every space of our universe can be found in this cultivation energy. It is more appropriate for us to call it an energy field, and so we normally call it an energy field.

So what can this field do? As you all know, our practitioners of the orthodox Fa have this feeling: Because it comes from cultivation of the orthodox Fa, it is benevolent and assimilated to Zhen-Shan-Ren, the characteristic of the universe. Therefore, all of our practitioners can feel it while sitting here in this field, and their minds are free of bad thoughts. In addition, while sitting here many practitioners do not even think of smoking. They feel an atmosphere of serenity and peace, which is very comfortable. This is the energy carried by a practitioner of the orthodox Fa, and that is what it does within the scope of this field. Later, after this class, most of our practitioners will have gong—the truly developed energy. Because what I am teaching you is something from cultivation of the orthodox Fa, you should also apply this xinxing standard to yourself. As you continually practice and follow our xinxing requirements in cultivation practice, your energy will gradually become more powerful.

We teach salvation of both ourselves and others, as well as of all beings. Thus, Falun can save oneself by turning inward and save others by turning outward. While turning outward, it gives off energy and can benefit others. This way, within your energy-covering field others will benefit, and they may feel very comfortable. Whether you are on the street walking, in the workplace, or at home, you can have this effect on others. People within your field may unintentionally have their illnesses healed since this field can rectify all abnormal conditions. A human body should not become ill, and being ill is an abnormal state. It can rectify this abnormal state. When an evil-minded person is thinking of something bad, this person might change his mind due to the powerful effect of your field; he might then no longer want to commit the wrongdoing. Perhaps a person wants to swear at someone. Suddenly, he may change his mind and will not want to swear. Only the energy field from cultivation practice in an orthodox Fa can produce this effect. Therefore, in the past there was this saying in Buddhism: "The Buddha-light illuminates everywhere and rectifies all abnormalities." This is what it means.

How Should Falun Dafa Practitioners Spread the Practice?

After the class, many of our practitioners think that this practice is very good, and they want to pass it on to their relatives or friends. Yes, all of you can spread it and pass it on to anyone. But, there is one thing that we must declare to everyone. We have given everyone so many things that cannot be measured or valued with money. Why do I give them to everyone? They are for your cultivation practice. Only if you practice cultivation, can you be given these things. In other words, when you spread the practice in the future, you cannot use these things to seek fame and self-interest. Thus, you cannot hold a class and collect fees as I do. Because we need to print books and materials and travel around to teach the practice, we need to cover the costs. Our fees are already the lowest in the country, yet the things imparted are the most numerous. We are truly bringing people toward high levels; everyone knows this point themselves. As a Falun Dafa practitioner, when you spread the practice in the future, we have two requirements for you.

The first one is that you cannot collect a fee. We have given you so many things, but they are not for you to make a fortune or seek fame. Rather, they are for saving you and enabling you to practice cultivation. If you collect a fee, my fashen will take back everything given to you, and you will no longer be a practitioner of our Falun Dafa. What you have spread would not be our Falun Dafa. When you spread it, you should not pursue fame and personal gain, but should serve others voluntarily. All practitioners are doing it this way nationwide, and assistants from different regions have also set this example themselves. If you want to learn our practice, you may come as long as you want to learn it. We can be responsible to you and will not charge you a penny.

The second requirement is that you should not add personal things to Dafa. In other words, during the course of teaching the exercise, regardless of whether your tianmu is opened, you have seen something, or you have developed some supernormal capabilities, you cannot use what you have seen to explain our Falun Dafa. That little bit that you have seen at your level is nothing and far from the actual meaning of the Fa that we teach. So when you spread the practice in the future, you ought to be very careful with this issue. Only by doing so can we ensure that the original things in our Falun Dafa remain unchanged.

In addition, nobody is permitted to teach the practice in the manner that I do, nor is anyone allowed to teach the Fa in this large-scale lecture format that I use. You are unable to teach the Fa. This is because what I am teaching has very profound implications, and it incorporates something of high levels. You are practicing cultivation at different levels. In the future after you make progress, you will continue to improve when you again listen to this recording. As you constantly listen to it, you will always gain new understanding and new results. It is more so reading this book. This teaching of mine is taught by incorporating something very profound at high levels. Therefore, you are unable to teach this Fa. You are not allowed to say it, using my original words as yours, or else it is an act of plagiarizing the Fa. You can only use my original words to say it, adding that this is how Teacher says it or how it is written in the book. You can only say it this way. Why? Because when you say it this way, it will carry the power of Dafa. You cannot spread the things that you know as Falun Dafa. Otherwise, what you pass on is not Falun Dafa, and what you do is the same as undermining our Falun Dafa. If you say something according to your ideas and your mind, it is not the Fa and cannot save people; nor will it have any effect. Therefore, nobody else can teach this Fa.

The way you transmit this practice is by playing the audiotapes or the videotapes for practitioners at the exercise sites or instructional sites, and assistants may then teach them the exercises. You can use the seminar form to have everyone communicate with one another, and you may discuss and share things with one another. We require that you do it this way. At the same time, you cannot call a practitioner (the disciple) who passes on Falun Dafa "Teacher" or "Master," for there is only one master in Dafa. All practitioners are disciples, no matter when they begin the practice.

When you spread the practice, some people may think, "Teacher can install Falun and adjust one's body, but we can't do that." It does not matter. I have already told you that behind every practitioner there is my fashen, and not just one. Accordingly, my fashen will take care of these things. When you teach a person the practice, he will obtain Falun right then if he has a predestined relationship. If he does not have a good predestined relationship, he can obtain it gradually after a period of practice and after his body is adjusted. My fashen will help him adjust his body. Besides these things, I am telling you that if a person learns the Fa and the practice by reading my book, watching my videotapes, or listening to my recordings, and if he truly treats himself as a practitioner, he can also get these things that he deserves.

We do not allow practitioners to see patients, as Falun Dafa practitioners are absolutely prohibited from treating illnesses for other people. We are teaching you to ascend in cultivation, rather than letting you develop any attachments or ruin your own body. Our exercise sites are better than any other qigong exercise sites. As long as you go to our exercise sites for practice, it is much better than your treating your own illness. My fashen sit in a circle, and above the exercise site is a shield on which there is a big Falun. A large fashen guards the site above the shield. This site is not an ordinary site, nor is it a site for an ordinary qigong practice: It is a site for cultivation practice. Many of our practitioners with supernormal capabilities have seen that this Falun Dafa site is shielded with red light, and it is red all over.

My fashen can also directly install Falun for a practitioner, but we do not encourage one's attachment. When you teach a person the exercises, he may say, "Oh, I have Falun now." You wrongly think that it is installed by you, when it is not. I am telling you this so that you will not develop this attachment. It is all done by my fashen. This is how our Falun Dafa practitioners should spread the practice.

Anyone who tries to change the Falun Dafa exercises is undermining Dafa and this school of practice. Some people have turned the exercise instructions into rhymes, and that is absolutely not permitted. A genuine cultivation way is always passed down from a prehistoric time. It has been preserved from quite a remote age and has successfully cultivated numerous great enlightened people. No one dares to change a bit of it. Such a thing can only take place in this Dharma-ending Period of ours. These things have never occurred throughout history. Everyone must be very careful with this issue.

LECTURE FOUR

Loss and Gain

In the community of cultivators, the relationship between loss and gain is frequently brought up. Among everyday people, it is also discussed. How should our practitioners treat losses and gains? It is different from ordinary people. What everyday people want is personal gain and how to live well and comfortably. Our practitioners are not this way, but exactly the opposite. We do not seek what everyday people want. Instead, what we get is something everyday people cannot obtain—even though they want to—except through cultivation practice.

The loss we normally refer to is not loss in a narrow scope. When one speaks of loss, one will think of donating some money, giving a hand to those in need, or feeding a beggar on the street. Those are also a form of giving and a form of loss. Yet, this only refers to being less concerned about the sole issue of money or possessions. Giving up wealth is, of course, an aspect of loss, and a relatively major aspect as well. But the loss we refer to is not limited to this narrow scope. As practitioners, in the course of cultivation there are so many attachments to be relinquished, such as the mentality of showing off, jealousy, the competitive mentality, and zealotry. Many different attachments must be discarded, for the loss we discuss is one in a broad sense. During the entire course of cultivation, we should lose all everyday people's attachments and various desires.

One may wonder: "We're practicing cultivation among

everyday people. If we lose everything, aren't we the same as monks or nuns? It seems impossible to lose everything." In our school of practice, those who practice cultivation among everyday people are required to practice cultivation precisely in ordinary human society, and to conform to everyday people as much as possible. You are not really asked to lose anything materially. It does not matter how high your position ranks or how much wealth you own. The key is whether you can abandon that attachment.

Our school of practice directly targets one's mind. The key issue is whether you can take lightly and care less about the issues of individual gain and interpersonal conflicts. Cultivation practices in temples or in remote mountains and woods completely sever your access to ordinary human society, forcing you to lose everyday people's attachments and denying you any material benefits so that you can lose them. A practitioner among everyday people does not follow this path. This person is required to take them lightly in this everyday human environment. Of course, this is very difficult. It is also the most crucial aspect of our school of practice. Therefore, the loss we refer to is loss in a broad sense instead of a narrow one. Let us talk about doing good deeds and donating some money or goods. Nowadays, some of the beggars that you see on the street are professional and they may even have more money than you. We should focus on a broader spectrum instead of minor trivia. Cultivation practice should focus with openness and dignity on a broad perspective. In the course of our losses, what we actually lose are the bad things.

Human beings often believe that everything they pursue is good. In fact, from a high-level perspective, these are to satisfy those bits of vested interests among everyday people. It is said in religion that regardless of how much money you have or how

145

high your position ranks, it is good for only a few decades. One cannot bring it along at birth or carry it after death. Why is gong so precious? It is precisely because it grows right on the body of your yuanshen and can be carried at birth and taken forth after death. In addition, it directly determines your Fruit Status in cultivation, and it is therefore difficult to cultivate. In other words, what you lose is something bad. Thus, you can return to your original, true self. So what do you gain? The improvement of your level; eventually you achieve the Right Fruit and complete cultivation, solving the fundamental issue. Certainly, it will not be easy for you to immediately lose all sorts of everyday people's desires and reach the standard of a true practitioner, as it takes time to make it. When you hear me say that it takes time, you might say that Teacher has told us to take time, and so you will take time in doing so. That will not be permitted! You should be strict with yourself, though we allow you to improve gradually. If you could do it all at once today, you would be a Buddha today. Thus, it is not realistic. You will be able to achieve this gradually.

What we lose is actually something bad. What is it? It is karma, and it goes hand in hand with different human attachments. For example, everyday people have all kinds of bad thoughts. For self-interest, they commit various wrong deeds and will acquire this black substance, karma. This directly involves our own minds. In order to eliminate this negative thing, you must first change your mind.

Transformation of Karma

There exists a transformation process between the white substance and the black substance. After a conflict takes place between one another, there occurs this process of transformation. When one does a good deed, one acquires the white substance, de. When one does a bad deed, one obtains the black substance, karma. There is also an inheriting process. One may ask, "Is this because one did bad things early in one's life?" It might not be completely so because this karma is not accumulated in only one lifetime. The community of cultivators believes that yuanshen does not become extinct. If yuanshen does not become extinct, one probably had social interactions before this life. So one might have owed something to someone, bullied someone, or done other bad things, such as killing, which would induce this karma. These things add up in another dimension, and one always carries them; the same is also true with the white substance. This is not the only source, as there is also another situation. Throughout the generations in the family, ancestors may also accumulate karma for later generations. In the past, the elderly had this saying: "One should accumulate de, and one's ancestors have accumulated de. This person is giving away de and abusing de." That was said very correctly. Nowadays, average people no longer listen to this saying. If you tell those young people about losing de or lacking de, they will not take it to heart at all. In fact, its meaning is indeed very profound. It is not merely the ideological and spiritual standard of modern people, but also an actual material existence. Our human bodies have both of these kinds of substances.

Someone asked, "Is it that if one has too much black substance one is unable to practice to the high level?" One could say so, as with a lot of black substance, one's enlightenment quality will be affected. Because it forms a field around one's body and wraps a person up right in the middle, one is cut off from Zhen-Shan-Ren, the characteristic of the universe. Thus, this person's enlightenment quality may be poor. When people talk about cultivation practice and qigong, this person will consider all of them superstitious, and he will not believe them at all. He will find them ridiculous. It is usually this way, but not absolute. Is it that it's too difficult for this person to practice cultivation, and that he is unable to achieve high-level gong? It is not so. We have said that Dafa is boundless, and it is completely up to your heart to practice cultivation. The master takes you through the entrance, and it is up to you, yourself to practice cultivation. It all depends upon how you, yourself practice cultivation. Whether you can practice cultivation all depends upon whether you can endure, sacrifice, and suffer. If you can commit your mind, no difficulties can stop you. I would say that there is not a problem.

A person with a lot of the black substance will usually have to sacrifice more than a person with a lot of the white substance. Because the white substance is directly assimilated to the characteristic of the universe, Zhen-Shan-Ren, as long as a person upgrades his xinxing in conflicts, his gong will increase. It is that simple. One with much de has good enlightenment quality. He can suffer and endure physical as well as mental hardships. Even if this person suffers more physically and less mentally, his gong still increases. This is not the case for a person with a lot of the black substance, as he must first go through this process: He must transform the black substance into the white substance. This process is also quite painful. Therefore, a person with poor enlightenment quality usually must suffer more tribulations. With a lot of karma and poor enlightenment quality, it is more difficult for this person to practice cultivation.

Take a specific case, for example. Let us see how this person practices cultivation. The sitting meditation requires putting up both legs on top of each other for a long period of time. The legs will be painful and numb after assuming the posture. As time passes by, one will begin to feel quite uneasy and then become rather restless. Suffering physically and mentally can make both the body and the mind quite uncomfortable. Some people cannot bear the pain in sitting with the legs like that, and they want to give up by putting the legs down. Some people cannot bear it anymore after sitting a little longer. Once the legs are put down, one's practice is in vain. Once the legs are in pain, one will do some warm-ups before resuming the sitting position. We find that this serves no use whatsoever. This is because we have seen that when the legs are painful, the black substance moves to the legs. The black substance is karma that can be eliminated through suffering; it can then be transformed into de. Once the pain is felt, karma begins to be eliminated. The more karma that comes, the more pain the legs feel. Therefore, the pain in the legs does not arise without reason. Usually, one's legs in the sitting meditation will feel the pain intermittently. After a moment of very uncomfortable pain, it is over and there is some relief. Soon the pain starts all over again. It usually happens this way.

As karma is eliminated piece by piece, the legs will feel a little better after a piece is eliminated. Soon another piece comes up, and the legs will feel the pain again. After the black substance is eliminated, it does not dissipate, as this substance does not become extinct. Upon being eliminated, it is directly transformed into the white substance, which is de. Why can it be transformed this way? This is because this person has suffered, sacrificed, and endured tribulations. We have said that de is obtained through enduring and suffering hardships, or by doing good deeds. Therefore, this situation will occur in the sitting meditation. Some people quickly take the legs down once they begin to ache, and they will do some warm-ups before resuming the sitting position. That will achieve nothing whatsoever. While doing the standing exercise, one's arms may get tired from doing the holding-wheel posture. When one cannot bear it anymore and puts down the arms, this will not serve any purpose at all. What does that bit of pain account for? I would say that it is simply too easy if one can succeed in cultivation by just holding the arms up like that. This is what will happen when people practice the sitting meditation.

Our school of practice does not proceed primarily this way, though a part of it also plays a role in this regard. In most cases, one transforms karma through xinxing conflicts among one another, and this is where it manifests itself. While one is in a conflict, the clashes between each other even surpass the physical pains. I would say that the physical pains are the easiest thing to endure, as they can be overcome by biting the teeth tightly. When a conflict takes place between one another, the mind is the hardest thing to control.

For instance, upon arriving at the workplace, a person will become furious when he overhears two people denigrating him very badly. We have said, however, that as a practitioner one should not fight back when being punched or insulted, but should conduct oneself with a high standard. Thus, he thinks that Teacher has said that as practitioners we should not be the same as others and must conduct ourselves better. He will not quarrel with those two persons. But normally when a problem arises, if it does not irritate a person psychologically, it does not count or is useless and cannot make him or her improve. Accordingly, his mind cannot get over it and is still bothered by it. It could be that his mind is hooked on it. He always wants to turn around to look at the faces of those two people. Upon looking back, he sees the two wicked-looking faces in a heated conversation. He can no longer take it and becomes very upset. He may even pick a fight with them right away. When a conflict occurs among one another, it is very difficult to control one's mind. I say that it would be easy if everything could be taken care of in the sitting meditation; however, it will not always be this way.

Accordingly, in your future cultivation practice you will run into all kinds of tribulations. How can you practice cultivation without these hardships? If everyone is good to one another without conflict of interests or interference from the human mind, how can your xinxing make progress by your only sitting there? That is impossible. One must truly temper and upgrade oneself through actual practice. Someone asks, "Why do we always have tribulations in cultivation practice? Those problems aren't much different from those of everyday people." It is because you are practicing cultivation among everyday people. You will not be suddenly turned upside down with your head facing the ground, flying up there and suffering in the air—it won't be like that. Everything will assume the form of everyday situations, such as someone may have irritated you today, someone has upset you, someone has mistreated you, or someone suddenly speaks to you with no respect. It is to see how you will react to these issues.

Why do you encounter these problems? They are all caused by your own karma. We have already eliminated for you many, numerous pieces of it, leaving only that tiny bit which is divided into tribulations at different levels for upgrading your xinxing, tempering your mind, and removing your different attachments. These are all your own tribulations that we use to improve your xinxing, and you will be able to overcome them. As long as you upgrade your xinxing, you can overcome them. Unless you,

151

yourself do not want to do so, you can make it, provided you want to overcome them. Therefore, from now on when you come across a conflict you should not consider it a coincidence. This is because when a conflict occurs, it will take place unexpectedly. But that is not a coincidence—it is for improving your xinxing. As long as you treat yourself as a practitioner, you can handle it properly.

Of course, you will not be informed of a tribulation or conflict ahead of time. How can you practice cultivation if you are told everything? It will not serve any use. They usually occur unexpectedly so that they can test one's xinxing and make one's xinxing truly improve. Only then can it be seen whether one can maintain one's xinxing. Therefore, when a conflict arises, it does not occur accidentally. This issue will be present during the entire course of cultivation practice and in the transformation of karma. Unlike what everyday persons imagine, it is much more difficult than suffering physically. How can you increase gong simply by practicing the exercises a bit longer when the arms are sore from being raised and the legs are tired from standing? How can you increase gong with only a few more hours of exercise? That only serves to transform one's benti, but it still needs to be reinforced with energy. It does not help upgrade one's level. Mentally overcoming tribulations is the key to truly improving one's level. If one can make progress just by suffering physically, I would say that Chinese farmers suffer the most. Shouldn't they all become qigong masters, then? No matter how much you suffer physically, you do not suffer as much as they do, who work both hard and painstakingly in the field everyday under the baking sun. It is not that simple a matter. Therefore, we have said that to truly improve oneself, one should genuinely upgrade one's mind. Only then can one truly upgrade oneself.

During the process of transforming karma, to keep yourself under control—unlike an everyday person who would mess things up—you should always maintain a heart of benevolence and a mind of kindness. If you suddenly bump into a problem, you will be able to take care of it properly. When you always maintain a heart of benevolence and compassion, you will have time or room to buffer the confrontation and think should a problem arise suddenly. If you always think about competing with others and fighting back and forth, I would say that you will start a fight with others whenever there is a problem—this is guaranteed. Thus, when you encounter a conflict, I would say that it is to transform your black substance into the white substance, de.

When our humankind evolves to this extent today, almost everyone is born with karma built upon karma, and everyone's body has quite a lot of karma. In transforming karma, therefore, this situation will usually occur: While your gong increases and your xinxing improves, your karma is eliminated and transformed. When one runs into a conflict, it may manifest in a xinxing tribulation between one another. If you can endure it, your karma will be eliminated, your xinxing will improve, and your gong will increase as well. All of these will come together. People in the past had a lot of de and good xinxing to begin with. As long as they suffered a little bit of hardship, they could increase their gong. People are not like that today. As soon as they suffer, they do not want to practice cultivation. Furthermore, they have become less enlightened, making it harder for them to practice cultivation.

In cultivation practice, there may be two scenarios when dealing with specific conflicts or when others treat you badly.

One is that you might have treated this person badly in your previous life. You feel in your heart that it is unfair, "How can this person treat me like this?" Then why did you treat this person that way in the past? You might claim that you actually did not know it at that time, and this life has nothing to do with the other life. That does not work. There is another issue. In conflicts, the issue of transforming karma is involved. Therefore, in dealing with specific conflicts we should be forgiving instead of acting like ordinary people. This should apply to the workplace or other work environments. The same is true as well with self-employed people, for they also have social interactions. It is impossible not to interact with society, as at least there is contact among neighbors.

In social interactions one will come across all kinds of conflicts. For those who practice cultivation among everyday persons, what type of business you are in does not matter. Regardless of how much money you have, how high your position ranks, or what kind of private enterprise or company you run, it makes no difference as you should trade fairly and maintain a righteous mind. All professions in human society should exist. It is the human heart that is indecent, rather than one's occupation. There was a saying in the old days: "Nine out of ten merchants are fraudulent." That is a saying made by everyday people. I would say that it is a matter of the human heart. As long as your heart is righteous and you trade fairly, you deserve to earn more money if you make more effort. That is because you are rewarded for the effort you have put in among everyday people. No loss, no gain. You have worked for it. With any social status, one can still be a good person. There are different conflicts for people of different social classes. The upper-class society has conflicts of the upper-class society, all of which can be properly dealt with.

In any social class, one can be a good person and care less for different desires or attachments. One can prove oneself a good person at different strata, and one can practice cultivation at one's own social level.

Nowadays, whether in a state-run company or in other enterprises in this country, interpersonal conflicts have become very unique. In other countries and throughout history, this phenomenon has never occurred. Consequently, conflicts over self-interest are shown to be particularly intense. People play mind games and compete for a tiny bit of personal gain; the thoughts they have and the tricks they use are very vicious. Even being a good person is difficult. For instance, you arrive at your workplace and find the atmosphere there not right. Later, a person tells you that so-and-so has publicized you badly and reported on you to the boss, putting you in an awful situation. Others all stare at you with an unusual look. How can an ordinary person tolerate that? How can one put up with that? "If someone makes trouble for me, I'll return the same. If he has supporters, I do, too. Let's fight." If you do this among everyday people, they will say that you are a strong person. As a practitioner, however, that is completely awful. If you compete and fight like an ordinary person, you are an ordinary person. If you outdo him, you are even worse than that ordinary person.

How should we deal with this issue? Upon running into this conflict, we should, first of all, keep a cool head, and we should not behave the same as that person. Of course, we can explain the matter kindly, and it is not a problem if we clarify the issue. But you should not become too attached to it. If we encounter these problems, we should not compete and fight like others. If you do what that person did, aren't you an ordinary person? Not only should you not compete and fight like him, but also you should not resent that person in your mind. Really, you should not hate that person. If you hate that person, aren't you upset? You have not followed forbearance. We practice Zhen-Shan-Ren, and you would have even less compassion to speak of. So you should not be like him or become really upset with him, despite his putting you in this awful situation where you cannot even raise your head. Instead of being angry with him, you should thank him in your heart and thank him sincerely. An ordinary person may think this way: "Isn't that being like Ah Q?"[1] I am telling you that it is not so.

Think about it, everyone: You are practitioners. Shouldn't you be required to meet a high standard? The principles of everyday people should not apply to you, right? As a practitioner, isn't what you get something of high levels? Accordingly, you must follow the high-level principles. If you do what that person did, aren't you the same as he? Why should you thank him, then? Think about it: What will you obtain? In this universe, there is a principle which says: "no loss, no gain." To gain, one must lose. That person puts you in an awful situation among everyday people, and he is the party that has gained at your expense. The worse the situation he puts you in and the greater its impact, the more you will endure and the more de he will lose. Such de will all be given to you. While you are enduring all that, you might care less for it and not take it seriously in your mind.

In this universe, there is another principle: If you have suffered a lot, the karma in your body will be transformed. Because you have sacrificed, however much you have endured

---

[1] Ah Q (ah cue)—a foolish character in a Chinese novel.

will all be transformed into an equal amount of de. Isn't this de what a practitioner wants? You will gain in two ways, as your karma is also eliminated. If the person did not create this situation for you, how could you upgrade your xinxing? If both you and I are nice to each other and sit there in harmony, how can it be possible to increase gong? It is precisely because that person has created this conflict for you that there is this opportunity to improve xinxing, and you can make use of it to upgrade your own xinxing. Isn't your xinxing raised this way? You have gained in three ways. You are a practitioner. With xinxing upgraded, won't your gong also increase? You have gained four ways in one shot. Why shouldn't you thank that person? You should sincerely thank him from the bottom of your heart—it is actually so.

Of course, that person's thought was not decent, or else he would not have given you de. But he has indeed created an opportunity to upgrade your xinxing. In other words, we must pay attention to cultivating xinxing. At the same time xinxing is cultivated, karma is eliminated and transformed into de so that you can ascend to a higher level; these go hand in hand. From the high-level perspective, these principles are all changed. An ordinary person will not understand it. When you look at these principles from the high level, everything will be different. Among everyday people you may find these principles correct, but they are not actually right. Only what is seen from the high level is truly right. It is usually like this.

I have thoroughly explained the principles to everyone, and I hope that in future cultivation practice everyone will treat himself as a practitioner and truly practice cultivation since the principles are already presented here. Perhaps some people, because they live among everyday people, still think that in the face of actual material interests, being everyday people is practical. Amid the current of everyday persons they still cannot conduct themselves with the high standard. Actually, for being a good person among everyday people there are heroes who serve as models, but those are models among everyday people. If you want to be a practitioner, it all depends on cultivating your heart and on you, yourself being enlightened since there are no role models. Fortunately, today we have made public this Dafa. In the past, if you wished to practice cultivation nobody would teach you. This way, you can follow Dafa and perhaps you will do better. Whether you can practice cultivation or make it and what level you can reach all depend on you, yourself.

Of course, the way karma transforms does not take place completely as I have just described; it can manifest in other areas. It can happen either in society or at home. While walking on a street or in another social environment, one may come across some trouble. You will be made to abandon all those attachments that cannot be given up among everyday people. As long as you have them, all of those attachments must be removed in different environments. You will be made to stumble, whereby you will become enlightened to the Tao. This is how one goes through cultivation practice.

Typically there is another situation. In the course of cultivation practice many of you will find that when practicing qigong, your spouses will often become very unhappy. As soon as you begin the exercises, your spouse will throw a fit at you. If you do something else, your spouse will not mind. No matter how much time you waste playing Mah Jong,[2] your spouse might

---

[2] Mah Jong—traditional Chinese game played by four people.

be unhappy, but not as much as if you practice qigong. Your qigong practice does not bother your spouse, and what a good thing it is since you exercise the body to keep fit, and you are not disturbing your spouse. Yet once you start practicing qigong, your spouse will throw things around and start a fight. Some couples almost get divorced because of disputes over qigong practice. Many people have not thought about why this situation takes place. If you ask your spouse later: "Why do you get so upset if I practice qigong?" he or she cannot explain it and will really be out of reasons. "Really, why did I become so angry and worked up at that time?" Actually, what's the matter? While one is practicing qigong, one's karma must be transformed. You will not gain without loss, and what you lose are bad things. You must sacrifice.

Perhaps, as soon as you step in the door, your spouse will throw a fit right in your face. If you endure it, your effort of practicing qigong today is not in vain. Some people also know that in qigong practice one should value de. Therefore, this person usually gets along very well with his spouse. He thinks, "Usually, if I say 'one,' she doesn't say 'two.' Today she's overruling me." He cannot control his temper and will start a fight. With this, today's practice ends up in vain. Because karma was there, she was helping him remove it. But he would not accept it and started a fight with her. The karma thus could not be eliminated. There are a lot of these instances and many of our practitioners have experienced them, but they have not thought about why they were this way. Your spouse would not care if you were to do something else. Qigong practice should actually be a good thing, but she always finds fault with you. In fact, your wife is helping you eliminate karma, though she does not know it herself. She is not fighting with you only superficially and still good to you in her heart—it is not so. It is real anger from the bottom of her heart, because whoever has acquired the karma feels uncomfortable. It is guaranteed to be this way.

Upgrading Xinxing

Because many people could not maintain good xinxing in the past, many problems occurred. After their practice reached a certain level, they could not make further progress. Some people have a high xinxing level to begin with. Their tianmu are opened at once with the practice and can reach a certain realm. Because this person has relatively good inborn quality and a high xinxing level, his gong increases rapidly. By the time the gong reaches his xinxing level, the gong has also increased up to that level. If he wants to continue increasing his gong, the conflict will also become very serious, as it requires him to keep upgrading xinxing. This is particularly true for a person with good inborn quality. He may think that his gong has been increasing well and the practice also goes very well. Why are there suddenly so many problems? Everything goes wrong. People mistreat him, and his boss also does not favor him. Even the situation at home becomes very tense. Why are there so many problems all of a sudden? This person himself might not get it. Because of his good inborn quality, he has reached a certain level that brings about this situation. Yet how can that be a practitioner's final criterion for completing cultivation? It is far from the end of cultivation practice! You must continue to upgrade yourself. Because of that little amount of your inborn quality you have reached this state. In order to ascend further, the standard must be raised as well.

Someone may say, "I'll earn some more money to settle my

family down well so I won't have to worry about anything. Afterwards, I'll practice cultivation." I would say that this is your wishful thinking. You are unable to interfere with the lives of others, nor can you control others' fates, including those of your wife, sons, daughters, parents, or brothers. Can you decide those things? Furthermore, how will you practice cultivation if you do not have any worries or troubles? How can you do the exercises comfortably and restfully? How can there be such a thing? That is what you think, from the perspective of everyday people.

Cultivation practice must take place through tribulations so as to test whether you can part with and care less about different kinds of human sentimentality and desires. If you are attached to these things, you will not succeed in cultivation. Everything has its karmic relationship. Why can human beings be human? It is because human beings have sentimentality. They live just for this sentimentality. Affection among family members, love between a man and a woman, love for parents, feelings, friendship, doing things for friendship, and everything else all relate to this sentimentality. Whether a person likes to do something or not, is happy or unhappy, loves or hates something, and everything in the entire human society comes from this sentimentality. If this sentimentality is not relinquished, you will be unable to practice cultivation. If you are free from this sentimentality, nobody can affect you. An everyday person's mind will be unable to sway you. What takes over in its place is benevolence, which is something more noble. Of course, it is not easy to abandon this sentimentality right away. Cultivation practice is a long process and a process of gradually giving up one's attachments. Nonetheless, you must be strict with yourself.

As practitioners, you will suddenly come across conflicts.

What should you do? You should always maintain a heart of compassion and kindness. Then, when you run into a problem, you will be able to do well because it gives you room to buffer the confrontation. You should always be benevolent and kind to others, and consider others when doing anything. Whenever you encounter a problem, you should first consider whether others can put up with this matter or if it will hurt anyone. In doing so, there will not be any problems. Therefore, in cultivation practice you should follow a higher and higher standard for yourself.

Some people often do not understand these issues. When a person's tianmu is open and sees a Buddha, he will go home and worship the Buddha, praying in his mind, "Why don't you help me out? Please solve this problem for me." That Buddha, of course, will not do anything for this person because that problem is arranged by the Buddha, intending to improve his xinxing and upgrade him by way of the tribulation. How can the Buddha take care of the problem for you? He will not solve the problem for you at all. How can you increase your gong and upgrade your xinxing and level if he solves your problem? The key is to increase your gong. To the great enlightened people, living as a human being is not the purpose, and one's life is not meant for being human—it is meant for you to return to the origin. Human beings suffer a lot. The enlightened people think that the more one suffers, the better, as one should speed up repaying one's debts. This is what they think. Some people do not understand it and begin to complain to the Buddha if their praying does not work, "Why don't you help me? I burn incense and kowtow to you everyday." Because of this, one may throw the Buddha statue to the ground and start to condemn Buddha thereafter. As a result of this condemnation, one's xinxing drops, and one's gong disappears. The person knows that everything is gone, so he resents Buddha

162

even further, believing that the Buddha is ruining him. The person measures Buddha's xinxing with an ordinary person's criteria. How can that comparison be made? How can it work if a person views high-level things with the standard of everyday people? Therefore, a lot of these cases often take place when people regard their suffering in life as being unfair. Many people drop down this way.

In the past few years, many grand qigong masters, including the well-known ones, have fallen to become nobody. Of course, those genuine qigong masters have already left upon accomplishing their missions in history. Only some are left behind and become lost among everyday people, being still active with a lowered xinxing level. These people have already lost their gong. A few qigong masters who were well-known in the past are still active in society. When their masters found that they were lost among everyday people and could not free themselves from obsessing over fame and personal gain, after they had become hopeless, their masters took away their fu yuanshen. All of the gong was developed in the body of fu yuanshen. There are quite a lot of these typical examples.

In our school of practice, these cases are quite few. Even if there are some, they are not as notable. There are many outstanding examples in terms of xinxing improvement. One practitioner works in a textile factory in X city of Shandong Province. After studying Falun Dafa, he taught other coworkers to practice. As a result, the factory has taken on a new look. He used to take home pieces of towels from the textile factory, and so did the rest of the employees. After practicing Dafa, instead of taking things home he brought back to the factory what he took home before. When others saw his actions, nobody would take things home anymore. Some employees also returned to the factory what they previously took home. This situation occurred throughout the entire factory.

One volunteer director at a city's Dafa instruction center went to a factory to see how Falun Dafa practitioners were doing with their practice. The factory manager came out to meet him in person: "Since studying Falun Dafa, these workers have been coming to work early and going home late. They work very diligently and will do any assignment the boss gives. They also no longer compete for personal gain. By doing so, they've made the whole factory take on a new look, and the factory's economic returns have also improved. Your practice is so powerful. When is your teacher coming? I'd also like to attend his lectures." The main purpose of our cultivating Falun Dafa is to bring people toward the higher level. While it does not intend to do such a thing, it can nonetheless assume a great constructive role by promoting spiritual civilization in society. If everyone searches internally and considers how to conduct himself or herself well, I would say that society will stabilize and the human moral standard will rise again.

When I was teaching the Fa and the practice in Taiyuan,[3] there was a practitioner over fifty years old. She and her spouse had come to attend my lectures. When they walked into the middle of the street, a car drove by very fast, and its rearview mirror caught the elderly lady's clothes. With her clothes caught by the car, the lady was dragged for a distance of over ten meters and brought down to the ground. The car stopped after moving beyond twenty meters. The driver was very upset after getting out of the car: "Hey, you weren't watching where you were walking."

---

[3] Taiyuan (tie-yu-en)—capital city of Shangxi Province.

164

Nowadays, people behave this way and will first of all shirk responsibility upon coming across a problem, regardless of whether they are at fault. The passengers inside the car said: "Find out how badly the lady was hit. Let's take her to a hospital." The driver came to his senses and rushed to say: "How is everything, ma'am? Are you hurt? Let's go to a hospital and take a look." This practitioner slowly got up from the ground and said: "There's nothing wrong. You can leave." She scrubbed off the dirt on her clothes and left with her husband.

She came to the class and told me this story, and I was very pleased. Our practitioners' xinxing have indeed improved. She said to me: "Teacher, I studied Falun Dafa today. If I hadn't studied Falun Dafa, I wouldn't have treated the accident this way today." Think about it, everyone: For a retired person, the prices of merchandise are so high these days and there is no welfare benefit. A person over fifty years old was dragged that far by a car and knocked down to the ground. Where could her body be injured? Everywhere. She could have stayed on the ground without having to get up. Go to the hospital? Fine. She could have stayed at the hospital and would not move out. An everyday person might be that way, but she is a practitioner and did not do that. We have said that good or evil comes from a person's spontaneous thought, and the thought at that moment can bring about different consequences. With her old age, if she were an everyday person, how could she not be injured? Yet, her skin was not even scratched. Good or evil comes from that instant thought. If she were lying down there claiming, "Ugh, I feel terrible. Something is wrong here and there." Then, her bones might really have been fractured, and she would be paralyzed. No matter how much money she was paid, how could she be comfortable being hospitalized for the rest of her life? Those bystanders even found it strange that the elderly woman did not blackmail him and ask him for money. Nowadays, human moral values have been distorted. The driver indeed drove the car too fast, but how could he possibly hit someone on purpose? Didn't he do it unintentionally? But, people are like this today. If he were not blackmailed, even the bystanders would find it unfair. I have said that now people cannot distinguish good from bad. If one tells another person that he is doing something wrong, he will not believe it. Because human moral values have changed, some people seek nothing but self-interest and will do anything for money. "If a person is not after self-interest, heaven and earth will kill him"—this has already become a motto!

One practitioner in Beijing took his child to Qianmen[4] for a walk after dinner and saw a commercial vehicle promoting lottery tickets. The child became interested and asked to play the lottery. He gave the child one yuan to play, and the child ended up with the second prize, a luxury junior bike. The child was very delighted. At once an idea flashed into his mind: "I'm a practitioner. How can I go for such a thing? How much de must I give away if I get something that isn't paid for?" He said to the child: "Let's not take it. We can buy one ourselves if you want it." The child became upset: "I've begged you to buy one, and you didn't do it. Now, you won't let me keep it when I get one on my own." The child cried and screamed terribly. This man could not do anything about it but take the bike home. At home, the more he thought about it, the more uneasy he felt. He thought about sending the money to those people. Then he figured: "The lottery tickets are gone, and won't they divide the money among themselves if I send it to them? I should donate the money to my workplace."

---

[4] Qianmen (chyen-mun)—one of the major shopping districts in Beijing.

Fortunately, there were quite a few Falun Dafa practitioners in his workplace, and his boss could understand him. If it occurred in a typical environment or a typical workplace, where you said that you were a practitioner who did not want a lottery bike and wanted to donate the money to the workplace, even the boss would think that you had some mental problems. Others would also make some comments: "Has this person gone astray in qigong practice or developed cultivation insanity?" I have said that the moral values have been distorted. In the 1950's and 1960's, this would be no big deal and quite common—nobody would find it odd or strange.

We have said that no matter how much human moral values have changed, this characteristic of the universe, Zhen-Shan-Ren, will forever remain unchanged. If someone says that you are good, you may not really be good. If someone says that you are bad, you may not really be bad. This is because the criteria that evaluate good and bad are distorted. Only one who complies with this characteristic of the universe is a good person. It is the sole criterion which determines a good or bad person, and it is recognized by the universe. Although great changes have taken place in human society, human moral values have declined tremendously. Human morality is deteriorating daily, and profits have become the sole motivation. Yet, changes in the universe do not occur according to changes in humankind. As a practitioner, one cannot conduct oneself based on the standard of everyday people. It is not permitted if you go do things simply because everyday people consider them right. When everyday people say that it is good, it may not be good. When everyday people say that it is bad, it may not be bad, either. In this time when the moral values are distorted, if you tell someone that he is doing something bad, he will not believe it! As a practitioner, one must assess things with the characteristic of the universe. Only then can one distinguish what is genuinely good and what is truly bad.

Guanding

In the community of cultivators, there is this circumstance called guanding. Guanding is a religious ritual from the cultivation way of Tantrism in the Buddha School. Its purpose is that, through the procedure of guanding, a person will no longer follow other schools of cultivation and will be accepted in this particular school as a true disciple. Now, what's so strange about this? This religious formality is also being applied to qigong practices. Not only is it practiced in Tantrism, but also in the Tao School. I have said that all those who teach in society the practice of Tantrism under the banner of Tantrism are shams. Why is it put this way? It is because Tang Tantrism has already disappeared from our country for over one thousand years, and it no longer exists. Because of the language barrier, Tibetan Tantrism has never been able to be entirely introduced to the *Han*[5] regions. Particularly, because it is an esoteric religion, it must be secretly practiced in monasteries. It must also be secretly taught by the master, and the master has to take the person to practice secretly. If this cannot be done, it absolutely cannot be taught.

Many people who go to Tibet to study qigong have this agenda: They want to find a master and study Tibetan Tantrism in order to become qigong masters in the future and to become rich and famous. Think about it, everyone: A true, living Buddhist

---

[5] *Han* (hahn)—the majority ethnicity of Chinese people.

lama who has received genuine teaching has very powerful supernormal capabilities and can read such a person's mind. Why does the person come here? He will know it right away by reading the person's mind: "You come here wanting to study the practice and to become a qigong master for money and fame, undermining this school of Buddha cultivation." For such a serious practice in Buddhahood cultivation, how can it be casually ruined by your pursuit of becoming a qigong master for fame and money? What's your motivation? Therefore, he will not teach this person anything at all, nor will this person get any real teachings. Of course, with so many monasteries around, one may learn some superficial things. If one's mind is not right, one will acquire futi when one tries to be a qigong master and then commits wrongdoings. Futi animals also have energy, but it is not from Tibetan Tantrism. Those who go to Tibet sincerely in search of the Dharma may settle down there once they arrive—those are true practitioners.

It is strange that now many Taoist practices also perform guanding. The Tao School uses energy channels. Why should it practice the so-called guanding? I have been to the South to give lectures. According to what I know, there are over ten heterodox practices that do guanding, particularly in the region of Guangdong. What are they trying to do? If the master does guanding to you, you will become his disciple and cannot learn any other practice. If you do, he will punish you, as that is what he does. Isn't that doing an evil practice? What he teaches is something for healing and fitness. People are learning it simply because they want to have healthy bodies. Why should he do these things? Someone claims that if people practice his qigong, they cannot practice any other qigong. Can he save people toward completion of cultivation? That is misleading disciples. Many people do things this way.

The Tao School never teaches guanding, but now it also has the so-called guanding. I have found that the qigong master who makes the loudest noise about the practice of guanding has a gongzhu only as high as a two or three-story building. I think that for a well-known qigong master, his gong has decreased quite pitifully. Hundreds of people are lining up for him to do guanding. His gong is limited to that height and will soon fall to nothing. What can he use to do guanding then? Isn't he deceiving people? When seen from another dimension, genuine guanding makes one's bones look like white jade from the head to the feet. It is through gong or the high-energy matter that one's body is purified from the head to the feet. Can this qigong master do that? He cannot. What does he do? Of course, he probably will not try to start a religion. His goal is that once you study his practice, you belong to him. You must attend his classes to study his things. The goal is to earn your money. He will not make any money if no one studies his practice.

Like disciples in other cultivation practices of the Buddha School, disciples of Falun Dafa will experience many times guanding by the master in other dimensions; but you will not be told about it. Those with supernormal capabilities or those who are sensitive may feel it during sleep or at another time, when a warm current suddenly comes down from the top of the head to all over the body. The purpose of guanding is not to add higher gong to yours, as it must be developed through your own cultivation practice. Guanding is a reinforcing method for purifying and further cleaning up your body. One will go through guanding many times—your body must be cleaned up at every level. Because cultivation depends on one's own efforts while the transformation of gong is done by the master, we do not practice the ritual of guanding.

There are some people who also practice so-called "worshipping the master." Speaking of this, I would like to mention something. Many people want to worship me as the master. This period of ours in history is different from that of Chinese feudal society. Do kneeling down and kowtowing stand for taking someone as the master? We do not practice this ritual. Many people think: "If I kowtow, burn incense, and worship Buddha with a sincere heart, my gong will increase." I find this quite ridiculous. Genuine cultivation practice depends entirely upon a person him or herself, so it is useless to pray for something. You do not have to worship a Buddha or burn incense. As long as you really practice cultivation according to the standard of a practitioner, Buddha will be very pleased to see you. If you always do bad deeds outside, he will be disgusted to see you although you burn incense and kowtow to him. Isn't this the truth? Genuine cultivation practice depends upon the person him or herself. What's the use of your kowtowing and worshipping the master if you do whatever you want today upon stepping outside this door? We do not care for this formality at all. You could even damage my reputation!

We have given everyone so many things. For all of you, as long as you truly practice cultivation and conduct yourselves strictly according to Dafa, I will treat you as my disciples. As long as you practice Falun Dafa, we shall treat you as disciples. If you do not want to practice it, we cannot do anything for you. If you do not practice cultivation, what's the use of carrying that title? It does not matter whether you are from the first session of classes or the second session. How can you be our practitioners by doing the exercises alone? To attain a healthy body and truly make progress toward the high levels, you must practice cultivation by truly following our xinxing standard. Therefore, we do not care for those formalities. As long as you practice cultivation, you are a practitioner in our school of practice. My fashen know everything—they know everything on your mind, and they can do anything. They will not take care of you if you do not practice cultivation. If you practice cultivation, they will help you all the way to the end.

In some qigong practices, practitioners who have never seen their masters claim that if they pay a few hundred yuan and kowtow to a certain direction, that will be good enough. Isn't that self-deception and deceiving others? Additionally, these people are very devoted thereafter and begin to defend or protect their practices and masters. They also tell others not to study other practices. I find it quite ridiculous. Also, someone does something called *mo ding*.[6] Nobody knows what effect there is after his touch.

Not only those who teach their practices under the banner of Tantrism are phony; all those who teach qigong in the name of Buddhism are the same as well. Think about it, everyone: For several thousand years, cultivation methods in Buddhism have been in those forms. How can it still be Buddhism if someone alters it? Cultivation methods are for serious Buddha cultivation, and they are extremely complex. A tiny change will cause a mess. Because the transformation of gong is very complex, what one feels accounts for nothing. One cannot practice cultivation based on how one feels. The religious form for monks is a cultivation method; once it is changed, it will not be something from that

---

[6] *mo ding*—as claimed by some qigong masters, touching the top of one's head to give energy.

school. There is a great enlightened person in charge of each school, and each school has produced many great enlightened persons. Nobody dares to casually change the cultivation method in that school. For a petty qigong master, what mighty virtue does he have to dare offend the master and change a practice of Buddhahood cultivation? Will it still be that school if it's really changed? Phony qigong can be distinguished.

Xuanguan Shewei[7]

Xuanguan shewei is also called *xuanguan yiqiao*.[8] These terminologies may be found in the books of <u>Dan Jing</u>, <u>Tao Tsang</u>, and <u>Xingming Guizhi</u>.[9] So, what's it all about? Many qigong masters cannot explain it clearly. This is because at the level of an average qigong master, one is unable to see it, nor is one allowed to see it. If a practitioner wants to see it, this person must reach the upper level of Wisdom Eyesight or higher. An ordinary qigong master cannot reach this level; thus, he cannot see it. Throughout history, the community of cultivators has been discussing what is xuanguan, where is yiqiao, and how to place xuanguan in position. In the books of <u>Dan Jing</u>, <u>Tao Tsang</u>, and <u>Xingming Guizhi</u>, you can find them all discussing the theories without telling you the substance. From one discussion to another, they confuse you. They do not explain things clearly because the substance cannot be known by everyday people.

---

[7] Xuanguan Shewei (shwen-gwan shuh-way)—"placement of the mysterious pass."

[8] *Xuanguan Yiqiao* (shwen-gwan yee-chyow)—one aperture of the mysterious pass.

[9] <u>Xingming Guizhi</u>—classic Chinese texts for cultivation practice.

Furthermore, I am telling you that because you are Falun Dafa disciples, I will tell you these words: "Never read those heterodox qigong books." I am not referring to the foregoing classic texts, but to those sham qigong books written by people today. You should not even open them. If the idea flashes in your mind that "well, this sentence seems reasonable," with this, the futi in the book will attach to your body. Many books were written under the control of futi which manipulate human attachments for fame and fortune. There are a lot—quite a lot—of phony qigong books. Many people are being irresponsible and writing books with futi and chaotic things in them. Usually, it is better not to even read the classic books mentioned above or other related classic scriptures, as it involves the issue of being single-minded in one practice.

One official from the China Qigong Science Research Society told me a story which really made me laugh. He said that there was a person in Beijing who often went to qigong seminars. After listening to many speeches, he felt that qigong was nothing more than what was said there. Because everyone was at the same level, they all talked about the same things. Not unlike other sham qigong masters, he thought that the content of qigong was not more than that! Then he also wanted to write a book on qigong. Think about it, everyone: A non-practitioner would write a qigong book. Nowadays, qigong books are copied from one another. As his writing progressed, he stopped on the issue of xuanguan. Who understands what xuanguan is? Even among genuine qigong masters, few understand it. He went to ask a phony qigong master. He did not know that the person was phony, as he did not understand qigong anyway. But if this phony qigong master could not respond to the question, wouldn't others realize that he was a fake? Therefore, he dared to make it up and said that xuanguan yiqiao is at the tip of one's penis. It sounds quite funny. Do not laugh, for this book is already published in society. This is to say that qigong books today have reached such a ridiculous extent. What is the use of your reading those books? It serves no use and can only be harmful.

What is xuanguan shewei? In the Shi-Jian-Fa practice, when a person's cultivation is beyond the middle-level or at the high-level Shi-Jian-Fa, this person starts to grow yuanying. The yuanying and *yinghai*[10] that we refer to are two different things. Yinghai are tiny and playful, and run around joyfully. Yuanying does not move. If yuanshen does not take control of it, yuanying will sit still on a lotus flower with two legs folded on top of each other and with both hands conjoined. Yuanying grows up from dantian and can be seen at the microscopic level, even when it is smaller than the point of a needle.

Additionally, another issue should be clarified. There is only one genuine dantian, and it is the *tian*[11] in the lower abdominal area. It is above the *huiyin*[12] point and below the belly inside one's body. Many forms of gong, many supernormal capabilities, many abilities, fashen, yuanying, yinghai, and a lot of beings all grow up from this tian.

In the past, a few practitioners talked about the upper dantian, the middle dantian and the lower dantian. I would say that they were wrong. Some people also claim that their masters have taught them this way for generations, and that the books have said so as

[10] *yinghai* (ying-high)—cultivated infant(s).

[11] *tian* (t'yen)—"field."

[12] *huiyin* (hway-yeen)—An acupuncture point in the center of the perineum.

well. Let me tell everyone that there was dross even in ancient times. Though some things may have been inherited for years, they might be incorrect. Some minor cultivation ways in the world have always been passed down among everyday people, but they are not for cultivation and are good for nothing. When they call it the upper dantian, the middle dantian, and the lower dantian, they are saying that dantian is wherever dan can grow. Isn't this a joke? When a person's mind focuses on somewhere in the body for a long time, an energy cluster will develop and form dan. If you do not believe it, keep your mind focused on your arm and keep it that way for a long time and dan will form there. Therefore, some people have seen this situation and declare that dantian is everywhere. This sounds even more ridiculous. They think that dantian is wherever dan forms. Actually, it is a dan, but not a tian. You may say that dan is everywhere, or that there is the upper dan, the middle dan, and the lower dan. However, there is only one actual tian that can develop numerous Fa, and it is the one in the lower abdominal area. Therefore, the sayings of the upper dantian, the middle dantian, and the lower dantian are wrong. Wherever one's mind concentrates for a long period of time, dan will form.

Yuanying grows up slowly from dantian in the lower abdominal area to become larger and larger. When it grows to be the size of a ping-pong ball, the shape of its whole body will be very visible with the nose and eyes formed. At the same time when yuanying is as big as a ping-pong ball, a small round bubble will be born beside it. After birth, the bubble will grow along with yuanying. When yuanying reaches four inches tall, a lotus flower petal will appear. When yuanying grows to be five or six inches, the petals of the lotus flower will basically be formed, and a layer of lotus flower will appear. A shining, golden yuanying will sit on a golden lotus flower plate, looking very beautiful. This is the never-degenerated Vajra body, which is called "the Buddha-body" in the Buddha School, or "yuanying" in the Tao School.

Our school of practice cultivates and requires both forms of the bodies; benti must be transformed as well. It is known to everyone that a Buddha body is not allowed to manifest among everyday people. With much effort, it can show its shape and its light can be seen with an everyday person's eyes. Upon transformation, however, the physical body appears to be the same as an average person's body among everyday people. An everyday person cannot tell the difference, though this body can travel between dimensions. When yuanying reaches four to five inches, the air bubble will also grow to that height, and it is transparent like an air balloon. Yuanying sits still there in the meditation position. By this time the air bubble will leave dantian. As it is grown and mature, it will therefore move up. The process of its moving up is very slow, but its motion can be observed daily. It gradually moves up higher and higher. With meticulous attentiveness, we are able to feel its existence.

When the air bubble reaches one's *tanzhong* point,[13] it will stay there for a while. Because there is a lot of the human body's essence there (the heart is also there), a system of things will be formed in the air bubble. This essence will be supplied into the air bubble. After a while, it will again move up. When it passes through the throat, one will feel suffocated as though the blood vessels are all blocked, and one will feel quite uncomfortably swollen. This will last only a couple of days. Then the air bubble

---

[13] *tanzhong* (tahn-jong) point—acupuncture point on the anterior midline of the chest.

will move up to the top of one's head, and we call it "reaching niwan." It is said that it has reached niwan while, in fact, it is as big as your whole head. Your head will feel swollen. Because niwan is a very important place for a human being, its essence must also be formed in the air bubble. Then the air bubble will try to squeeze out from the tianmu tunnel, and this feels quite uncomfortable. One's tianmu will be squeezed to the point of soreness, and one's temples will feel swollen while the eyes feel like they are digging inward. This feeling will last until the air bubble makes its way out of the tianmu tunnel and hangs in front of one's forehead. That is called xuanguan shewei, and it hangs there.

By this time, those with open tianmu are unable to see anything. This is because in cultivation practice in the Buddha School or the Tao School, its door is shut to speed up the formation of things inside xuanguan. There are two front doors and two rear doors, and they are all closed. Like the gateways of Tiananmen in Beijing, there are two big doors on each side. In order to make xuanguan quickly formed and substantiated, the doors are not opened except under very special circumstances. One who can see things with tianmu cannot see things at this point, as that is not allowed. What's the purpose of it hanging there? Because hundreds of energy channels in our body meet there, at this point they must all circle through xuanguan and then move out of it. They must go through xuanguan, and the goal is to lay some additional foundations and to form a system of things inside xuanguan. Because the human body is a small universe, it will form a small world with all of the essential things of the human body formed in it. Yet, it is still only a facility that cannot be fully operational.

In the Qimen School's cultivation practice, xuanguan is open. When xuanguan is ejected to the outside, it is like a cylinder, but it will gradually become round. Its doors on both sides are thus open. Because the Qimen School does not cultivate Buddhahood or the Tao, one must protect oneself. There are many masters in the Buddha School and the Tao School, all of whom can safeguard you. You do not need to see things, nor will you have any problems. It, however, is not so in the Qimen School, as one must protect oneself. Therefore, one must maintain the ability to see things. At that time, one's tianmu sees things like a telescope. After this system is formed, in a month or so, it begins to return to the inside. Upon returning inside the head, this is called the shift of xuanguan positions.

When xuanguan returns to the inside, one's head will also feel swollen and uncomfortable. Then it will squeeze out from one's *yuzhen* point.[14] This squeezing out also makes one feel uncomfortable, as though one's head were split open. Xuanguan will come out all at once, and then one will right away feel relieved. Upon coming out, xuanguan will hang in a very deep dimension and exist in the body form of a very deep dimension. Therefore, one will not rub against it during sleep. But, there is one thing: When xuanguan shewei occurs for the first time, one feels something in front of the eyes. Though it is in another dimension, one always feels that the eyes are blurred as if something is covering them, making one feel very uncomfortable. Because the yuzhen point is a very important pass, xuanguan must also form a system of things there. Then it returns inside one's body again. Xuanguan yiqiao, in fact, does not refer to one xuanguan position, for it must change positions multiple times.

---

[14] *yuzhen* (yu-jhun) point—acupuncture point in the lower rear side of one's head.

179

When it returns to niwan, it begins to descend in the body until reaching the *mingmen* point.[15] At the mingmen point, it will come out again.

The mingmen point in the human body is an extremely important and major point. It is called "aperture" in the Tao School and *"guan"*[16] by us. It is a major pass which truly resembles an iron gate, and it has numerous layers of iron gates. It is known that a human body has many layers. Our flesh cells are one layer, and the molecules inside are another. There is a gate placed at each layer of atoms, protons, electrons, the very microscopic particles, the infinitesimal microscopic particles, and from the infinitely microscopic particles down to the extremely infinite microscopic particles. Therefore, there are numerous supernormal capabilities and many special capabilities locked up inside the gates of different layers. Other practices cultivate dan. When dan is about to explode, the mingmen point must first be blasted open. If it is not blasted open, the supernormal capabilities cannot be released. After xuanguan forms a system at mingmen point, it will again return inside the body. Then it returns to the lower abdominal area. This is called xuanguan returning to the position.

Upon its return, xuanguan does not return to its original place. By now, yuanying has grown to be quite big. The air bubble will cover yuanying and envelop it. As yuanying grows, so grows xuanguan. In the Tao School, usually when yuanying grows to be about a six or seven-year-old child, it will be allowed to leave one's body; this is called yuanying coming to birth. Under the control of one's yuanshen, it can move around outside one's body.

[15] *mingmen* (ming-mun) point—"Gate of life"; an acupuncture point on the lower back and on the posterior midline.

[16] *guan* (gwan)—"pass."

One's physical body does not move, and one's yuanshen will come out. Normally in the Buddha School, yuanying will be out of any danger when it is cultivated to be as big as the person. At this time, it is usually allowed to leave the body and come out of the body. By now yuanying has grown to be as big as the person him or herself, and its cover is also big. The cover has already expanded outside one's body, and that is xuanguan. Because yuanying has grown to be so big, xuanguan will certainly expand outside the body.

Perhaps you have seen the Buddha statues in temples and find that Buddhas are always inside a circle. In particular, a Buddha's portrait always has a circle in which the Buddha sits. A lot of Buddha portraits are like that, and especially those in old temples are all like that. Why does a Buddha sit inside a circle? Nobody can explain it clearly. Let me tell you that it is this xuanguan, but at this time it is no longer called xuanguan. It is called a "paradise," though it is actually not yet a paradise, as it only has this facility. It is like a factory with the facility, but without the capability for production. There must be energy resources and raw materials before it can produce. A few years ago, many practitioners said: "My gong level is higher than that of a Bodhisattva," or "My gong level is higher than that of a Buddha." Upon hearing this, others would find it quite inconceivable. In fact, what they said was not at all inconceivable, for one's gong must indeed be cultivated to a very high level in the human world.

Then why is there this situation that one has become higher than a Buddha in cultivation? It cannot be understood so superficially. This person's gong is indeed at a very high level. That is because when his cultivation reaches a very high level and the moment of complete enlightenment, his gong level will indeed be very high. Just moments prior to the complete enlightenment, eight-tenths of his gong will be taken down together with his xinxing standard, and this energy will be used to substantiate his paradise—a paradise of his own. Everyone knows that in addition to this xinxing standard, a practitioner's gong is cultivated through suffering numerous lifelong tribulations and experiencing difficult environments. It is therefore extremely precious. Eight-tenths of this precious stuff is used to substantiate his paradise. Therefore, when he succeeds in cultivation in the future, he will get whatever he wants just by holding out his hands, and he will have anything he desires. He can do anything he wants, and there is everything in his paradise. That is his mighty virtue that is cultivated through his own suffering.

This person's energy can be transformed into anything at will. Therefore, if a Buddha wants to have something, eat something, or to play with something, he can do it. They come from his own cultivation achievement, which is *fowei*.[17] Without it, a person cannot succeed in cultivation. By this time it can be called one's own paradise. This person will only have two-tenths of his remaining gong to complete cultivation and attain the Tao. Though only two-tenths of his gong is left, his body is not locked. He can either give up this body or keep it, but this body will have already been transformed by the high-energy matter. At this time, he can exercise his great divine powers, which have unmatchable might. But when a person practices cultivation among everyday people, he is usually locked up without any major capabilities. No matter how high his gong level, he is still restricted. Now it is different.

---

[17] *fowei* (fwuo-way)—the Buddha status.

LECTURE FIVE

The Falun Emblem

The symbol of our Falun Dafa is Falun. Those with supernormal capabilities can see that this Falun is rotating. The same is true for our small Falun badges, which are also rotating. Our cultivation practice is guided by Zhen-Shan-Ren, the characteristic of the universe, and by the principles of the cosmos' evolution. Therefore, what we cultivate is quite immense. In a sense, this Falun emblem is a miniature of the universe. The Buddha School conceptualizes the universe as a world of ten directions with four faces and eight sides. Perhaps some people can see a vertical energy column above and below it. With its top and bottom, Falun exactly makes up the ten-directional world and constitutes this universe. It represents the Buddha School's summary of the universe.

This universe, of course, consists of numerous galaxies including our Milky Way. The whole universe is in motion, and so are all galaxies within it. Therefore, the Taiji symbols and the small 卐 symbols in the emblem are also rotating. The entire Falun is rotating, and the large 卐 symbol in the center is rotating as well. In a sense, it symbolizes our Milky Way. Because we are of the Buddha School, the center retains the symbol of the Buddha School; this is how its surface looks. All different substances have their forms of existence in those other dimensions where they have very substantial and very complex processes of evolution and forms of existence. This Falun emblem is the miniature of the universe. It also has its own form of existence

183

and process of evolution in all other dimensions, so I call it a world.

When Falun rotates clockwise, it can automatically absorb energy from the universe. Rotating counter-clockwise, it can give off energy. Inward (clockwise) rotation offers self-salvation while outward (counter-clockwise) rotation offers salvation to others—this is a feature of our practice. Some people have asked: "Since we're of the Buddha School, why is there also Taiji? Doesn't Taiji belong to the Tao School?" It is because what we cultivate is very immense, which is the same as cultivating the entire universe. Then think about it, everyone: This universe consists of two major schools, the Buddha School and the Tao School. With either of them excluded, it will not constitute a complete universe, nor can it be called a complete universe. Consequently, we have included things from the Tao School. Also, some people have said that in addition to only the Tao School, there are also Christianity, Confucianism, other religions, etc. Let me tell you that after its cultivation reaches a very high level, Confucianism belongs to the Tao School; when many Western religious cultivation practices reach higher levels, they are classified as belonging to the same system of the Buddha School. There are only two such major schools.

Then why do two of the Taiji patterns have red color at the top and blue color at the bottom, and the other two Taiji patterns have red color at the top and black color at the bottom? What we generally understand is that Taiji is made of the two substances of black and white, the qi of yin and yang. That notion comes from a very low level, as Taiji has different manifestations in different dimensions. At the highest level, its colors manifest in this way. The Tao that we commonly understand has this red color at the top and this black color at the bottom. For instance, some of our practitioners' tianmu are open, and they have discovered that the red color they see with their flesh eyes is green in the adjacent dimension. The golden color is seen as purple in another dimension, as it has this inversion. In other words, colors change from dimension to dimension. The Taiji with the red color at the top and the blue color at the bottom belongs to the Great Pre-Taoism, which includes the cultivation practices from the Qimen School. The four smaller 卐 symbols are from the Buddha School. They are the same as the one in the middle, which is also from the Buddha School. The Falun in these colors is relatively bright, and we use it as the symbol of Falun Dafa.

The Falun that we see through tianmu is not necessarily in these colors, because its background color can change, although its pattern does not change. When the Falun that I have installed in your lower abdominal area rotates, your tianmu may see it as red, purple, green, or perhaps colorless. Its background color keeps changing in the order of red, orange, yellow, green, sky-blue, blue, and purple. As a result, what you see may be different colors, but the svastikam[1] symbols or the Taiji's colors and pattern within it will remain the same. We find that this background color looks relatively good, so we have adopted it. Those with supernormal capabilities can see a lot of things beyond this dimension.

Some people say: "This symbol 卐 looks like Hitler's stuff." Let me tell you that this symbol itself does not connote any

---

[1] svastikam—"Wheel of light" from Sanskrit, the symbol dates back over 2,500 years and has been unearthed in cultural relics in Greece, Peru, India, and China. For centuries it has connoted good fortune, represented the sun, and been held in positive regard.

concepts of class. Some people say: "If its corner tilts to this side, it'll be Hitler's stuff." It is not so, because it rotates both ways. Our human society began to know this symbol widely twenty-five hundred years ago in Sakyamuni's time. It has only been several decades since Hitler's time during World War II. He appropriated it, but the color he used was different from ours. It was black and pointing upwards, and was used in the upright position. I will only address so much regarding this Falun, though I have only mentioned its superficial form.

Then what does this svastikam 卐 symbolize in our Buddha School? Some people say that it stands for good fortune, which is an interpretation of everyday people. Let me tell you that 卐 signifies a Buddha's level. It only exists at the Buddha level. A Bodhisattva or an Arhat does not have it. But senior Bodhisattvas, the Four Senior Bodhisattvas, have it. We have found that these Senior Bodhisattvas have far surpassed the level of ordinary Buddhas, and they are even higher than a Tathagata. Beyond the level of Tathagata, there are numerous Buddhas. A Tathagata has only one 卐 symbol. Those who have reached beyond the level of Tathagata will have more 卐 symbols. A Buddha whose level is twice as high as a Tathagata has two 卐 symbols. For those who are still higher, they have three, four, five svastikams, and so on. Some have so many svastikams that they are all over their bodies, including on their heads, shoulders, and knees. When there are too many of them, they will even appear on their palms, fingers, foot arches, toes, etc. As one's level continually increases, one will have more and more 卐 symbols. Therefore, the 卐 symbol represents a Buddha's status. The higher a Buddha's status, the more 卐 symbols a Buddha has.

The Qimen School[2]

In addition to the Buddha School and the Tao School, there is the Qimen School, which calls itself the Qimen cultivation practice. With regard to cultivation practices, everyday people have this perception: From ancient China to this day, people have regarded the Buddha School and the Tao School as orthodox cultivation ways, and they also call them the orthodox schools of cultivation practice. This Qimen School has never been made public, and very few people have heard about its existence, except from literary works.

Is there a Qimen School? Yes. During the course of my cultivation practice, particularly in the later years, I came across three highly-accomplished masters from the Qimen School, who imparted to me the essence of their practices, which is very unique and very good. Simply because it is very unique, what it cultivates is quite unusual and cannot be understood by most people. In addition, they state that they are neither of the Buddha School nor of the Tao School. They do not cultivate Buddhahood or the Tao. Upon learning that they do not cultivate Buddhahood or the Tao, people call them *pangmen zuodao*.[3] They call themselves the Qimen School. Pangmen zuodao has a deprecating connotation, but here it is not in a negative sense, as it does not accuse the school of being an evil practice—that is for sure. The term's literary definition also does not imply an evil practice. In history, the Buddha School and the Tao School have been called the orthodox schools of cultivation practice. When this practice

---

[2] Qimen (chee-mun) School—"unconventional School."

[3] *pangmen zuodao* (pahng-mun zuoh-dow)—"the side door and clumsy way."

187

cannot be understood by the public, people call it "pangmen" or a side door and an unorthodox school. What is "zuodao" about? "Zuo" implies clumsiness or a clumsy way. A classical term in China, zuo often referred to being clumsy. Pangmen zuodao carries this implication.

Why isn't it an evil practice? This is because it also has strict xinxing requirements. Its cultivation practice also follows the characteristic of the universe. It does not violate the characteristic or the law of the universe, nor does it engage in committing wrong deeds. Therefore, it cannot be called an evil practice. The Buddha School and the Tao School are orthodox schools, not because the characteristic of the universe conforms to their practices, but because the practices of both the Buddha School and the Tao School observe the characteristic of the universe. If the Qimen School's cultivation practice also complies with the characteristic of the universe, it is not an evil practice, but a righteous school as well. This is because the criterion for discerning good or bad and benevolence or evil is the characteristic of the universe. Its cultivation abides by the characteristic of the universe, so it is also an orthodox way, despite that its requirements differ from those in the Buddha School and the Tao School. It does not widely teach disciples, and it is taught to a very small population. The Tao School teaches a lot of disciples, but only one disciple receives the genuine teachings. The Buddha School believes in salvation of all beings, so whoever can practice cultivation may do it.

A Qimen School practice cannot be inherited by two persons, for it is passed down to only one chosen person over a long period of time in history. Therefore, throughout history it could not be seen by everyday people. Of course, when qigong was popular, I found that a few people from this school also came out to teach.

After some public teaching, however, they realized that it was not feasible because the master forbade some of it from being imparted to the public. If you want to teach it to the public, you cannot select students. Those who come to learn it will bring different xinxing levels and different mentalities, as they are people of all different kinds. You will be unable to select disciples for teaching. Therefore, the Qimen School cannot be widely taught in public. Doing so can easily cause danger because its practice is very unique.

Some people wonder that while the Buddha School cultivates Buddhahood and the Tao School cultivates the Tao, what will a Qimen School practitioner become after completing cultivation? This person will be a wandering god without a definite boundary in the universe. It is known to everyone that Tathagata Sakyamuni has the Saha Paradise, Buddha Amitabha has the Paradise of Ultimate Bliss, and Medicine Buddha has the Glazed Paradise. Every Tathagata or great Buddha has his or her own paradise. Every great enlightened person constructs a paradise of his or her own, and many of his or her disciples live there. Yet one from the Qimen School does not have a designated boundary in the universe, and this person will be like a wandering god or lonesome immortal.

Practicing Evil Cultivation

What is "practicing evil cultivation?" It has several forms. There are people who specialize in practicing evil cultivation, since throughout history there have been people who pass down these things. Why are they being passed down? It is because they seek fame, personal gain, and money among everyday people; those are what they want. Of course, such a person does not have a high xinxing level and cannot get gong. What can he get then? Karma. If one has a lot of karma, it can also become a form of energy. But this person does not have any status and he cannot be compared with a practitioner. In comparison with everyday people, however, he can restrain them because karma is also a form of energy. When its density becomes very high, it can also strengthen the supernormal capabilities in one's body and produce such an effect. Therefore, throughout history some people have taught this. Such a person claims: "By doing bad deeds and by swearing, I can increase my gong." He is not increasing gong. Actually, he is increasing the density of this black substance, since doing bad deeds can bring about the black substance, karma. Therefore, this person's petty inborn supernormal capabilities can be reinforced by this karma. He can also develop some minor supernormal capabilities, though they are incapable of doing anything significant. These people hold that by doing bad deeds, they can also increase gong—that is what they say.

Some people say: "When a Tao is one *chi*[4] tall, a demon would be one *zhang*[5] high." That is a false statement made by everyday people. A demon will never be higher than a Tao. There is this fact that the universe we know as human beings is a tiny one among numerous universes, and we call it the universe for short. Every time our universe goes through a period of a great many years, it always experiences a great catastrophe which destroys everything in the universe, including planets and all lives. The motion of the universe follows a law. In our universe of this time, the human race is not the only species that has become

---

[4] *chi* (chr)—a Chinese unit of length (=1/3 meter).

[5] *zhang* (jahng)—a Chinese unit of length (=3 1/3 meters).

corrupt. Many lives have already observed the situation that, as far as the present time is concerned, a big explosion occurred long ago in the space of this universe. Today, astronomers cannot observe it because what we can now see through the most powerful telescopes are things 150 thousand light years back. In order to see the changes of the present cosmic body, we must wait for 150 thousand years to pass. That is quite a distant age.

At present, the entire universe has already undergone a great change. Whenever such a change takes place, all lives in the whole universe will be completely destroyed and lie in ruins. Every time this situation occurs, the characteristic and all the matter inside the previous universe must be blown up. Usually, all lives will be killed from the explosion. Yet, not everyone has been wiped out from the blast each time. After the new universe is reconstructed by the great enlightened beings at an extremely high level, there are still some that survive the explosion. The great enlightened beings build the universe according to their own characteristics and standards. Therefore, it has a different characteristic from that of the previous universe.

Those who have survived the explosion will continue to hold onto the previous characteristic and principles to do things in this universe. The newly constructed universe will observe the characteristic and principles of that new universe in its operation. Thus, those who escaped the explosion have become the demons that interfere with the principles of the universe. Nonetheless, they are not that bad since they are only abiding by the characteristic of the previous period's universe. They are what people refer to as the heavenly demons. However, they are no threat to everyday people, nor do they harm people. They only stick to their principles to do things. In the past, this was not supposed to be known by everyday people. I have said that there are many Buddhas beyond the level of Tathagata. What do those demons account for? They are very minute in comparison. Old age, illness, and death are also forms of demons, but they are also created to maintain the characteristic of the universe.

Buddhism believes in samsara, which mentions the issue of *asura*.[6] In fact, it refers to living beings in different dimensions, but they do not bear the human, inborn nature. To a great enlightened person, they are at a very low level and are quite incompetent. Nevertheless, they are scary in the eyes of everyday people since they have a certain amount of energy. They regard everyday people as animals, so they enjoy feeding on people. In recent years, they also came out to teach qigong. What sorts of things are they? How can they look like human beings? They look very scary. Once you learn their things, you will have to go with them and become their species. In qigong practice, if some people have bad thoughts that agree with their mentality, they will come to teach these people. One righteous mind can subdue one hundred evils. If you do not pursue anything, no one will dare to bother you. If you develop an evil thought or go after something bad, they will come to give you a hand, and you will be following a demonic cultivation way. This problem can take place.

Another situation is called unknowingly practicing an evil cultivation way. What is "practicing an evil cultivation way unknowingly?" It is when someone practices an evil way without realizing it. This problem is very common and simply too widespread. As I said the other day, many people practice qigong

---

[6] *asura*—"malevolent spirits" (from Sanskrit).

with wrong thoughts on their minds. Though they are practicing a standing exercise there with their hands and legs shaking from fatigue, their minds are not at rest. One is thinking: "Prices are going up. I have to go shopping after finishing the exercise. If I don't hurry up, things will be more expensive." Another person thinks: "The workplace is now assigning apartment units. Will I get one? The person in charge of assigning apartment units is always at odds with me." The more this person thinks about it, the angrier he becomes: "He won't assign me a unit for sure. How should I fight him... " All thoughts crop up. As I said earlier, they make comments from family issues to state affairs. When they speak of unpleasant topics, they become even angrier.

Qigong practice requires one to value de. In doing the exercises, if you do not think about good things, nor should you think about bad things. It is best if you do not think about anything. This is because during low-level qigong practice, a foundation must be laid. This foundation will play a critical role, for human mind activities have quite a part to play. Think about it, everyone: What're you adding to your gong? How can what you are practicing be good? How can it not be black? How many people who practice qigong are without these kinds of ideas? Though you practice qigong all the time, why haven't your illnesses gone away? Though some people do not have those bad thoughts at the exercise sites, they always practice qigong with an attachment to supernormal capabilities, the pursuit for this or that, different mentalities, and a variety of strong desires. Actually, they have already practiced evil cultivation unknowingly. If you say that this person is practicing an evil way, he or she will be unhappy: "I was taught by a well-known qigong master." But that well-known qigong master asks you to value de. Have you done it? During qigong practice, you always pitch in some bad thoughts.

How can you say that you will emerge from the practice with good things? This is the problem, and it is unknowingly practicing evil cultivation—something very common.

Double Cultivation of a Man and a Woman

In the community of cultivators, there is a cultivation practice called double cultivation of a man and a woman. Perhaps, you have seen the cultivation practices of Tibetan Tantrism where, in a Buddha sculpture or portrait, a male figure holds a female body, practicing cultivation. The male figure sometimes looks like a Buddha, and he holds a naked woman. Some may be transformations of Buddha in the appearance of a Vajra with the cow-head and horse-face, carrying an undressed female body as well. Why is it like this? We will first explain this matter to everyone. On our planet, it is not only China that has been influenced by Confucianism. A few centuries back our entire human race had similar moral values. Therefore, this cultivation practice actually did not come from this planet of ours. It came from another planet, but this method can indeed enable one to practice cultivation. When this cultivation practice was introduced to China at that time, it was unacceptable to the Chinese people precisely due to its portions of double cultivation of man and woman and of its secret practices. Therefore, during the Huichang period of the Tang Dynasty it was banned in the Han regions by the emperor. It was prohibited from being taught in the Han regions and was at that time called Tang Tantrism. Yet, it was passed down in the unique environment of Tibet, a special region. Why do they practice cultivation this way? Double cultivation of a man and a woman is for collecting yin to supplement yang and vice versa with mutual complement for mutual cultivation, enabling the goal of balancing yin and yang to be achieved.

It is known that according to either the Buddha School or the Tao School, particularly according to the Taoist theory of yin and yang, a human body inherently has yin and yang. Because a human body has yin and yang, it can develop through cultivation practice a variety of supernormal capabilities and living beings like yuanying, yinghai, fashen, etc. Because of the existence of yin and yang, one can develop many living beings through cultivation; the same is true either for a male body or a female body, and they can all grow in dantian. This theory really makes sense. The Tao School usually regards the upper body as yang and the lower body as yin. Some people also regard the back of the body as yang and the front of the body as yin. Others regard the body's left side as yang and its right side as yin. In China, we have a saying that the left side of the body is male and the right side female, and this is also derived from that with very sensible reasons. Because a human body inherently has yin and yang, with the interactions of yin and yang, it can itself achieve a balance of yin and yang; it can thus give birth to many living beings.

This then clarifies an issue: Without applying the method of the double cultivation of a male and a female, we can still reach a very high level in cultivation. In employing the method of male and female double cultivation, if it is used improperly, one will incur demonic interference, and it will become an evil practice. In Tantrism, if double cultivation of a male and a female is to be used at a very high level, the monk or lama must have reached a very high cultivation level. At that time, the master can guide a person in this type of cultivation practice. Because this person's xinxing level is quite high, he can conduct himself well without turning wicked. But, one with a low-level xinxing absolutely should not resort to this method. Otherwise, the person is bound to follow an evil practice. Because of a limited xinxing level and because he has not relinquished everyday people's desires and lust, that is where his xinxing's yardstick is, and it is bound to be evil if used. Therefore, we have said that when casually promoted at the low level, this is teaching an evil practice.

In recent years, quite a few qigong masters have been teaching double cultivation of a male and a female. What's so odd about it? Double cultivation of a man and a woman has also appeared in practices of the Tao School. In addition, it did not begin today, but started in the Tang Dynasty. How can the Tao School have double cultivation of a male and a female? According to the Taiji theory in the Tao School, a human body is a small universe that inherently has yin and yang. All genuine, great orthodox teachings have been passed down from a remote age. Any casual alternation or casual addition will mess up that particular school of practice and make it unable to achieve the goal of completing cultivation practice. So if your practice does not have double cultivation of a male and a female, you should never do that in cultivation. Otherwise, you will go wrong and run into problems. Particularly in our school of Falun Dafa, there is no double cultivation of a man and a woman, nor do we need it. That is how we look at this issue.

Cultivation of Mind and Body

The issue of cultivating mind and body has already been explained to all of you. Cultivating mind and body refers to cultivating one's xinxing at the same time that one's body is cultivated. In other words, benti is being transformed. In the process of

196

transformation, human cells will be gradually replaced by the high-energy matter, and aging will slow down. One's body will appear to gradually return to youth and experience gradual transformation until, in the end, it is completely replaced by the high-energy matter. By then, this person's body will have already been converted to a body of another type of matter. That body, as I said earlier, will transcend the Five Elements. Since it is no longer confined to the Five Elements, this person's body will no longer degenerate.

The cultivation practice in temples only deals with mind cultivation, so it does not teach exercises or cultivate the body. It requires nirvana, as the method that Sakyamuni taught requires nirvana. In fact, Sakyamuni himself had great, high-level Dharma, and he was able to completely transform his benti into the high-energy matter and take it away with him. In order to leave this cultivation method, he, himself took the path of nirvana. Why did he teach it this way? He did so to have people give up, to the greatest extent, attachments and everything, even including finally their physical bodies; all attachments were to be abandoned. In order to have people achieve this as much as possible, he took the path of nirvana. Therefore, Buddhist monks throughout history have all taken the path of nirvana. Nirvana means that when a monk dies he abandons his flesh body, and his own yuanshen will ascend with gong.

The Tao School emphasizes cultivating the body. Because it selects disciples and does not offer salvation to all beings, it has very outstanding pupils. Therefore, it teaches techniques and matters of how to cultivate life. Yet in this special cultivation practice of the Buddha School, and with Buddhism in particular, these are not taught. Not all practices in the Buddha School do not teach it. Many high-level practices in the Buddha School also teach it. Our school of practice teaches it. Our Falun Dafa requires both benti and yuanying; these two are different. Yuanying is also a body made of the high-energy matter, but it cannot be casually shown in this dimension of ours. In order to keep the appearance of an everyday person in this dimension over a long period of time, we must have our benti. Therefore, upon the transformation of this benti, its molecular combinations do not change even though its cells are replaced by the high-energy matter. Thus, this body will not look much different from that of an everyday person. Yet, there is still a difference: Namely, this body can enter other dimensions.

Those practices that cultivate both mind and body make one look very young in appearance, and one looks quite different from one's actual age. One day a person asked me: "Teacher, how old do you think I am?" As a matter of fact, she was approaching seventy years old, but she looked only over forty. Her face was without wrinkles, glowing with a fair and rosy complexion. She did not look like a person approaching seventy. This will happen to our Falun Dafa practitioners. To tell a joke, young ladies always like to apply facial makeup and want to make their complexion fairer and better. I would say that if you truly follow a cultivation practice of mind and body, you will naturally achieve that goal. It is guaranteed that you will not need to use cosmetics. We will not give more of these sorts of examples. In the past, because there were relatively more elderly comrades in different professions, I was treated as a young man. Things are getting better nowadays, and there are relatively more young people in every profession. Actually, I am not young anymore. I am heading toward fifty, as I am already forty-three years old now.

Fashen

Why is there a field around a Buddha statue? Many people cannot explain it. Some people say: "A Buddha statue has a field because monks chant scriptures to it." In other words, the field comes from monks' cultivation practice in front of it. Whether it is from the cultivation practice of monks or others, this energy should be scattered and not directional. The floor, the ceilings, and the walls of the entire temple should have the same field. Then why should the field on the Buddha statue be so powerful? Particularly for a Buddha statue in a remote mountain, in a cave, or on a rock, there is usually a field. Why is there this field? Some people have explained it this way or that way and still cannot explain it clearly. Actually, a Buddha statue has a field because it has a great enlightened person's fashen. Because the great enlightened person's fashen is there, it has energy.

Whether it is Sakyamuni or Bodhisattva Avalokitesvara,[7] if they really existed in history—think about it, everyone—weren't they also practitioners during their cultivation practice? When a person practices cultivation at a very high level beyond Shi-Jian-Fa, he or she will develop fashen. Fashen is born in one's dantian area and is made of Fa and gong. It manifests in other dimensions. Fashen has much of a person's power, but its mind and thoughts are controlled by that person. Yet, fashen itself is also a complete, independent, and realistic individual life. Therefore, it can do anything independently on its own. What fashen does is exactly the same as what the person's main consciousness wants it to do.

---

[7] Bodhisattva Avalokitesvara—known for her compassion, she is one of the two senior Bodhisattvas in the Paradise of Ultimate Bliss.

If a person does something in a certain way, his or her fashen will do it likewise; this is the fashen to which we refer. What I want to do can all be done by my fashen, such as adjusting the bodies of true practitioners. Because fashen does not carry an everyday person's body, it manifests itself in other dimensions. Its body is not a fixed one that cannot change; instead, it can become large or small. Sometimes, it becomes very large, so large that one cannot see its entire head. Sometimes, it becomes very tiny, even tinier than a cell.

Kaiguang[8]

A Buddha statue manufactured in a factory is only a piece of art. "Kaiguang" is to invite a Buddha's fashen to a Buddha statue that will then be worshipped as a tangible body among everyday people. In cultivation practice, when a practitioner has this heart of respect, the fashen on the Buddha statue will safeguard the Fa for this person, looking after and protecting him or her. That is the actual purpose of kaiguang. This can be done only with righteous thoughts expressed at the formal kaiguang ceremony, with the help of a great enlightened person at a very high level, or with the help of a practitioner at a very high level of cultivation who has this power.

A temple requires its Buddha statue to go through kaiguang, and people say that without kaiguang, a Buddha statue will serve no use. Today, the monks in temples—those genuine great masters—have all departed. Since the "Great Cultural Revolution," some of those junior monks who did not receive

---

[8] kaiguang (kye-gwang)—"light-opening"; in Buddhism, it is a consecration ritual to invite a Buddha to a Buddha statue or a Buddha portrait.

any real teachings have now become abbots. A lot of things have not been passed down. If you ask one of them: "What's the purpose of kaiguang?" He will say: "The Buddha statue will work after kaiguang." He cannot explain clearly why it is useful specifically, so he only holds the ceremony. He will put a Buddhist scripture inside a Buddha statue. Then he will seal the statue with paper and chant the scripture to it. He calls this kaiguang, but can the goal of kaiguang be achieved? That depends on how he chants the scripture. Sakyamuni said that one should chant the scripture with a righteous mind and undivided attention in order to shake the paradise of his cultivation practice. Only then can a great enlightened person be invited. And only when one of the great enlightened person's fashen arrives on the Buddha statue can the goal of kaiguang be achieved.

While chanting the scripture over there, some monks are thinking in their minds: "After kaiguang, how much money will I be paid?" Or while chanting the scripture, one thinks: "So-and-so treats me so badly." They also have personal conflicts. Now is the Dharma-ending Period. It cannot be denied that this phenomenon exists. We are not criticizing Buddhism here. Some of the temples are just not peaceful in the Dharma-ending Period. If one's mind is full of these things and expresses such ill thoughts, how can that great enlightened person come? The goal of kaiguang then cannot be achieved whatsoever. But it is not absolute, as there are a few good temples and Taoist monasteries.

In city "X," I saw a monk who had very dark hands. He put the scripture inside a Buddha statue and sealed it carelessly. After he mumbled a few words, the kaiguang procedure was over. Then he fetched another Buddha statue and mumbled a few words again. He charged forty yuan each time for kaiguang. Nowadays, monks

201

have commercialized kaiguang and made money off it. Upon taking a look at it, I found that kaiguang was not achieved as he could not do it at all. Nowadays monks even do such a thing. What else have I seen? A person who seemed to be a lay Buddhist was supposedly conducting kaiguang for a Buddha statue in a temple. He held a mirror in the sun to reflect sunlight on the Buddha statue. Then he claimed that kaiguang was done. It has become so ridiculous! Today, Buddhism has developed to this point, and it is a very common phenomenon.

A big bronze Buddha statue was made in Nanjing,[9] and it was put on Lantau Island in Hong Kong. It is a huge Buddha statue. Many monks from all over the world came to conduct kaiguang for it. One of the monks held a mirror in the sun to reflect the sunlight on the face of the Buddha statue and called it kaiguang. In a grand ceremony as solemn as this, such an act could even take place. I find it really lamentable! No wonder Sakyamuni said: "By the Dharma-ending Period, monks will have trouble saving themselves, let alone offering salvation to others." In addition, many monks interpret the Buddhist scriptures from their own perspectives. Even the scripture of the Lady Queen Mother has found its way into temples. Many things that are not of Buddhist classical materials have also entered temples, making these places quite chaotic and messy now. Of course, there are monks who still genuinely practice cultivation and are quite good. Kaiguang is actually to invite the fashen of a great enlightened person to stay on the Buddha statue. This is kaiguang.

So if this Buddha statue has not gone through kaiguang successfully, it should not be worshipped. If it is worshipped, serious consequences will occur. What are the serious

[9] Nanjing (nahn-jing)—capital of Jiangsu province.

consequences? Today, those who study the human body have discovered that our human mind activities or human thoughts can generate a substance. At a very high level, we have found that it is indeed a substance, but this substance is not in the form of the brain waves as we have discovered in research today. Instead, it is in the form of a complete human brain. Typically, when an everyday person thinks about something, what he or she generates is something in the form of the brain. Because it does not have energy, it will disperse shortly afterwards. A practitioner's energy, on the other hand, can be preserved much longer. This is not to say that this Buddha statue has a mind after being manufactured in the factory. No, it does not. Some Buddha statues have not been through the process of kaiguang, and neither was the goal of kaiguang achieved after they were taken to temples. If kaiguang is done by a phony qigong master or a person from an evil practice, it will be even more dangerous, as a fox or a weasel will sneak onto the Buddha statue.

For a Buddha statue that has not been through the procedure of kaiguang, if you worship it, it will be too dangerous. How dangerous will it be? I have said that as humankind evolves to this day, everything is deteriorating. The whole society and everything in the entire universe are becoming corrupt in succession. Everything that happens to everyday people is caused by them, themselves. It is very difficult to find an orthodox Fa or follow an orthodox way, owing to interference from various respects. One wants to find a Buddha, but who is a Buddha? It is very difficult to find one. If you do not believe it, let me spell it out. It will be terrible when the first person worships a Buddha statue that has not been through the procedure of kaiguang. How many people now worship a Buddha to attain the Right Fruit in cultivation? There are too few such people. What are most people's motivations for worshipping a Buddha? They seek to eliminate tribulations, solve problems, and make a fortune. Are these things from the Buddhist scriptures? They do not include these things whatsoever.

Suppose a Buddha worshipper who is after money prostrates himself before a Buddha statue or that of Bodhisattva Avalokitesvara or a Tathagata and says: "Please help me make some money." Well, a complete mind will form. Since this request is made to a Buddha statue, it is instantly projected onto the Buddha statue. In another dimension, an entity can become big or small. When this thought arrives on this entity, the Buddha statue will have a brain and mind, but it does not have a body. Other people also come to worship the Buddha statue. With this type of worship, they will gradually give it some amount of energy. It will be more dangerous if a practitioner worships it, for this worship will gradually give it energy and enable it to form a tangible body. Yet this tangible body is formed in another dimension. After it is formed, it exists in another dimension and can also learn some truths of the universe. Therefore, it can do some things for people. In this way, it can also develop some gong. But it helps people conditionally and for a price. It moves freely in another dimension and can control everyday people quite easily. This tangible body appears exactly the same as the Buddha statue. So it is human worshipping that creates a phony Bodhisattva Avalokitesvara or a fake Tathagata, which looks just like the Buddha statue with a Buddha's appearance. But the mind of the phony Buddha or phony Bodhisattva is extremely bad and is after money. It is born in another dimension. With a mind, it knows a little truth and does not dare to commit major wrongdoings, but it does dare to do minor bad deeds. Sometimes it also helps people; otherwise it is completely evil and will be killed. How does it help people? When someone prays: "Buddha, please help me because someone at home is ill," well, it will give you a hand. It will make you donate money in the donation box because its mind is after money. The more money you put in the donation box, the quicker the illness will be healed. Since it has some energy, it can, from another dimension, manipulate an everyday person. It will be particularly dangerous if a practitioner goes to worship it. What does this practitioner pray for? Money. Think about it, everyone: Why should a practitioner go after money? Praying to eliminate misfortune and illnesses for family members is the attachment of sentimentality to one's family. Do you want to change other people's fate? Everyone has his or her own fate! If you worship it and mumble: "Please help me make some money," well, it will help you. It would like you to go after more money, for the more you want it, the more things it can take from you. That is a fair trade. Other worshippers have put plenty of money in the donation box, and it will let you get some. How is it done? You may find a wallet after walking out the door, or your workplace may give you a bonus. Anyway, it will arrange for you to get money. How can it help you unconditionally? No loss, no gain. It will take some of your gong if it needs it, or it will take away the dan that you have cultivated. It wants these things.

These phony Buddhas are very dangerous sometimes. Many of our practitioners with tianmu open think that they have seen a Buddha. One might say that a group of Buddhas came to this temple today, with a Buddha called so-and-so leading a group of them. This person will describe what the group was like yesterday, what the group is like today, and that shortly after one group leaves, another arrives. Who are they? They just belong to this category—they are not genuine Buddhas, but sham ones. These cases are quite numerous.

It is more dangerous if this occurs in a temple. If monks worship it, it will take charge of them: "Aren't you worshipping me? And you are doing it with a clear mind! Well, don't you want to practice cultivation? I'll take care of you and tell you how to practice cultivation." It will make arrangements for them. Where will they go if they complete cultivation? Since cultivation practice is arranged by it, no schools of practice at higher levels will accept you. Since it arranges everything for you, you will have to follow it in the future. Won't your cultivation end up in vain? I have said that now it is very difficult for humankind to achieve the Right Fruit in cultivation. This phenomenon is quite common. Many of you have seen the Buddha-light in well-known mountains and along major rivers. The majority of it belongs to this category. It has energy and can manifest itself. A true great enlightened person does not casually reveal him or herself.

In the past, there were relatively fewer so-called earthly Buddhas and earthly Taos. Now, however, there are many. When they commit wrongdoings, the higher lives will kill them. When this is about to happen, they will run and get on the Buddha statues. Usually, a great enlightened person does not casually interfere with the principles of everyday people. The higher a great enlightened person's level is, the less he or she would bother to interfere with the principles of everyday people, not even a bit. After all, this higher being will not suddenly shatter a Buddha statue with lightening, for he or she will not do such a thing. The higher being will thus leave them alone if they climb onto Buddha statues. They know if they are to be killed, so they will try to escape. Consequently, is what you see the actual Bodhisattva Avalokitesvara? Is what you see a real Buddha? It is hard to tell.

Many of you may think of this issue: "What should we do with the Buddha statues at home?" Perhaps a lot of people have thought of me. In order to help practitioners in cultivation practice, I am telling you that you may do it this way. While holding the Buddha statue in hand, you can take my book (because the book has my photo) or my photo. Then you make the Big Lotus Flower Hand Sign[10] and make a request to Teacher for kaiguang, just as though you are requesting it to me. It will be done in half a minute. Let me tell everyone that this can only be done for our practitioners. This kaiguang does not work for your relatives or friends, since we only take care of practitioners. Some people say that they will take my photo to the homes of their relatives or friends to keep evil spirits away. I am not here to keep away evil spirits for everyday people—that is the worst disrespect for Teacher.

Speaking of the earthly Buddhas and earthly Taos, there is another issue. In ancient China, there were many people practicing cultivation in remote mountains and deep forests. Why aren't there any today? In fact, they have not disappeared. They just do not let everyday people know, and not even one of them is missing. These people all have supernormal capabilities. It is not that they are no longer around these years—they are still around. There are still several thousand of them in the world today. There are relatively more of them in our country, particularly in those famous big mountains and along the major rivers. They are also around in some high mountains, but they seal their caves with supernormal powers so that you cannot see them. Their cultivation progress is relatively slow, and their methods are relatively clumsy since they have not grasped the essence of cultivation. We, on the other hand,

---

[10] Big Lotus Flower Hand Sign—a hand posture for kaiguang.

directly target one's mind and practice cultivation according to the universe's highest characteristic and to the universe's form. Naturally, gong increases quite quickly. This is because the ways of cultivation practices are like a pyramid; only the central path is the main route. On those side and small paths, one's xinxing level in cultivation practice may not be high. One may become enlightened without achieving a high level of cultivation. They are, however, far inferior to the main road of genuine cultivation practice.

One from such a school of practice also takes disciples. Because this practice can only reach so high a cultivation level and one's xinxing level can only grow so high, all the disciples practice cultivation only towards this level. The closer a side-path practice is to the outskirts of cultivation, the more requirements it will have and the more complicated its cultivation practice will be, since it cannot grasp the essence of cultivation. In cultivation, one should mainly cultivate one's xinxing. They still do not understand this and believe that they can practice cultivation only by suffering hardships. Therefore, after a lengthy period of time and having practiced cultivation for several hundred years or more than one thousand years, they have obtained but a little bit of gong. In fact, it is not through suffering that they have gained gong. How do they get it? It is like with a normal person: One has a lot of attachments in youth, but by the time one becomes old, with the passage of time one's future seems hopeless. Those attachments are naturally relinquished and worn out. These side-path practices also use this method. They find that when one relies on sitting meditation, trance, and suffering hardships to progress in cultivation, one can also increase gong. Yet they do not know that their attachments of everyday people are slowly worn out over a long and harsh period of time, and that it is through slowly giving up those attachments that gong is increased.

Our practice has a focus and truly points out those attachments. By abandoning them, one will make very rapid progress in cultivation. I have been to some places where I would often run into those people who have practiced cultivation for many years. They said: "Nobody knows we are here. With regard to what you are doing, we won't interfere with it or cause any trouble." These persons belong to the ranks of those who are relatively good.

There have also been some bad ones that we have had to deal with. For instance, when I gave a class in Guizhou[11] for the first time, someone came to find me during the class and said that his grand master wanted to see me. He described his grand master and how he had practiced cultivation for many years. I found that this person carried negative qi and looked very vicious with a yellowish face. I said that I did not have time to see him and turned him down. Consequently, his old master was upset and began to make trouble for me, persisting to make trouble for me everyday. I am a person who dislikes fighting with others, nor was it worth a fight with him. Whenever he brought some bad things upon me, I would just clear them up. Afterwards, I would resume my lecturing.

There was a Taoist in the Ming Dynasty,[12] who was possessed by a snake at the time of his Taoist cultivation. Later, this Taoist died without completing his cultivation. The snake took over the Taoist's body and cultivated a human form. That man's grand

---

[11] Guizhou (gway-jhoe)—a province in the Southwest China.

[12] the Ming Dynasty— a period between 1368 A.D. and 1644 A.D. in Chinese history.

master was that snake in human form. Because his nature had not changed, he transformed himself into a big snake to make trouble for me. I thought that he went too far, so I caught him in my hand. I used a very powerful gong called "the dissolving gong" to dissolve his lower body and turn it into water. His upper body ran back home.

One day, the volunteer director at our instruction center in Guizhou was contacted by that person's disciple who said that his grand master wanted to see her. The director went there and entered a dark cave where she could not see anything except for a shadow sitting there with eyes beaming with green light. When he opened his eyes, the cave would be bright. The cave would be dark again if his eyes closed. He said in a local dialect: "Li Hongzhi will be coming again, and none of us will again cause those troubles this time. I was wrong. Li Hongzhi comes to offer salvation to people." His disciple asked him: "Grand Master, please stand up. What's wrong with your legs?" He answered: "I can no longer stand up as my legs were injured." When asked how they were injured, he began to describe his trouble-making process. At the 1993 Oriental Health Expo in Beijing, he again meddled with me. Because he always committed bad deeds and interfered with my teaching of Dafa, I then eliminated him completely. After he was eliminated, his fellow sisters and brothers all wanted to take action. At that point, I said a few words. They were all shocked and became so scared that none of them dared to do anything. They also came to understand what was going on. Some of them were still completely ordinary people though they had practiced cultivation for a long time. These are a few examples that I give you in addressing the issue of kaiguang.

Zhuyou Ke[13]

What is zhuyou ke? In the community of cultivators, in the course of teaching qigong many people teach it as a category of cultivation. In actuality, it is not something that belongs to the category of cultivation practice. It is taught as knack, incantations, and techniques. It utilizes the forms of drawing symbols, burning incense, burning papers, chanting incantations, etc. It can heal illness, and its treatment methods are very unique. For instance, if someone has grown a boil on her face, the practitioner will draw a circle on the ground with a brush-pen dipped in cinnabar ink and draw a cross in the middle of the circle. He will ask her to stand in the center of the circle. Then he will start to chant the incantations. Later he will use the brush-pen dipped in cinnabar ink to draw circles on her face. While drawing, he will chant the incantations. He will keep drawing until he makes a dot on the boil with the brush-pen, and the chanting of incantations is over. He will tell her that it is now well. When she feels the boil, she will find it indeed smaller and no longer painful, for this can be effective. He can heal minor illnesses, but not major ones. What will he do if your arm aches? He will begin to chant the incantations while asking you to hold out your arms. He will give a puff to the *hegu* point[14] of this hand of yours and have it exit from the hegu point of your other hand. You will feel a waft of air, and when you touch your arm, it will not feel as painful as before. In addition, some people use the methods of burning papers, drawing symbols, posting symbols, etc. They do these things.

---

[13] Zhuyou Ke (jew-yo kuh)—the practice of supplication.

[14] *hegu* (huh-goo) point—acupuncture point on the dorsum of the hand.

The worldly side-path practices in the Tao School do not cultivate life. They are entirely devoted to fortune-telling, *fengshui*,[15] exorcising evil spirits, and healing illness. Most of these are used by the worldly side-path practices. They can heal illnesses, but the methods employed are not good. We will not point out what they use to heal illness, but practitioners of our Dafa should not use them since they carry very low and very bad messages. In ancient China, healing methods were classified into subjects, for instance, fracture-setting methods, acupuncture, massage, chiropractic, acupressure, qigong healing, herb treatments, and so on. They were classified into many divisions. Each healing method is called a subject. This zhuyou ke has been classified as the thirteenth subject. Therefore, its full name is "The Number Thirteen Subject of Zhuyou." Zhuyou ke is not something within our cultivation category, for it is not gong attained through cultivation practice. Instead, it is something like a technique.

---

[15] *fengshui* (fung-shway)—Chinese geomancy, a practice of reading landscapes.

LECTURE SIX

Cultivation Insanity

In the community of cultivators, there is this term called cultivation insanity. It has had a very big impact on the public. In particular, some people have publicized it so much that some people become afraid of practicing qigong. When people hear that practicing qigong can lead to cultivation insanity, they will be too scared to try it. In fact, let me tell you that cultivation insanity does not exist whatsoever.

Quite a few people have acquired futi because their minds are not righteous. Their zhu yishi are unable to control themselves and regard it as gong. Their bodies are dictated by futi, making them mentally disoriented or making them yell and scream. When people see that qigong practice is like that, they are too scared to practice. Many of you think that this is qigong, but how can this be qigong practice? This is only the lowest state of healing and fitness, yet it is very dangerous. If you are accustomed to this way, your zhu yishi will always be unable to control yourself. Then your body might be dominated by fu yishi, foreign messages, futi, etc. You might engage in some dangerous acts and cause great damage to the community of cultivators. This is caused by one's immoral mind and the attachment to showing oneself off—this is not cultivation insanity. No one knows how some people have become so-called qigong masters, as they also believe in cultivation insanity. Actually, qigong practice cannot lead one to cultivation insanity. Most people learn this terminology from literary works, martial arts novels, and so on. If you do not believe

213

it, you can look into ancient books or cultivation books, where there are no such things. How can there be cultivation insanity? It is impossible for such a thing to occur.

It is usually believed that cultivation insanity has several forms. What I just mentioned is also one of its forms. Because one's mind is not righteous, one obtains futi and has various mentalities such as pursuing some qigong state to show off. Some people go right after supernormal capabilities or have practiced sham qigong. When they practice qigong, they are used to abandoning their zhu yishi. They lose their awareness of everything and give away their bodies to others. They become mentally disoriented and let their bodies be dictated by their fu yishi or foreign messages. They exhibit some strange behavior. Such a person will jump out of a building or dive into water if he is told to do so. He himself will not even want to live and will give away his body to others. This is not cultivation insanity, but it is going astray in qigong practice, and it is caused by one's acting that way intentionally at the beginning. Many people think that swinging their bodies around unconsciously is qigong practice. Actually, if one really practices qigong in this state, it can lead to serious consequences. That is not qigong practice, but a result of everyday people's attachments and pursuits.

Another case is that in qigong practice, one will be scared when qi is congested somewhere in the body or when qi cannot come down from the top of the head. A human body is a small universe. Particularly in a Taoist practice, when qi is going through a pass, one will run into these problems. If qi cannot go through the pass, it will stay there. It can occur not only in the head, but also in other parts of the body; however, a person's most sensitive place is the head. Qi will ascend to the top of the head and then

214

come down. If qi cannot go through a pass, one will experience such a sensation that the head feels heavy and swollen as if wearing a thick hat of qi, etc. But qi cannot control anything, nor can it cause any trouble or bring about any illness whatsoever. Some people do not know the truth about qigong and make some mysterious comments, and this has led to a chaotic situation. Accordingly, people think that if qi ascends to the top of the head and cannot come down, one will have cultivation insanity, go wrong, and so forth. As a result, many people themselves are scared.

If qi ascends to the top of the head and cannot come down, it is only a temporary state. For some people, it may last a very long time or half a year, and it still will not come down. If that is the case, one can find a real qigong master to guide the qi down, and it can come down. In qigong practice, those of you whose qi cannot go through a pass or come down should look for reasons within your xinxing to determine if you are stuck at that level for too long and whether you should upgrade your xinxing! Once you truly upgrade your xinxing, you will find that qi coming down. You cannot only pursue transformation of gong in the physical body without emphasizing improvement of your xinxing. It is waiting for you to upgrade your xinxing—only then will you make a holistic change. If qi is indeed blocked, it still will not cause any trouble. It is usually our own psychological factors at play. Besides, one will be scared upon learning from a phony qigong master that when qi moves to the top of the head, one will go awry. With this fear, it may indeed bring this person some trouble. Once you are scared, it is an attachment of fear. Isn't that an attachment? Once your attachment surfaces, shouldn't it be removed? The more you fear it, the sicker you will look. This attachment of yours must be removed. You will be made to learn from this lesson so that your fear can be removed, and you can advance.

Practitioners will not feel physically comfortable in their future cultivation, as their bodies will develop many kinds of gong, all of which are very powerful things moving around inside their bodies; they will make you feel uncomfortable one way or another. The reason for your discomfort is principally that you always fear catching some illness. In fact, the things that are developed in your body are quite powerful, and they are all gong, supernormal capabilities, and many living beings. If they move around, you will feel physically itchy, painful, uncomfortable, etc. The tips of the nervous system are particularly sensitive, and there will be all kinds of symptoms. As long as your body is not completely transformed by the high-energy matter, you will feel this way. It should be seen as a good thing anyway. As a practitioner, if you always treat yourself like an everyday person and always think that you have illnesses, how can you practice cultivation? When a tribulation comes in cultivation practice, if you still treat yourself as an everyday person, I would say that your xinxing at that moment has dropped to the level of everyday people. At least on this particular issue, you have dropped to the level of everyday people.

As true practitioners, we should look at issues from a very high level instead of from the perspective of everyday people. Should you believe that you are ill, this may really cause you to be sick. This is because once you assume that you are ill, your xinxing level will be as high as that of everyday people. Qigong practice and true cultivation practice will not lead to illness, particularly under this condition. It is known that what actually causes people to become ill is seventy percent psychological and thirty percent physiological. Typically, one first has a mental breakdown and cannot handle it, as this is a very heavy burden. That will quickly worsen the illness' condition; it is usually like this. For instance, there once was a person who was tied to a bed. They took one of his arms and claimed that they would slit it to make it bleed. Then they blindfolded his eyes and scratched his wrist once. (He was not at all cut and bleeding.) A water faucet was turned on so that he could hear water dripping, and he thus thought that it was his blood that was dripping. The man died shortly afterwards. In fact, he was not cut and bleeding—it was running water that was dripping. His psychological factors caused his death. If you always believe that you are ill, you will probably make yourself sick as a result. Because your xinxing has dropped to the level of everyday people, an average person will, of course, have illnesses.

As a practitioner, if you always think that it is an illness, you are actually asking for it. If you ask for an illness, it will come inside your body. As a practitioner, your xinxing level should be high. You should not always worry that it is an illness, for this fear of illness is an attachment and it can bring you trouble just the same. In cultivation practice one needs to eliminate karma, and that is painful. How can one increase gong comfortably? How can one otherwise remove one's attachments? Let me tell you a story from Buddhism. There once was a person who became an Arhat after much effort in cultivation. As he was just about to attain the Right Fruit in cultivation and become an Arhat, how could he not be happy? He was going to transcend the Three Realms! Yet this excitement is an attachment, an attachment of elation. An Arhat should be free of attachments, with a heart that cannot be affected. But he failed, and his cultivation ended up in vain. Since he failed, he had to start all over again. He resumed his cultivation, and after much painstaking effort he again made it in his cultivation. This time he became scared and reminded himself in his mind: "I shouldn't get excited. Otherwise, I'll fail again." With this fear, he failed again. Fear is also a kind of attachment.

There is another situation: When a person becomes mentally ill, this person will be labeled as having cultivation insanity. There are some people who even wait for me to treat their mental illnesses! I hold that a mental illness is not an illness, and I do not have time to take care of such things, either. Why? This is because a patient with mental illness does not have any virus, and his body has neither pathological changes nor infections; it is not an illness in my view. A mental illness occurs when a person's zhu yishi becomes too weak. How weak can it become? It is like a person who can never take charge of himself. A mentally ill patient's zhu yuanshen is just like that. It no longer wants to be in charge of this body. It is always in a daze and cannot lift up its spirit. At this point, the person's fu yishi or foreign messages will interfere with him. There are so many levels in each dimension. All sorts of messages will disturb him. Besides, one's zhu yuanshen might have committed some wrongdoings in previous lives, and the creditors may want to harm him. All kinds of things can transpire. We would say that this is what mental illness is all about. How can I cure it for you? I would say that this is how one actually acquires a mental illness. What can be done about it? Educate the person and help him lift up his spirit— but it is very difficult to do that. You will find that when a doctor at a psychiatric hospital picks up an electric-shock club in his or her hand, immediately the patients will be too scared to utter anything absurd. Why is it? At that moment, this person's zhu yuanshen becomes alert, and it fears the electrical shock.

Usually, once a person enters the door of cultivation practice, he will want to continue. Everyone has Buddha-nature and the heart for cultivation. Therefore, upon learning it, many practitioners will practice cultivation for the rest of their lives. It does not matter whether he can succeed in cultivation or obtain the Fa. This person nonetheless has the heart for following the Tao and always wants to practice it. Everyone knows that this person does qigong practice. People in his workplace know it, and it is known throughout the neighborhood as well as by those who live next door. But, think about it, everyone: In terms of true cultivation practice, who did such a thing a few years ago? Nobody did. Only if one truly practices cultivation can one's journey of life be changed. But as a regular person, this person is practicing qigong only for healing and fitness. Who will change his path of life? As an ordinary person, he will catch an illness one day or come across some trouble on another day. He might become mentally ill someday or drop dead. An ordinary person's whole life is just like that. Though you find a person practicing qigong in a park, in actuality, he is not truly practicing cultivation. Though he wishes to practice cultivation toward the high level, he cannot make it without receiving the orthodox Fa. He has only a desire to practice cultivation toward the high level. This person is still a qigong practitioner at the low level of healing and fitness. No one will change his path of life, so he will have illnesses. If one does not value virtue, one's illness will not even be healed. It is not true that once a person practices qigong, he will not catch any illness.

One must truly practice cultivation and pay attention to one's xinxing. Only by truly practicing cultivation, can one's illness be eliminated. Because qigong practice is not a physical exercise but something beyond everyday people, there must be a higher principle and standard for practitioners. One must follow that in order to achieve the goal. Yet, many people have not done so and remain everyday people. Therefore, they will still be ill when the time is due. This person may one day suddenly suffer a cerebral thrombosis, suddenly catch this or that disease, or become mentally ill. Everyone knows that he practices qigong. Once he becomes mentally ill, people will say that he has cultivation insanity, and that label will be affixed. Think about it, everyone: Is it reasonable to do this? A layperson does not know the truth. It is difficult even for the professionals or many practitioners to know the truth of it. If this person becomes mentally ill at home, it may be less problematic, though others will still say that he got it from qigong practice. If the person becomes mentally ill at an exercise site, it will be terrible. A big label will be imposed and will be impossible to remove, despite one's efforts. Newspapers will report that qigong practice has led to cultivation insanity. Some people oppose qigong without even looking at it: "Look, he was fine doing qigong exercise there a while ago, and now he has turned out like this." As an everyday person, whatever should happen to him will occur. He might have other illnesses or encounter other troubles. Is it reasonable to blame qigong practice for everything? It is like a doctor in a hospital: Because one is a doctor, one should never be ill in this life—how can it be understood like that?

It can, therefore, be said that many people make mindless comments without knowing the actual truth about qigong or the principles behind it. Once there is a problem, all kinds of labels are imposed on qigong. Qigong has been popular in society for a very short period of time. Many people hold stubborn views and always deny it, slander it, and reject it. No one knows what kind of mindsets these people have. They are so sick of qigong, as if it has anything to do with them. Once the word qigong is brought up, they will call it idealistic. Qigong is a science, and it is a higher science. This happens because those people's mentalities are too stubborn and their knowledge is too narrow.

There is another situation called the "qigong state" in the community of cultivators. Such a person has mental illusions, but not cultivation insanity. A person in this state is unusually rational. Let me first explain what the qigong state is all about. It is known that qigong practice involves the issue of one's inborn quality. There are people from every country in the world who believe in religion. For several thousand years there have been people in China believing in Buddhism or Taoism. They believe that doing good deeds is met with good rewards, and being evil is met with evil returns. But some people do not believe this. Particularly during the time of the "Great Cultural Revolution," this was criticized and labeled as superstition. Some people regard as superstition all of what they cannot understand, what is not learned from textbooks, what modern science has not yet developed, and what has not yet been understood. There were a lot of these people a few years ago, but now there are relatively fewer of them. Though you may not acknowledge some phenomena, they have actually manifested in our dimension already. You do not dare to recognize them, but now people have the courage to speak out about them. They have also learned some facts regarding qigong practice through hearing about them or witnessing them.

Some people are so stubborn that once you mention qigong, they will laugh at you from deep down inside. They think that you are being superstitious and too ridiculous. As soon as you

221

bring up the phenomena in qigong practice, they will regard you as being all-too-ignorant. Though such a person is prejudiced, his inborn quality might not be bad. If he has good inborn quality and wants to practice qigong, his tianmu may be opened at a very high level, and he may also have supernormal capabilities. He does not believe in qigong, but he cannot guarantee that he will not become ill. When he becomes ill, he will go to the hospital. When a doctor of Western medicine cannot cure him, he will go to see a doctor of Chinese medicine. When the doctor of Chinese medicine also cannot cure the illness and when no special prescription works, he will then think of qigong and ponder: "I'll try my luck to see whether qigong can actually heal my illness." He will come with much hesitation. Because of his good inborn quality, as soon as he practices qigong, he will be very good at it. Perhaps a master will be interested in him or maybe a higher life in another dimension will give him a hand. All of a sudden, his tianmu opens, or he is in a state of semi-enlightenment. With his tianmu open at a very high level, he can all of a sudden see some truth of the universe. Furthermore, he will have supernormal capabilities. Would you say that when such a person sees this type of situation his brain can take it? What kind of mental state do you think he'll be in? What was once regarded as superstitious, absolutely impossible, and ridiculous when others talked about it is actually lying right before his eyes, and he is indeed in contact with it. This person's mind will then be unable to take it, as the mental pressure is simply too great. What he says will not be understood by others, though his mind is rational. But he just cannot balance the relationship between both sides. He has discovered that what humankind does is wrong, while what is done on the other side is usually right. If he does things according to the way it is done over there, people will say that he is wrong. They cannot understand him, so they will say that he has cultivation insanity.

In fact, this person does not have cultivation insanity. Most of you who practice qigong will not become this way at all. Only those very prejudiced people will experience the qigong state. Many people in the audience here have their tianmu opened—quite a number of people. They have indeed observed things in other dimensions. They are not surprised, feel quite well, and their brains are not shocked, nor are they in this qigong state. After a person is in the qigong state, he is very rational and speaks very reasonably with very sensible logic. It is only that everyday people will not believe what he says. He may sometimes tell you that he saw someone who has passed away, and that this person told him to do something. How can everyday people believe this? Later, this person understands that he should keep those things to himself instead of talking about them. After he can properly deal with the relationship between both sides, everything will be all right. Typically, these people also carry supernormal capabilities, but this is not cultivation insanity, either.

There is another situation called "true insanity," and it is rarely seen. The "true insanity" to which we refer does not involve a person who is actually insane. Instead of having that meaning, it denotes "the cultivation of truth." What's true insanity? I would say that among practitioners, such a person is rarely seen, perhaps being but one out of a hundred thousand people. As a result, it is not common and does not have any impact on society, either.

Usually, there is a prerequisite for "true insanity." It is that this person must have superb inborn quality and must be quite elderly. Being of old age, it would be too late for the person to practice cultivation. Those with superb inborn quality are usually here on a mission and come from high levels; everyone is scared of visiting this ordinary human society, as one will be unable to recognize anyone after one's brain is washed. After a person comes to this social environment of everyday people, human interference will make her pursue fame or fortune and she will eventually drop to the level of everyday people. There will never be a day for her to escape from here. Therefore, nobody dares to come here, as everyone will be afraid. Yet there are such people who have come here. Upon arrival, they indeed cannot conduct themselves well among everyday people. They will indeed stumble to low levels and commit many wrongdoings in their lifetimes. When one lives to compete for personal gain, one commits a lot of bad deeds and owes others a great deal. Her master sees that she is about to fall down. Yet she is someone with Fruit Status, so the master will not let her drop down so easily! What can be done? Her master will be very worried and will have no other ways to let her practice cultivation. Where at this time could one find a master? She will have to return to the origin by practicing cultivation from scratch. But how can this be done easily? Being old, it would be too late for her to practice cultivation. Where could she find a cultivation practice of mind and body?

Only if she has superb inborn quality, and under this very unusual circumstance, could the method of true insanity be applied to her. In other words, when there is absolutely no hope for this person to return to the origin on her own, this method may be used to make her insane. Some functions in her brain will be switched off. For instance, as human beings we fear cold and filth, and so these portions of the brain that fear cold and filth will be switched off. After some functions are disabled, she will appear to have mental problems and act like one who is really mentally insane. But she usually does not commit any wrongdoings, nor does she insult or punch people. Instead, she often does good deeds, but she is very cruel to herself. Because she is unaware of being cold, in winter she will run around in the snow with bare feet and wear thin clothes. Her feet will be frozen to the point of heavy bleeding. Because she is unaware of filth, she dares to eat human excrement and drink human urine. I once knew such a person who would eat horse excrement as if it was tasty, though it was frozen very hard. She could suffer hardships that an everyday person would not suffer with a conscious mind. Just imagine how much this insanity made her suffer. Of course, such people usually have supernormal capabilities; most of them are elderly women. In the past, an elderly woman had her feet bound to make them smaller, but she could still jump effortlessly over a wall of two or more meters. When her family saw that she was insane and always ran out of the house, they would lock her up in the house. Once her family members left the house, she would unlock the door just by pointing her fingers at the lock. Then she would run off. Later, they would restrain her with iron chains. When everyone left home, she would shake off the chains with ease. It was impossible to restrain her. With this, she would suffer quite a lot of hardships. Because she suffered much and quite harshly, she would soon repay the debts from her wrongdoings. It would take three years at most, and usually only one or two years, as that suffering was quite tremendous. Afterwards, she would understand at once what had transpired. Because she completed her cultivation, she would become kaigong right away with a variety of divine powers emerging. These cases are very rarely seen, but there have been some throughout history. People with average inborn quality will not be allowed to do it this way. It is known that in history there have indeed been documented insane monks or insane Taoists, such as the insane monk who drove Qin Hui[1] out of a temple with a broom, and other stories about insane Taoists. There are many such classic stories.

With regard to cultivation insanity, we can say that it definitely does not exist. If someone can produce fire,[2] and if it is really like that, I would say that this person is quite awesome. If a person can light a fire by opening the mouth or by extending a hand, or can light a cigarette with a finger, I would call it a supernormal capability!

Demonic Interference in Cultivation

What is demonic interference in cultivation? It is the interference that we often run into in qigong practice. How does qigong practice invite demonic interference? There is actually much difficulty when one wants to practice cultivation. One simply cannot succeed in genuine cultivation without the protection of my fashen. As soon as you step out the door, your life may be in danger. One's yuanshen does not become extinct. Then, in your social activities in past lives, you might once have owed others, bullied others, or committed other wrongdoings. Those creditors will look for you. It is said in Buddhism that one lives because of karmic retribution. If you owe someone something, he will find you for the repayment. If he gets too much repayment, he will

---

[1] Qin Hui (chin hway)—a wicked official of the royal court in the Southern Song Dynasty (1127 A.D.-1279 A.D.).

[2] "to produce fire"—a Chinese term also meaning "cultivation insanity"; this can be understood both figuratively and literally here.

have to return the surplus to you the next time around. If a son disrespects his parents, they will trade places in the next life. This is how it cycles on and on. But we have indeed observed demonic interference, which prevents you from practicing qigong. All these have karmic relationships and are not without reasons. It will not be allowed to be so without a reason.

The most common form of demonic interference occurs as follows. Before you practice qigong, your environment is relatively peaceful; because you have learned qigong, you always like to practice it. As soon as you begin the sitting meditation, however, it suddenly becomes noisy outside the room. There are sounds of car horns, walking in the hallway, chatting, doors slamming, and a radio from outside. It is suddenly no longer quiet. If you do not practice qigong, the environment is quite peaceful, but once you begin the qigong practice, it is like this. Many of you have never thought about it further. What's really going on? You only find it odd and feel quite disappointed about being unable to practice qigong. This "oddness" will stop your practice. It is a demon interfering with you, as it manipulates people to disturb you. This is the simplest form of interference, and it can achieve the goal of stopping your qigong practice. If you practice qigong and achieve the Tao, what about those unpaid debts you owe others? They will not allow it, so they will not let you practice qigong. Yet, it is also an indication of a certain level. After a period of time, this phenomenon will no longer be allowed to exist. In other words, after these debts are worn out, they will not be allowed to come and interfere again. This is because those who practice cultivation in our Falun Dafa make rapid progress, and they also make quick breakthroughs in their levels.

There is another form of demonic interference. You know

227

that through qigong practice our tianmu can open. With tianmu open, some people may see some frightening scenes or scary faces while practicing qigong at home. Some have messy, long hair, and some want to fight you or even make various moves, which are quite frightening. Sometimes one will see them all crawling outside the window and appearing very scary. Why can this situation occur? This is a form of demonic interference. In our Falun Dafa school, however, this case is very rarely seen. Perhaps, it happens to one out of a hundred people. Most people will not encounter this situation. Because it does not have any benefit for your practice, it is not allowed to interfere with you like this. In other conventional practices, this kind of interference is the most common phenomenon, and it will last quite a long period of time. Some people cannot practice qigong and become frightened simply for this reason. One usually chooses to practice qigong in a quiet environment at night. If one sees a person standing before one's eyes, who looks half-ghost and half-human, one will be too scared to practice qigong. Usually, there is no such phenomenon in our Falun Dafa. But there are a few extremely rare exceptions, as some people have very special situations.

Another kind of practice is one of both internal and external cultivation. It requires the practice of martial arts and internal cultivation. This kind of practice is commonly seen in the Tao School. Once a person studies this practice, he will often run into this demonic interference that is not encountered in ordinary practices, except for the practices of both internal and external cultivation, or those of martial arts. That is, there will be people who seek him for a fight. There are many Taoist practitioners in the world; many of them are students of martial arts or of internal and external cultivation. A student of martial arts can also develop gong. Why is it? If a person removes desires, fame, and profits among other attachments, he can also increase gong. Yet, his attachment to competitiveness will take time to abandon, and it will be abandoned quite slowly. Therefore, he will easily do such a thing, and it can even happen at certain levels. While sitting in trance, he will know who is practicing martial arts. His yuanshen will leave his body to challenge another person for a fight to determine whose martial arts are better, and this fight will then break out. These things also occur in another dimension where someone may also come to him for a fight. If he refuses, the other person will really kill him. A fight will thus break out between the two. Once this person falls asleep, someone will seek him for a fight, and this makes his night restless. Actually, this is the time to remove his attachment to competitiveness. If this competitive mentality is not relinquished, he will always be this way. As time passes, he still cannot move beyond this level after several years. He will be rendered unable to continue qigong practice. With too much energy consumed, his physical body also can no longer bear it and may easily be disabled. Thus, in practices of both internal and external cultivation, one may encounter this situation, and it is also quite common. In our practice of internal cultivation, there is no such situation, nor is it allowed to occur. These several forms that I just addressed exist quite commonly.

There is yet another form of demonic interference that everyone, including each person in our school of practice, will encounter: It is the demon of lust. This is something very serious. In ordinary human society, because of this marital life, humankind can produce its descendants. The human race just evolves this way, and there is sentimentality in human society. Thus, such a thing is perfectly justified for everyday people. Since human beings have sentimentality, being upset is sentimentality, so are happiness, love, hatred, enjoying doing one thing, resenting doing another thing, preferring one person to another, hobbies, and dislikes. Everything belongs to sentimentality, and everyday people just live for it. Then, as a practitioner and one who rises above and beyond, one should not use this approach to judge things, and one should break away from them. Therefore, as to the many attachments that come from sentimentality, we should take them lightly and eventually abandon them. Desires, lust, and things of these sorts are all human attachments, and all of them should all be given up.

For those practitioners who practice cultivation among everyday people, our school of practice does not ask you to become a monk or nun. Young practitioners should still have families. So how should this issue be treated? I have said that our school of practice directly targets one's mind. It does not make you actually lose anything in terms of material benefits. Instead, you are to temper your xinxing amidst the material benefits of everyday people. What is truly upgraded is your xinxing. If you can give up the attachment, you are able to abandon everything; when you are asked to give up material benefits, you will certainly be able to do it. If you cannot let the attachment go, you will not be able to discard anything. Therefore, the real purpose of cultivation is to cultivate your heart. The cultivation practices in temples force you to lose these things so as to get rid of this attachment of yours. By not letting you think about it, they force you to completely reject them; and they have adopted such a method. But we do not require you to do so. We ask you to care less about the material interests that lie right before you. Thus, those who go through their cultivation in our school of practice are most solid. We do not ask you to become monks and nuns. As our practice is spread more widely in the future, those practitioners of ours who practice cultivation among everyday people should not all be turned into quasi-monks. It is not allowed for every Falun Dafa practitioner to become this way. In the course of practice, we require the following of everyone: Even though you practice and your spouse might not, it is not permitted for you to get a divorce because of the practice. In other words, we should take this matter lightly, and you should not attach as much importance to it as do everyday people. In particular, the so-called sexual freedom and pornography of today's society are interfering with people. Some people are very interested in such things. As practitioners, we should attach little importance to them.

From the high-level perspective, everyday people are playing with mud while in society without realizing that it is dirty. They are playing with mud on earth. We have said that you should not cause disharmony in your family because of this issue. Therefore, at the present stage, you should care less about it. It is good to keep a normal and harmonious marriage life. In the future when you reach a certain level, there will be another situation at that level. At present, it should be this way, and it would be fine if you meet this requirement. Of course, you should not follow what is going on in society. How can that be allowed?

There is another factor involved in this issue. You know that our practitioners' bodies carry energy. Now, eighty to ninety percent of the people from this class will not only have their illnesses healed, but will also have their gong developed. Thus, your body carries very powerful energy. Your gong and your present xinxing level are not proportionate. Your gong is temporarily greater, having been suddenly upgraded, and now your xinxing is being upgraded. Gradually, your xinxing will catch up. It is guaranteed that within this period of time it will catch up. Thus, we have done this ahead of time. In other words, you have some amount of energy. Because the energy cultivated from an orthodox Fa is purely righteous and benevolent, everyone sitting here feels an atmosphere of serenity and compassion. I have cultivated myself this way and carry these things with me. Everyone sitting here is harmonious without ill thoughts in mind, and no one even thinks about smoking a cigarette. In the future, you should also follow the requirements of our Dafa, and the gong that you develop through cultivation practice will also be this way. With your ever-increasing energy potency, the energy scattered from the gong in your body will also be quite powerful. Even if it is not that powerful, an everyday person within your field will still be restrained. Or if you are at home, you will also restrain others, and your family members may be restrained by you. Why is this so? You do not even have to use your mind to do this. This field is one of pure harmony, compassion, and righteous faith. Therefore, people are unlikely to think of bad things or commit bad deeds. It can have this effect.

The other day I said that the Buddha-light illuminates everywhere and rectifies all abnormalities. In other words, the energy scattered from our bodies can rectify all abnormal conditions. Therefore, under the effects of this field, if you do not think about these things, you will unintentionally restrain your spouse as well. If you do not and will not think of them, your spouse will not think of them, either. But it is not absolute, for in the present environment there are all kinds of things on television that, if it is turned on, can easily stimulate one's desires. But, under normal conditions, you have this restraining effect. In the future when you reach high-level cultivation practice, without my telling you, you will know what to do. By then there will be another state to ensure a harmonious life. You, therefore, should not concern yourself with this too much, as being overly concerned is also an attachment. There is not an issue of eroticism between husband and wife, but there is lust. As long as you can take it lightly and feel right in your mind, it will be fine.

So what kinds of demons of lust will one encounter? If your ability of *ding*[3] is not adequate, it will appear in your dreams during sleep. While you are sleeping or sitting in meditation, it will suddenly show up. If you are male, a beauty will appear. If you are female, the man of your dreams will show up. Yet they will be naked. Once your mind thinks about it, you will ejaculate and make it a reality. Think about it, everyone: In our cultivation practice, the essence of the body is used to cultivate one's life; you cannot always ejaculate like this. Meanwhile, you have not passed the lust test. How can it be permitted? Therefore, I am telling you that everybody will come across this issue, and it is guaranteed. While teaching the Fa, I am imprinting very powerful energy in your mind. You may not recall specifically what I have said after stepping outside the door, but when you actually encounter this issue, you will remember what I said. As long as you regard yourself as a practitioner, you will remember it right away and be able to restrain yourself, and you will then be able to pass this test. If you fail the test the first time, it will be difficult to pass it the second time. Yet there is also the case where when one fails the first test, one will regret it very much upon waking from sleep. Perhaps, this mentality and state of mind will reinforce your thoughts about it. When the issue again arises, you will be able to control yourself and pass the test. If one who fails the test does not care about it, it will be harder to pass later. It is definitely this way.

This form of interference can come from either demons or

[3] *ding* (ding)—a state of empty, yet conscious mind.

from the master, who transforms one object into another to test you. Both forms exist because everyone must pass this test. We begin cultivation practice as everyday people. The first step is this test, and everyone will run into it. Let me give you an example. When I was teaching a class in Wuhan,[4] there was a thirty-year-old young man there. Right after I gave this lecture, he went home and sat in meditation. He achieved the state of ding right away. After that, he suddenly saw Buddha Amitabha appearing on one side and Lao Zi on the other. This is what he said in his experience report. After showing up, both looked at him without saying a word and then disappeared. Later, Bodhisattva Avalokitesvara showed up with her hands carrying a vase from which a white smoke emerged. As he sat there and saw everything very vividly, he became quite pleased. Suddenly, the smoke transformed into a few beauties; beauties are those flying heavenly girls who are very attractive. They danced for him with very graceful movements. He thought to himself: "Because I'm practicing here, Bodhisattva Avalokitesvara is rewarding me by transforming a few beauties for me to watch and is sending the flying heavenly girls to dance for me." As he was becoming delighted by this thought, these beauties suddenly became naked and made different moves towards him, coming to hug his neck and caress his waist. This practitioner's xinxing had improved very quickly. At that point, he became alarmed right away. The first thought that came to his mind was: "I'm not an ordinary person. I'm a practitioner. You shouldn't treat me this way, for I'm a Falun Dafa practitioner." Once this thought emerged, everything suddenly disappeared since they were all transformed anyway. Then Buddha Amitabha and Lao Zi showed up again. Lao Zi pointed to this practitioner and said to Buddha Amitabha with a smile: "This kid is teachable." It means that this fellow is good and can be taught.

---

[4] Wuhan (woo-hahn)—capital of Hubei Province.

Throughout history, or from the perspective of higher dimensions, the issues of one's desire and lust have been very critical in determining whether one can practice cultivation. So we must really regard these things with indifference. However, we practice cultivation among everyday people, and so we do not ask you to give it up completely. At least at the present stage, you should take it lightly and not resemble how you were in the past. As a practitioner, one should be this way. Whenever there is interference of one kind or another in qigong practice, you should look for reasons within yourself and determine what you still have not let go.

Demonic Interference From One's Own Mind

What is "demonic interference from one's own mind?" A human body has a physical field in every level's dimension. Within a special field, everything in the universe can be reflected into your dimensional field, like a shadow. Although they are shadows, they are of material existence. Everything within the field of your dimension is dictated by the thoughts in your brain. That is, if you calmly see things with tianmu and without using your mind, what you observe is true. If you start to think a little, what you see will be false. This is called demonic interference from one's own mind, or "transformation with mind-intent." This is because some practitioners cannot treat themselves as practitioners and are unable to handle themselves properly. They pursue supernormal capabilities and are attached to petty skills or even to listening to certain things from other dimensions. They are after these things. It is easiest for these people to develop demonic interference from their own minds and to drop to low levels. No matter how high one's cultivation level is, once this problem occurs one will fall all the way to the bottom and, in the end, be ruined—this is an extremely serious issue. It is unlike other areas where if one fails a xinxing test this time, one may rise from the fall and continue to practice cultivation. But it is not the case if demonic interference from one's own mind occurs, as this life of the person will be ruined. Particularly for those practitioners with tianmu open at certain levels, this problem can happen easily. Also, some people are always interfered with by foreign messages in their consciousness, and they believe whatever they are told by foreign messages; this problem can also take place. Therefore, some of you with tianmu open will be interfered with by different sorts of messages.

Let me give you an example. It is very difficult for one to keep one's mind undisturbed at a low level of cultivation. You may not be able to see clearly what your teacher looks like. One day you may suddenly see a large, tall immortal. He gives you a few complimentary words and teaches you something. If you accept it, your gong will be messed up. Once you become delighted and accept him as your master, you will go with him. But he has not attained the Right Fruit, either. In that dimension, his body can transform to be large or small. With this before your eyes and seeing this large immortal, you will be really excited. With this excitement, aren't you going to learn from him? It is very difficult to save a practitioner if he cannot conduct himself properly. He can easily ruin himself. The heavenly beings are all immortals, yet they, too, have not attained the Right Fruit and will continue to go through samsara just the same. If you casually take such a being as your master and follow him, where can he take you? He cannot even attain the Right Fruit. Won't your cultivation be in vain? Eventually, your own gong will be messed

236

up. It is very difficult for one's mind to stay undisturbed. I am telling everyone that this is a very serious issue, and many of you will have this problem later. I have taught you the Fa; it is up to you whether you can conduct yourself properly. What I have addressed is one of the situations. Don't let your mind be disturbed when you see an enlightened person from another school of practice. Stay with only one school of practice. Whether it is a Buddha, a Tao, an immortal, or a demon, they should not move your heart. In conducting oneself this way, success is bound to be in sight.

The demonic interference from one's mind also manifests in other forms. You may have seen interference from a relative who has passed away, and this person cries and begs you to do this or that. All kinds of things can happen. Will your mind stay unaffected? Suppose that you are very fond of this child of yours or love your parents, and your parents have passed away. They told you to do some things... all of which are things that you should not do. If you do them, it will be bad. It is just so tough to be a practitioner. It is said that Buddhism is in chaos. It has even absorbed from Confucianism things such as respecting parents and love for children. Buddhism did not have such content. What does it mean? Since one's real life is yuanshen, the one who gives birth to your yuanshen is your real mother. In the course of samsara, you have had mothers who were human and non-human, and there are too many of them to be numbered. It is also countless how many sons and daughters you have had throughout your different lifetimes. Who is your mother? Who is your son or daughter? No one knows it after one passes away. You still must repay what you owe others. Human beings live in delusion and just cannot give up these things. Some people cannot let go of their sons and daughters and claim how good they are, and then they pass away. One may speak of how good one's mother is, but then she also dies. This person grieves so much that he almost wants to follow her for the rest of his life. Why don't you think about it? Aren't they here to torment you? They use this form to make you unable to lead a good life.

Perhaps everyday people do not understand it. If you are attached to this, you cannot practice cultivation whatsoever. Buddhism therefore does not have such content. If you want to practice cultivation, human sentimentality must be relinquished. Of course, in practicing cultivation in ordinary human society, we should respect parents and educate our children. Under all circumstances, we must be good and kind to others, let alone to our family members. We should treat everyone in the same way. We must be good to our parents and children and be considerate of others in all respects. Such a heart is thus unselfish, and it is a heart of kindness and benevolence. Sentimentality is something of everyday people, and everyday people just live for it.

Many people cannot conduct themselves well, and this causes difficulties in cultivation practice. A person may claim that a Buddha has told him something. Unless danger threatens your life and you are told how to eliminate it, all those who tell you that you will have a tribulation today and how to avoid something about to occur, those who tell you the first-prize lottery ticket number and ask you to try it, and those who wish to have you get good things in ordinary human society, are demons. If you always get your way among everyday people and cannot pass this test, you will not make progress. If you live very well among everyday people, how can you practice cultivation? How can your karma be transformed? How will you have an environment to upgrade your xinxing and transform your karma? Everyone should be sure to keep this in mind. A demon can also praise you and tell you how high your level is, what a great Buddha or a great Tao you are, and that it thinks that you are terrific—those are all phony. As one who truly practices cultivation toward high levels, you should give up various attachments. When encountering these issues, you should all be on your guard!

During cultivation practice, your tianmu will be opened. With tianmu open, a person has his difficulties in cultivation. With tianmu closed, a person also has his difficulties in cultivation. In either case, it is not easy to practice cultivation. After your tianmu is open, with a variety of messages interfering with you, it will be indeed very difficult for you to conduct yourself well. In other dimensions, everything is dazzling to the eye, very beautiful and nice, all of which may lure your heart. Once you are moved by it, you might be interfered with and your gong will be messed up—it is usually this way. Thus, when a person with demonic interference from his own mind cannot conduct himself well, this situation may occur. For example, once a person develops a bad thought, it is very dangerous. One day his tianmu is opened, and he can see things quite clearly. He thinks: "At this exercise site, only my tianmu is openned very well. Am I perhaps an unusual person? I was able to learn Teacher Li's Falun Dafa and have studied it so well, better than all the others. Perhaps, I'm also not an ordinary person." This thought is already not right. He will wonder: "Maybe I'm a Buddha as well. Well, let me take a look at myself." When he looks at himself, he will find himself indeed a Buddha. Why is it? This is because everything within the dimensional field around his body will transform according to his thoughts, which is also called "transformation with mind-intent."

Everything reflected from the universe will transform with one's thoughts, because everything within a person's dimensional field is at his or her command. So are the reflected images, which are also material existence. This person thinks: "Maybe I'm a Buddha, and perhaps what I wear is also a Buddha's robe." Then he will find that what he wears is indeed a Buddha's robe. "Wow, I'm indeed a Buddha." He will be very excited. "Perhaps I'm not even a small Buddha." With another look, he will find himself a big Buddha. "Perhaps I'm even greater than Li Hongzhi!" He will take a look again: "Wow, I'm indeed greater than Li Hongzhi." Some people also hear this with their ears. A demon will interfere with him and say: "You're greater than Li Hongzhi. You're so much greater than Li Hongzhi." He will also believe it. Have you thought about how you are going to practice cultivation in the future? Have you ever practiced cultivation? Who has taught you cultivation? Even when a real Buddha comes here on a mission, he must also practice cultivation from scratch. His original gong will not be given to him, and it is only that he will progress quicker in practicing cultivation. Therefore, once this problem occurs to him, it will be difficult for him to help himself out; he will develop this attachment right away. After this attachment is developed, he will dare to say anything: "I'm a Buddha. You don't need to learn from others. I'm the Buddha, so I'll tell you what to do." He will begin to do these things.

Don't we have someone like that in Changchun? At the beginning he was quite good. Later, he started to do these things. He thought that he was a Buddha. In the end, he considered himself greater than everybody else. This was incurred when he could not conduct himself well and by the attachment that he developed. Why is there this phenomenon? Buddhism teaches that no matter what you see, you should ignore it, for it is all demonic illusion, and that one should just continue cultivation advancement through meditation. Why doesn't it allow you to see them and be attached to them? It cautions against the occurrence of this problem. In Buddhist cultivation practice, there is no reinforced cultivation method, nor is there any guidance in its scriptures to avoid these things. Sakyamuni did not teach such Dharma at that time. In order to avoid the problem of demonic interference from one's own mind or transformation with mind-intent, he called all of the scenes observed in cultivation practice demonic illusions. So, once an attachment is developed, it will lead to this demonic illusion. It is very difficult for one to stay away from it. If it is not dealt with properly, one will be ruined and follow a demonic path. Because he has called himself a Buddha, he has already demonized himself. In the end, he may get futi or other things and be totally ruined. His heart will also become immoral, and he will fall down completely. There are a lot of such people. Even in this class, there are people who think quite highly of themselves right now and talk with a different attitude. It is taboo even in Buddhism for one to find out what one is all about. What I just said is another form of demonic interference, which is called "demonic interference from one's own mind" or "transformation with mind-intent." Beijing has some practitioners like that, and there are also some in other regions. Further yet, they have caused very serious interference for practitioners.

Someone has asked me: "Teacher, why don't you eliminate this problem?" Think about it, everyone: If we clear all obstacles in your path of cultivation practice, how will you practice cultivation? It is under the circumstance of demonic interference that you can demonstrate whether you can continue your cultivation, be really enlightened to the Tao, be unaffected by

241

interference, and be sure-footed in this school of practice. The great waves shift the sand, and that is what cultivation practice is all about. What is left in the end will be genuine gold. Without this form of interference, I would say that it is too easy for one to practice cultivation. In my view, your cultivation is already too easy. Those high-level great enlightened beings may find it more unfair: "What are you doing? Are you saving people like this? There are no obstacles in the path of cultivation, and one can make one's cultivation directly to the end. Is this cultivation? As one proceeds in cultivation, one becomes increasingly more comfortable without any interference. How can this be allowed?" This is the issue, and I have been thinking about it as well. At the outset, I took care of many such demons. If I am to do that all the time, I also find it not right. I was also told: "You've made their cultivation too easy. People only have that little bit of hardship of their own. There is only that little bit of trouble among themselves. They have a lot of attachments that they still can't give up! It remains a question of whether they can understand your Dafa itself while they are in the midst of confusion and tribulations." It involves such an issue, so there will be interference and tests. I just said that this is a form of demonic interference. It is very difficult to truly save a person, yet so very easy to ruin a person. Once your mind is not righteous, you will be ruined at once.

Your Zhu Yishi Should Predominate

Because of some wrongdoings committed in different lifetimes, they have brought about disasters to people and have created karmic obstacles for the practitioner. Therefore, there will be birth, old age, illness, and death. These are ordinary karma. There is another powerful karma that greatly affects practitioners—it is called thought karma. People have to think in leading their lives. Because one is lost among everyday people, one will often develop in one's mind thoughts for fame, benefits, lust, anger, etc. Gradually, these thoughts become the powerful thought karma. Since everything in other dimensions has life, karma is also the same. When one begins to practice cultivation in an orthodox Fa, one must eliminate one's karma. Eliminating karma means having karma wiped out and transformed. Of course, karma will resist, and so one will have tribulations and obstacles. But, thought karma can directly interfere with one's mind. Therefore, one's mind has swear words that condemn Teacher and Dafa, and one may think of some evil thoughts or swear words. As a result, some practitioners do not know what is going on and think that these thoughts come from themselves. Some people also believe that they are from futi, but they are not from futi. Rather, they result from the reflection of thought karma on one's mind. Some people do not have a very strong zhu yishi and will comply with the thought karma to commit wrongdoings. Such people will be ruined and drop in levels. Most people, however, can remove and resist it with very strong subjective thoughts (a strong zhu yishi). With this, it indicates that this person can be saved and can distinguish good from bad. In other words, the person has good enlightenment quality. My fashen will help eliminate the majority of such thought karma. This situation is seen frequently. Once it transpires, one will be tested to see if one can overcome such bad thoughts on one's own. If one is determined, the karma can be eliminated.

Your Mind Must be Right

What's not a right mind? It refers to a person's inability to always treat himself as a practitioner. A practitioner will come across tribulations in cultivation practice. When a tribulation comes, it may manifest as an interpersonal conflict. There will be mind games and the like involved, which directly affect your xinxing. There will be many cases in this regard. What else will you encounter? Our bodies may suddenly feel uncomfortable. This is because repaying the karma will be manifested in different ways. At a certain point in time, you will be made unable to discern clearly whether something is true, whether your gong exists, whether you can practice cultivation and make it, or whether there are Buddhas and if they are real. In the future, these situations will surface again to give you this false impression and make you feel as though they do not exist and are all false—it is to see whether you are determined. You say that you must be firm and sure-footed. With this determination, if you can indeed be firmly resolute at that point, you will naturally do well because your xinxing will have already improved. But you are not yet that stable at the moment. If you are given this tribulation right away, you will not be enlightened to it at all, nor will you be able to practice cultivation whatsoever. Tribulations may take place in different respects.

In the course of cultivation practice, one must practice cultivation this way to ascend to higher levels. Thus, once some of you feel physical discomfort somewhere, you will think that you are ill. You always fail to treat yourselves as practitioners, for if this happens to you, you will consider it an illness. Why are there so many troubles? Let me tell you that a lot of it has already been removed for you, and your tribulations are already quite trivial. If it were not removed for you, you might already have dropped dead had you encountered this trouble. Perhaps you would never be able to get out of your bed. When you meet with a little trouble, you will feel uncomfortable. But how can it be that comfortable? For instance, when I taught a class in Changchun, there was a person with very good inborn quality, who was indeed a good prospect. I also found him to be very good and increased his tribulations a little bit so that he could quickly repay karma and become enlightened—I was preparing it this way. Yet, one day he suddenly seemed to suffer cerebral thrombosis and fell to the ground. He felt that he could not move and as though his four limbs were out of commission. He was sent to a hospital for emergency rescue. He was then able to walk again. Think about it, everyone: With cerebral thrombosis, how could one walk around and move both arms and legs again so quickly? Instead, he blamed Falun Dafa for making him go wrong. He did not think about it: How could he recover so quickly from cerebral thrombosis? If he had not practiced Falun Dafa at that time, he might have really died there when he fell. Perhaps, he would have become paralyzed for the rest of his life and would have indeed had cerebral thrombosis.

This is to say just how difficult it is to save a person. So much had been done for him, yet he still did not realize it; instead he said something like that. Some veteran practitioners say: "Teacher, why do I feel uncomfortable all over my body? I always go to the hospital to get injections, but it doesn't help. Taking medicine also doesn't help." They were not even embarrassed to say that to me! Of course, they would not help. Those are not illnesses. How could they help? You may go ahead and have a physical exam. There is not anything wrong, but you just feel uncomfortable. We have a practitioner who broke a few needles at a hospital. In the end, the liquid medicine spouted out, and the needle still would not penetrate. He came to understand: "Oh, I'm a practitioner, and I shouldn't take injections." He just realized that he should not take an injection. Therefore, whenever you come across tribulations, be sure to pay attention to this issue. Some people think that I just do not allow them to go to the hospital, so they think: "If you don't let me go to the hospital, I'll go see a qigong master." They still consider it an illness and want to see a qigong master. Where can they find a true qigong master? If you find a phony one, you will be ruined at once.

We have said: "How can you distinguish between a phony qigong master and a real one?" Many qigong masters are self-proclaimed. I have been verified and have in hand the documents of experiments from the scientific institutions involved. Many qigong masters are shams and are self-proclaimed. There are many of them who bluff and deceive people. Such a phony qigong master can also heal illnesses. Why can he do it? The person has futi without which he would not be able to deceive people! That futi can also give off energy and treat illnesses. Being a form of energy's existence, it can restrain everyday people quite easily. But I have said: "What will futi give you when it treats your illness?" At the very microscopic level, it is all the image of that futi. If it is given to you, what will you do? "It is easier to invite an immortal than to see one off."[5] We do not need to be concerned with everyday people, as they just want to be everyday people and find temporary relief. You, however, are a practitioner. Don't you want to continually purify your body? If it is attached to your body, when will you be able to get rid of it? In addition, it also has a certain amount of energy. Some people will wonder: "Why does Falun allow it to come? Don't we have Teacher's

---

[5] "It is easier to invite an immortal than to see one off."—a Chinese expression commonly used to describe a situation that is easy to fall into, but difficult to get out of.

fashen to safeguard us?" There is a principle in our universe: Nobody will intervene if you want something yourself. As long as it is what you want, nobody will intervene. My fashen will stop you and give you hints. If it finds out that you are always like that, it will no longer take care of you. How can one be forced to practice cultivation? You cannot be made or forced to practice cultivation. It is up to you to truly make progress. No one can do anything about it if you do not wish to upgrade yourself. You have been taught the principles and the Fa. Who can you blame if you still don't want to upgrade yourself? With regard to what you want, both Falun and my fashen will not intervene—this is for sure. Some people even went to other qigong masters' classes and after going home felt very uncomfortable. That is for sure. Why didn't my fashen protect you? What did you go there for? By going there to listen, didn't you want to seek something? If you did not listen with your ears, how could it get into your body? Some people have deformed their Falun. Let me tell you that this Falun is worth more than your life. It is a higher life that cannot be ruined at will. Now there are many phony qigong masters, and some of them are quite well-known. I have told the administrators at China Qigong Science Research Society that in ancient times, the royal court was once plagued by Da Ji.[6] That fox did a lot of vicious things, but was still not as bad as the phony qigong masters today who have simply brought damage to the entire country. How many people have become victimized?! You see that on the surface it appears to be quite good, but how many people are carrying those kinds of things on their bodies? If they give it to you, you will have it—they are simply too

---

[6] Da Ji (dah jee)— a wicked concubine of the last emperor in the Shang Dynasty (1765 B.C.-1122 B.C.). She is believed to have been possessed by a fox spirit and to have caused the fall of the Shang Dynasty.

rampant. It is therefore difficult for an ordinary person to discern from the appearance.

Some people may think: "After attending this qigong seminar and listening to what Li Hongzhi said today, I've realized how great and profound qigong is! If there are other qigong seminars again, I should attend them, too." I would say that you definitely should not go there. If you listen to them, bad things will enter your ears. It is very difficult both to save a person and to change his or her mind. To purify a person's body is also very difficult. There are too many phony qigong masters. As to even a genuine qigong master from an orthodox practice, is he really clean? Some animals are very vicious. Although those things cannot attach to his body, neither can he drive them away. This person, and particularly his students, do not have the ability to challenge these things on a large scale. When he gives off gong, there are all kinds of messy things interfused with it. Though he may be quite decent himself, his students are not righteous and have different futi—all kinds of them.

If you really want to practice cultivation in Falun Dafa, you should not go and listen to them. Of course, if you do not want to practice cultivation in Falun Dafa and want to practice everything, you may go ahead; I will not stop you, as you are not a Falun Dafa disciple, either. If something goes wrong, do not claim that it results from the Falun Dafa practice. Only when you follow the xinxing standard and practice cultivation according to Dafa, are you a genuine Falun Dafa practitioner. Someone has asked: "Can I associate with practitioners of other qigong practices?" Let me tell you that they are only practicing qigong while you are practicing cultivation in Dafa. After attending this class, you will leave them far behind in terms of levels. This Falun is formed through many generations' cultivation practice and is mighty powerful. Certainly, when you make contact with them, if you can manage not to receive or take anything from them and just be a normal friend, it will not matter much. If those people really carry something, however, it will be very bad, and it is better not to make any contact with them. In terms of a couple, I think that it will also not matter much if your spouse does another qigong practice. But there is one thing: Since you practice the orthodox Fa, your practice will benefit others. If your spouse does an evil practice, he or she may carry bad things on the body. In order to ensure your safety, he or she must also be cleaned up. Everything will be cleaned up for you in other dimensions. Your home environment will also be cleared. If your environment is not cleaned up and you have all sorts of things interfering with you, how can you practice cultivation?

Yet, there is one situation in which my fashen will not help clean things up. We have a practitioner who one day saw my fashen come to his home. He was very excited: "Teacher's fashen is here. Teacher, please come in." My fashen said: "Your room is too messy, and there are too many things." Then, it left. Usually, when there are too many evil spirits in other dimensions, my fashen will clean them out for you. His room, however, was full of different bad qigong books. He came to understand it and cleaned it up by burning the books or selling them. My fashen then returned. This is what this practitioner told me.

There are also people who see fortune tellers. Someone asks me: "Teacher, I'm practicing Falun Dafa now. I'm also very interested in Zhouyi or things like fortune-telling. Can I still use them?" Let me put it this way: If you carry a considerable amount of energy, whatever you say will have an impact. If something is not that way, but you have told someone that it is that way, you may have committed a bad deed. An everyday person is very weak. His messages are unstable and may change. If you open your mouth and say something to him, that tribulation may become true. If this person has a lot of karma that he must repay, and you keep telling him that he will have good fortune, will it be allowed, when he is unable to repay his karma? Aren't you doing harm to him? Some people just cannot let go of these things and are attached to them as though they have some talents. Isn't this an attachment? Besides, even if you really know the truth, as a practitioner you should maintain your xinxing and not casually unveil a heavenly secret to an everyday person. That is the principle. No matter how one uses Zhouyi to predict, some of it is already no longer true anyway. Predicting one way or another with some of it being true and some of it being false, this fortune-telling is allowed to exist in ordinary human society. Since you are someone with genuine gong, I would say that a true practitioner should follow a higher standard. Yet, some practitioners will find other people to tell their fortunes and ask: "Will you do some fortune-telling for me to see how I'm doing? How is my cultivation practice? Or do I have any tribulations?" They find others to predict these things. If that tribulation of yours is predicted, how can you upgrade yourself? The entire life of a practitioner has been rearranged. One's palm reading, face reading, birth data, and all messages in one's body are already different and have been changed. If you go to a fortune-teller, you will believe him. Why else would you do it? What he can tell are some superficial things about your past. Yet their substance has already changed. Then think about it, everyone: If you go to a fortune-teller, aren't you listening to and believing him? Then, doesn't it cause you a psychological burden? Isn't it an attachment if you burden yourself with thinking about it? So how can this attachment be removed? Haven't you self-imposed an additional tribulation on yourself? Won't you have to suffer more to give up this attachment? Every test or every tribulation is related to the matter of either progression or regression in cultivation. It is already difficult, yet still you add this self-imposed tribulation. How can you overcome it? You might come across hardships or troubles as a result of it. Your altered path of life is not allowed to be seen by others. If it is seen by others or if you are told when you will have a tribulation, how can you practice cultivation? Therefore, it is not permitted to be seen at all. Nobody from other schools of practice is allowed to see it, either. Even fellow disciples from the same school of practice are not allowed to see it. No one will be able to tell it correctly, because a life like that has been changed and is one for cultivation practice.

Someone asked me if he could read other religious books and other qigong books. We have said that religious books, particularly the Buddhist ones, all teach people how to cultivate their xinxing. We are also of the Buddha School, so there should not be any problem. But, there is one point to be made: Many things in the scriptures were mistranslated in the translation process. In addition, many interpretations of the scriptures were also made from perspectives at different levels, and the definitions were casually made. That is plundering the Dharma. Those people who casually interpreted the scriptures were too far away from the realm of Buddhas; they did not understand the scriptures' actual content. Therefore, they would also have different understandings of the issues. It will not be very easy for you to understand them thoroughly, and you will be unable to comprehend them on your own. But if you say: "I'm just interested in studying the scriptures," and you always study the scriptures, you will be practicing in that school of practice, since the scriptures have also integrated the gong and the Fa from that school of practice. Once you study it, you will be practicing in that school of practice. It involves this issue. If you study it in depth and follow that school of practice, you may have assumed that school of practice instead of ours. Throughout history, in cultivation practice one has been required not to undertake two schools of practice at the same time. If you really want to practice this school of practice, you should only read the texts in this school of practice.

As far as qigong books are concerned, you should not read them if you want to practice cultivation. Particularly with regard to qigong books published nowadays, you should not read them. The same is true for books such as <u>Huangdi Neijing,</u>[7] <u>Xingming Guizhi</u>, or <u>Tao Tsang</u>. Though they do not carry those bad messages, they also contain messages from different levels. They themselves are also ways of cultivation practice. Once you read them, they will give you something and interfere with you. If you find one of their sentences good, well, something will come to you and be added to your gong. Though it is not something bad, how will you practice cultivation when something else is suddenly given to you? Won't it cause problems as well? If you add an extra part to the electronic unit inside a television set, what do you think will happen to this television set? It will be out of order instantly. This is the principle. Additionally, many qigong books nowadays are false and carry a variety of messages. As one of our practitioners was turning the pages of a qigong book, a big snake jumped out of it. Of course, I will not discuss this in detail. What I just addressed are some problems resulting from practitioners' inability to conduct themselves properly; that is,

---

[7] <u>Huangdi Neijing</u> (hwang-dee nay-jing)—Yellow Emperor's scripture for internal cultivation.

those problems are caused by an incorrect mind. It is beneficial that we point them out and let everyone know what to do and how to distinguish them so that problems will not occur in the future. Though I did not overemphasize what I just said, everyone should be sure to pay attention to it because problems usually arise over this issue, and they normally surface here. Cultivation practice is extremely arduous and very serious. If you are being careless for a moment, you may stumble and become ruined at once. Therefore, one's mind must be right.

Martial Arts Qigong

In addition to internal cultivation practices, there is martial arts qigong. While speaking of martial arts qigong, I must stress an issue that now there are claims of many qigong forms in the community of cultivators.

There are now the so-called painting qigong, music qigong, calligraphy qigong, and dancing qigong—there are all sorts of them. Are they all qigong? I find it very odd. I would say that this is plundering qigong. It is not only plundering qigong, but also simply ruining qigong. What is their theoretical basis? It is said that while one is painting, singing, dancing, or writing, one should be in a state of trance or the so-called qigong state. Does that make it qigong? It should not be understood this way. Isn't that ruining qigong? Qigong is a broad and profound study of cultivation of the human body. Oh, how can being in the state of trance be called qigong? Then, what will it be called if we go to the restroom in a state of trance? Isn't that ruining qigong? I would call it qigong undermining. Two years ago at the Oriental Health Expo, so-called calligraphy qigong was there. What is calligraphy qigong? I went over there to take a look and saw a person there writing. Upon writing, he gave off his qi to each word with his hands, and the qi emitted was all black. His mind was preoccupied with money and fame. How could he have gong? His qi could not be good, either. His writings were hung up, with expensive price stickers. But they were all sold to foreigners. I would say that whoever bought them would be miserable. How could the black qi be good? That person's whole face looked dark. He was obsessed with money and only thought about money—how could he have any gong? Nonetheless, this person's business card carried a pile of titles, such as the so-called International Calligraphy Qigong. I would ask how such a thing could be called qigong?

Think about it, everyone: Eighty to ninety percent of the people from this class will not only have their illnesses healed, but will also develop gong—the genuine gong. What your body carries is already quite supernormal. If you practice cultivation on your own, even with a whole lifetime you will not develop it via cultivation. Even if a young person begins the practice right now, in this lifetime he will not be able to develop what I have given, and he will still need the guidance of a true, good master. It has taken us many generations to form this Falun and these mechanisms. These things are installed in your body all at once. Therefore, I am telling you not to lose it easily just because you have obtained it easily. They are extremely valuable and priceless. After this class, what you carry with you is the real gong, the high-energy matter. When you go home and write a few words— no matter how your handwriting is—it carries gong! Thus, should everyone from this class be entitled to the name of "master," and all become calligraphy qigong masters? I would say that it should not be understood this way. As a person with genuine gong and energy, you do not need to give it off intentionally; you will leave energy on whatever you touch, and it will all be shining brightly.

I also found in a magazine a piece of news which reported that a calligraphy qigong class was to be held. I read it briefly to see how it would be taught. It was written that one should first regulate one's breathing or inhale and exhale. Next, one should sit for fifteen to thirty minutes, focusing the mind on the qi in dantian and imagining lifting the dantian qi to the forearm. Then, one should pick up the brush-pen and dip it into black ink. After that, one should move the qi to the brush-pen point. When one's mind-intent reaches there, one may start to write. Isn't that deceiving people? Oh, if one can move the qi somewhere, that would be considered qigong? In that case, before we eat a meal we should sit in meditation for a while. We would then pick up chopsticks and move the qi to the tips of our chopsticks to have the meal. That would be called the dining qigong, wouldn't it? What we eat would all be energy as well. We are just commenting on this issue. I call that undermining qigong, as they take qigong as something so shallow. People therefore should not understand it in this way.

Martial arts qigong, however, can already be considered an independent qigong practice. Why is it? Because it has a heritage of several thousand years, a complete system of cultivation theories, and a complete system of cultivation methods, it can be regarded as a complete system. Despite that, martial arts qigong remains something at the lowest level of internal cultivation practices. The hard qigong is a form of clustered energy-matter that is solely intended for attacking. Let me give you an example. After attending our Falun Dafa class, a practitioner in Beijing could not press anything with his hands. When he was shopping for a baby carriage, he was surprised that the baby carriage would

255

collapse at the sound of "Pa" when he checked its sturdiness with his hands. When he went home and sat in a chair, he could not press it with his hands. If he did, the chair would break. He asked me what was going on. I did not tell him why because I did not want him to develop an attachment. I just said that it was all natural, let it be, and ignore it since it was all good. If that supernormal capability is used well, a piece of rock could be smashed into powder with a pinch of his hand. Isn't this the hard qigong? Nevertheless, he had never practiced the hard qigong. In internal cultivation practices, these supernormal capabilities can usually be developed. But, because it is difficult to handle one's xinxing well, one usually is not allowed to use them even if they have been developed. In particular, at the low level of cultivation practice, one's xinxing has not been upgraded. Thus, the supernormal capabilities that are developed at the low level will not be granted at all. As time goes by and your level is upgraded, these things will no longer be of any use and will not need to be provided.

How is martial arts qigong practiced specifically? In practicing martial arts qigong, one must regulate the qi, but it is not easy to regulate qi at the beginning. Though one may want to regulate qi, one might not be able to do so. What should one do, then? One must exercise his hands, both sides of his chest, his feet, legs, arms, and head. How does one exercise them? Some people punch a tree with their hands or palms, and some people slap a rock with their hands. How painful it must be for the bones to make such contact, as they will bleed with only a little effort! The qi still cannot be regulated. What should be done? One will start to swing one's arms and make the blood move backward to the arms, and one's arms and hands will thus swell. They will actually be swollen. After that, when one slaps a rock, the bones will be padded and will not make direct contact with the rock. Thus they will not feel the pain as much. As one continues to practice, the master will teach this person. As time passes, he will learn to regulate qi. Nevertheless, the ability to regulate qi alone is not good enough, for in an actual combat the opponent will not wait for you. Of course, when one can regulate qi, one is able to resist attacks and may not feel the pain after being hit with a very thick club. After directing qi to the arms, the arms will swell. But at the beginning, qi is the most primitive thing and can be transformed into the high-energy matter as one continues to practice. When it is transformed into the high-energy matter, it will gradually form an energy cluster of great density, and this energy cluster has intelligence. Therefore, it is also a supernormal capability cluster, or namely, a supernormal capability. Nevertheless, this supernormal capability is solely for attacking and attack protection. It will not work if used to treat illnesses. Because this high-energy matter exists in another dimension and does not travel in our dimension, its time travels faster than ours. When you punch someone, you do not need to direct qi or think about it as the gong will be there already. When you try to ward off someone's attack, the gong will also be there already. No matter how quickly you throw a punch, it will travel faster than you do as the time concepts are different on the two sides. Through practicing martial arts qigong, one can develop the so-called Iron Sand Palm, Cinnabar Palm, Vajra Leg, and Arhat Foot.[8] These are the skills of everyday people. Through practice, an ordinary person can achieve this level.

The biggest difference between martial arts qigong and the internal cultivation practices is that martial arts qigong requires

---

[8] Iron Sand Palm, Cinnabar Palm, Vajra Leg, Arhat Foot—types of Chinese martial arts techniques

practicing in motion; qi thus travels under the skin. Because it requires practicing in motion, one cannot achieve a state of tranquility, nor will one's qi enter dantian. One's qi will travel under the skin and through the muscles. Therefore, one cannot cultivate the body, nor can one cultivate the high-level abilities. Our internal cultivation practice requires practicing in a state of tranquility. Conventional practices require that qi enters dantian in the lower abdominal area. They require practice in a state of tranquility and the transformation of benti. They can cultivate the body and lead to practicing cultivation at higher levels.

You may have learned from novels martial arts techniques such as the so-called Golden Bell Shield, Iron Cloth Shirt, and striking through a poplar tree from one hundred paces away. With the light martial arts, one can travel back and forth in high locations. Some can even enter another dimension. Do such martial arts exist? Yes, that is for sure. Yet, they do not exist among everyday people. Those who have indeed cultivated such superb martial arts cannot show them off in public. Because such a person does not simply practice martial arts and is completely beyond the level of everyday people, he must practice cultivation by following an internal cultivation practice. The person must value and improve his xinxing. He must care little about things such as material interests. Though he can cultivate such martial arts, he can no longer casually use them among everyday people thereafter. It is permitted if he uses them with nobody around to see it. In reading those novels, you will find that a character will fight and kill for a secret sword art manual, treasure, or women. Everyone is portrayed to have great abilities, traveling back and forth mysteriously. Think about it, everyone: Don't those people who truly have these martial arts skills have to cultivate them through internal cultivation practice? They acquire them only through cultivating their xinxing, and they must have already long been disinterested in fame, profit, and various desires. How can they kill others? How can they care that much for money and wealth? It is absolutely impossible. Those are only artistic exaggerations. People just go after the mental stimulation and will do anything for that craving. The authors have capitalized on this point and try their best to write whatever you look for or find pleasing. The more inconceivable the writings, the more you want to read them. Those are only artistic exaggerations. Those who indeed have these martial arts abilities will not act like that. In particular, they will not demonstrate them in public.

The Mentality of Showing Off

Because of practicing cultivation among everyday people, a lot of our practitioners cannot release many of their attachments. Many attachments have already become second nature, and these people themselves cannot detect them. This mentality of showing off can manifest in any situation; it can also surface when doing a good deed. In order to gain fame, personal profit, and a little benefit, some people often brag about themselves and show off: "I'm very capable and a winner." We also have such cases where those who practice a little better than others, have better tianmu visions, or whose exercise movements look better, also like to show off.

One may claim: "I've heard something from Teacher Li." People will surround this person and listen to what he says. He will pass on the hearsay embellished with his own understanding. What is the purpose? It is to show himself off. There are some people who also spread the hearsay among one another with a great deal of interest, as though they are well informed, and as though so many of our practitioners do not understand or know as much as they do. It has become natural for them, and perhaps they do not realize it themselves. Subconsciously, they just have this mentality of showing off. Otherwise, what would be the purpose of circulating the hearsay? Some people gossip about when Teacher will return to the mountains. I am not from the mountains. Why should I return to the mountains? Still, others gossip that I have told someone something on a particular day, and that I treat that person very specially. What good will it do to spread these things? It will not serve any good at all. We have seen, however, that this is their attachment—the mentality of showing off.

Some people have come to me for my autograph. What is the purpose? It is an everyday people's custom to have someone's autograph as a souvenir. If you do not practice cultivation, my autograph will not serve any use for you. Every word in my book bears my image and Falun, and every sentence was spoken by me. What do you still need my autograph for? Some people presume: "With the autograph, Teacher's message will protect me." They still believe in things such as messages. We do not care about messages. This book is already invaluable. What else are you still looking for? All these are reflections of those attachments. Also, after seeing the demeanor of the disciples who travel with me, some people will imitate them without realizing whether they are good or bad. In fact, it does not matter who the person is—there is only one Fa. Only by observing this Dafa can one meet the genuine standard. The people who work by my side have not received any special treatment and are the same as everyone else; they are just staff members of the Research Society. Do not develop those attachments. Oftentimes, upon forming these attachments, you may play the role of unintentionally undermining Dafa. The sensational hearsay that you have invented may even lead to conflicts or stir up a practitioner's attachment to getting closer to Teacher in order to hear more things and so on. Aren't these all the same issue?

What else can this mentality of showing off easily lead to? I have been teaching the practice for two years. Some among our veteran Falun Dafa practitioners may soon become kaigong. Some will enter a phase of gradual enlightenment and suddenly reach it. Why didn't they have these supernormal capabilities earlier? This is because though I pushed you to such a high level all at once, doing that would not be allowed, for your attachments of everyday people had not been completely removed. Certainly, your xinxing had already improved remarkably, yet many attachments had not been released. Therefore, those supernormal capabilities were not given to you. After this phase is over and you become steady, you will at once be put in a state of gradual enlightenment. In this state of gradual enlightenment, your tianmu will be opened at a very high level and you will develop many supernormal capabilities. In fact, let me tell you that when you truly practice cultivation, you have already at the beginning developed many supernormal capabilities. You have already reached this high level, so you have many supernormal capabilities. This situation may have happened to many of you recently. There are also some people who cannot reach a high level in cultivation. What they have physically, along with their endurance, is predestined. Consequently, some people will become kaigong or enlightened—completely enlightened—at a very low level. There will be such people.

I am pointing out this issue to let everyone know that once

there is such a person, you must be sure not to regard him as a remarkable, enlightened person. This is a very serious issue in cultivation practice. Only through following this Dafa can you do things correctly. You should not follow or listen to him because he has supernormal capabilities, supernatural powers, or because he can see some things. You will do him harm, as he will develop the attachment of jubilation and end up losing everything and having them switched off. In the end, he will stumble. One who has become kaigong may also stumble. If one cannot conduct oneself well, one will also stumble even if one is enlightened. When things are not handled properly, even a Buddha can stumble, not to mention a practitioner like you among everyday people! Therefore, no matter how many supernormal capabilities you have developed, how great they are, or how powerful your divine power is, you must conduct yourself well. Recently, we had someone sitting here who could disappear at one moment and reappear the next. It is just like that. Even greater supernatural powers will be developed. What will you do? As our practitioners or disciples, whether these things happen to you or others in the future, you should not idolize them or pursue these things. Once your mind goes wrong, it will be all over, and you will stumble. Perhaps, you are at an even higher level than they are, only except that your supernatural powers have not yet emerged. At least, you have stumbled on this particular issue. Accordingly, everyone must be sure to pay particular attention to this matter. We have deemed this a highly important issue because such a matter will soon take place. Once it occurs, it is unacceptable if you cannot conduct yourself well.

A practitioner who has developed gong and become kaigong or truly enlightened should not take himself to be someone special. What he has seen are things limited to his own level. His cultivation has reached this level, because his enlightenment ability, xinxing standard, and wisdom have reached this level. With regard to things at higher levels, therefore, he might be in disbelief. Precisely because he does not believe them, he thinks that what he sees is absolute and that there are only these things. That is way off, because this person's level is just here.

Some people will become kaigong at this level since they cannot go any further in cultivation practice. As a result, they can become kaigong and enlightened only at this level. Among those of you who will complete cultivation in the future, some will be enlightened on the small worldly paths, some will be enlightened at different levels, and some will be enlightened with the Right Fruit. Only the enlightened people with the Right Fruit will achieve their highest levels, being able to see things and manifesting themselves at different levels. Even those who are enlightened on the worldly paths at the lowest level will be able to see some dimensions and some enlightened people, and they will be able to communicate with them as well. At that time, you should not become complacent because enlightenment on the small worldly paths at the lower levels cannot attain the Right Fruit—this is for sure. What can be done about it, then? One can only stay at this level. To practice cultivation toward a higher level will be a future matter. Since one's cultivation can only go so far, what should one do if one is not to become kaigong? Though you will keep cultivating yourself like this, your cultivation can no longer make progress, so you will become kaigong since you have reached the end of your cultivation; there will be many such people. No matter what happens, one must maintain good xinxing. Only through adhering to Dafa can one be truly right. Whether it is your supernormal capabilities or your kaigong, you achieve them through practicing cultivation in Dafa.

If you put Dafa in a secondary place and put your supernatural powers in the primary place, or as an enlightened person you believe that what you understand one way or another is correct, or if you even regard yourself as being great and beyond Dafa, I would say that you have already started to stumble. It would be dangerous and you would become ever worse. At that time, you would really be in trouble, and your cultivation would end up in vain. If things are not done right, you will stumble and fail in your cultivation.

Let me also tell you that the content of this book has combined the Fa that I have taught in several classes. Everything was taught by me, and every sentence was spoken by me. Every word was pulled from the tape recordings and transcribed word for word. My disciples and practitioners helped me transcribe everything from the tape recordings. I then revised it over and over again. It is all my Fa, and what I have taught is only this Fa.

LECTURE SEVEN

The Issue of Killing

The issue of killing is very sensitive. For practitioners, we have set the strict requirement that they cannot kill lives. Whether it is of the Buddha School, the Tao School, or the Qimen School, regardless of which school or practice it is, as long as it is an orthodox cultivation practice, it will consider this issue very absolute and prohibit killing—this is for sure. Because the consequence of killing a life is so serious, we must address it in detail. In the original Buddhism, killing mainly referred to taking a human life, which was the most serious act. Later, killing large-sized lives, large domestic animals, or relatively large animals were all considered very serious. Why has the issue of killing been taken so seriously in the community of cultivators? In the past, Buddhism held that lives that were not supposed to die would, if killed, become lonesome spirits and homeless ghosts. Before, rituals were performed to free these people's souls from misery. Without such services, these souls would suffer hunger and thirst, living in a very bitter situation. This is what Buddhism said in the past.

We believe that when one does something wrong to another person, one must give quite a lot of de as compensation. Here, we usually refer to one's having taken away things that belong to other people and so on. Yet, if a life is put to an end all of a sudden, whether it is an animal or another creature, this will generate quite a lot of karma. Killing once mainly referred to taking away a human life, and it would cause a great amount of karma. Yet, killing other ordinary lives is no lesser sin, for it also directly causes much karma. Particularly for a practitioner, in the course of cultivation practice you are given some tribulations at each different level. They all come from your own karma and are your own tribulations, which are placed at different levels for you to upgrade yourself. As long as you improve your xinxing, you will be able to overcome them. But if you suddenly obtain so much karma, how can you overcome it? With your xinxing level, you will not be able to make it at all. It may make you completely unable to practice cultivation.

We have found that when a person is born, there are many of him born simultaneously within a certain scope of this cosmic space. They all look alike with the same name, and they do similar things. Therefore, they can also be called part of his whole entity. This involves such an issue, for if one of them (as in the case of other large animals' lives) is suddenly dead while the rest of him in other different dimensions have yet to complete their predestined life journeys and still have many years to live, this dead person will be in a homeless situation and drift about in the cosmic space. The lonesome spirits and homeless ghosts who suffer from hunger, thirst, and other hardships as described in the past might be this way. But we have indeed observed the terrible situation in which this person suffers because he must wait for his final destiny when every one of him in each dimension completes his life journey. The longer it is, the more he suffers. The more he suffers, the more the karma created by his suffering will be added to the killer's body. Think about it: How much more karma might you accumulate? This is what we have observed through supernormal capabilities.

We have also observed this situation: When a person is born, a profile of his whole life will exist in a specific dimension. In other words, where his life is and what he should do are all included in it. Who has arranged his life? It is obviously done by a higher life. For instance, in our ordinary human society, after birth one belongs to a certain family, a certain school, and upon growing up a certain workplace; various contacts in society are made through a person's job. That is, the layout of the entire society has been planned this way. Yet, if this life suddenly dies and not according to the original, specific arrangement, or if things have been changed, the higher life will not forgive the meddler. Think about it, everyone: As practitioners, we want to practice cultivation toward higher levels. That high-level life will not even forgive the killer. Do you think that this person can still practice cultivation? The levels of some masters are not even as high as that of this higher life who has made this arrangement. Therefore, the person's master will also be punished and sent down to the low level. Just think about it: Is this an ordinary issue? So once a person does such a thing, it is very difficult for him or her to practice cultivation.

Among Falun Dafa practitioners, there may be some who have fought in times of war. Those wars were conditions brought about by greater cosmic changes on the whole, and you were only an element in that circumstance. Without human activities under the cosmic changes, such conditions would not have been brought to ordinary human society, nor would they be called the cosmic changes. Those events evolved according to greater changes and were not entirely your fault. What we are discussing here is the karma resulting from one's insisting on doing bad things in seeking personal gains, satisfying self-interest, or when one is somehow affected. As long as it involves changes in the entire immense space and major changes in society, it is not your fault.

Killing can bring about enormous karma. One may wonder: "We can't kill a life, but I'm the cook at home. What will my family eat if I can't take a life?" This specific issue does not concern me, as I am teaching the Fa to practitioners instead of casually telling everyday people how to live. With regard to how one should deal with specific issues, you should make a judgment according to Dafa. You should do things however you see fit. Everyday people will do whatever they want to, and that is their business; it is not possible for everyone to truly practice cultivation. As a practitioner, however, one should follow a higher standard, so I am hereby putting forward the requirements for practitioners.

In addition to human beings and animals, plants are also lives. Any matter's life can manifest in other dimensions. When your tianmu reaches the level of Fa Eyesight, you will find that rocks, walls, or anything can talk to you and greet you. Perhaps one may wonder: "The grains and vegetables that we eat are also lives. There are also flies and mosquitoes at home. What should we do?" It is quite uncomfortable to be stung by a mosquito in the summer, and one will have to watch it sting without reacting to it. If one sees that a fly is on one's food and making it dirty, one also should not kill it. Let me tell you that we should not casually kill a life without reason. But neither should we become overly-cautious gentlemen who always focus on these trifles; they watch each step they take and jump around fearing to step on an ant. I would say that you live a tiring life. Isn't that also an attachment? Though by jumping around you might have not killed the ant, you may have nonetheless killed a lot of microorganisms. There are many more microscopic lives at the microscopic level, including germs and bacteria; perhaps you have also stepped on and killed many of them. In that case, we should not live anymore. We do not want to become such people, as it makes cultivation practice impossible. One should focus on a broader perspective and practice cultivation in an upright and dignified manner.

As human beings, we have the right to maintain human lives. Therefore, our living environment should also meet the needs of human lives. We cannot harm or kill lives intentionally, but we should not be overly concerned with these trifles. For instance, the vegetables and grains that we grow are all lives. We cannot stop eating or drinking something because it has life, for how can we then practice cultivation? One should look beyond that. For example, while you are walking, some ants or insects may run under your feet and get killed. Perhaps they are supposed to die since you do not kill them intentionally. In the world of organisms and microorganisms, there is also the issue of ecological balance—too many of any species will be problematic. We should thus practice cultivation in a dignified and righteous way. When flies and mosquitoes are in the house, we may drive them out or install a window screen to keep them out. Sometimes, they cannot be driven out, and if they are then smashed, so be it. If they are going to sting and harm people in the space where human beings live, one should certainly drive them out. If they cannot be driven out, one cannot just watch them sting people there. As a practitioner, you do not mind them and you are immune to them, but your family members do not practice cultivation and are everyday people concerned with the problem of contagious diseases. We cannot watch and do nothing when a mosquito stings a child on the face.

Let me give you an example. There was a story about Sakyamuni in his early years. One day Sakyamuni was going to take a bath in a forest, and he asked a disciple to clean the bathtub. His disciple went to the bathtub and found it full of insects crawling everywhere. The insects would be killed if he cleaned the bathtub. The disciple came back to Sakyamuni and said: "The bathtub is full of insects." Sakyamuni did not look at him and replied: "You should go and clean the bathtub." The disciple went back to the bathtub and did not know how to clean it, as doing so would kill the insects. He again came back to Sakyamuni and said: "Master, the bathtub is full of insects. If I clean it, the insects will be killed." Sakyamuni looked at him and said: "What I asked you to do was to clean the bathtub." The disciple understood all of a sudden, and he went and cleaned the bathtub right away. This story tells a principle: We should not stop taking baths because there are insects, nor should we find another place to live because there are mosquitoes. We also should not tie up our necks and stop eating or drinking because both grains and vegetables are lives. It should not be this way. We should cope with this relationship properly and practice cultivation in a dignified way. It will be fine as long as we do not harm any life intentionally. Meanwhile, people also must have a human living space and living conditions, and these should also be maintained. Human beings still need to maintain their lives and live normally.

In the past, some phony qigong masters said: "One may kill lives on the first or the fifteenth of each lunar month." Some of them even claimed that it was fine to kill two-legged animals as though they were not lives. Is killing on the first or the fifteenth not considered taking a life? So that's just digging the earth, is it? Some sham qigong masters can be identified from their speeches and conduct, or by what they say and what they are after. All those qigong masters making such statements usually have futi. Just look at the way a qigong master possessed by a fox eats a chicken. When this person gobbles it up, he is not even willing to spit out the bones.

Killing does not only bring about a lot of karma, it also involves the issue of compassion. Shouldn't we have compassion as practitioners? When our compassion emerges, we can find all living beings and every person suffering. This will happen.

The Issue of Eating Meat

Eating meat is also a very sensitive issue, but eating meat is not killing a life. Though all of you have studied the Fa for so long, we have not required everyone to stop eating meat. Many qigong masters tell you to stop eating meat as soon as you walk into their classes. You may think: "I'm not yet mentally prepared to stop eating meat all of a sudden." The meal served at home today may be roasted chicken or fried fish. Though they smell quite good, you are not allowed to eat them. The same is true with religious cultivation practices that force one not to eat meat. Conventional practices in the Buddha School and some practices in the Tao School also say so and prohibit one from eating meat. We are not asking you here to do so, but we are also concerned with this issue. Then, what do we require? Because our practice is one in which the Fa cultivates practitioners, this means that some situations will arise from gong and the Fa. In the course of practice, different levels produce different situations. Someday or after my lecture today, some people may be in this state: They can no longer eat meat, and meat will smell sickening. If one eats it, one will want to throw up. You are not forced by anyone, nor do you force yourself not to eat the meat. Instead, this comes from your own mind. After reaching this level, you will not be able to eat meat, as it is being reflected from the gong. If you really swallow the meat, you will indeed throw up.

Our veteran practitioners all know that this situation will occur in Falun Dafa cultivation practice, as different levels present different situations. Some practitioners have a strong desire for and a strong attachment to eating meat—they usually eat a lot of meat. When others find meat very sickening, they do not feel so and can still eat it. In order to remove this attachment, what should be done? This person will have a stomachache upon eating meat. With abstention from meat, he or she will not have pain. This situation will happen, and it means that one should not eat meat anymore. Does it mean that thereafter our school of practice will have nothing to do with meat? It is not so. How should we deal with this issue? Being unable to eat meat comes from one's own heart. What is the purpose? Cultivation practices in temples force one to not eat meat. This, along with being unable to eat meat as reflected in our practice, both intend to remove this human desire for or attachment to eating meat.

If there is no meat in their bowls, some people simply will not have their meals. That is an everyday person's desire. One morning when I was passing the rear entrance of Triumph Park in Changchun, three people came out of the rear entrance, shouting loudly. One of them said: "What sort of qigong is it that's practiced and one can't even eat meat? I'd rather give up ten years of my life to eat meat!" What a strong desire that is! Think about it, everyone: Shouldn't this desire be removed? It definitely should. In the course of cultivation practice, one is to give up different desires and attachments. To put it plainly, if the desire to eat meat is not removed, isn't it that the attachment hasn't been abandoned? How can one complete cultivation? Therefore, as long as it is an attachment, it has to be removed. But this does not mean that one will never again eat meat. Giving up eating meat itself is not the purpose. The purpose is to not let you have this attachment. If you can give up the attachment during the time when you cannot eat meat, you might be able to eat it again later. Meat will not smell sickening or taste awful then. At that time, if you eat meat, it will not matter.

When you can eat meat again, both your attachment and desire for meat will have already been given up. A big change will occur, however, as meat will no longer be tasty to you. If it is cooked at home, you will eat it with your family. If it is not cooked at home, you will not miss it. If you eat it, it will not taste delicious. This scenario will occur. But, practicing cultivation among everyday people is quite complicated. If your family always cooks meat, over a period of time you will find it very tasty again. Such relapses will occur in the future, and they will repeat many times over the entire course of cultivation practice. You may suddenly be unable to eat meat again. You should not eat it when you cannot eat it. You will really be unable to eat it, and upon eating it you will throw up. Wait until you can eat meat again and follow the course of nature. Eating meat or not is not itself the purpose—the key is to give up that attachment.

Our Falun Dafa school enables one to make quick progress. As long as you upgrade your xinxing, you will make quick breakthroughs at each level. Some people are not attached to meat in the first place and do not care whether there is meat in their meal. It will take them a couple of weeks to wear out this attachment. Some people may take one, two, or three months, or perhaps half a year to do it. Except for in very unusual cases, it will not take more than a year for one to be able to eat meat again.

273

This is because meat has already become a staple food for people. Nonetheless, professional practitioners in temples should not eat meat.

Let us talk about how Buddhism regards eating meat. The earliest original Buddhism did not prohibit eating meat. When Sakyamuni took his disciples to the forest to practice cultivation through hardships, there was no such rule prohibiting the meat diet. Why wasn't there one? It was because when Sakyamuni taught his Dharma twenty-five hundred years ago, human society was very backward. Some regions had agriculture while others still did not. Cultivated farmlands were very few, and forests were everywhere. Grains were in short supply and extremely rare. Human beings had just emerged from primitive society and were living mainly on hunting; many regions fed mainly on meat. In order to abandon human attachments as much as possible, Sakyamuni forbade his disciples from having access to any wealth, materials, etc. He took disciples with him to beg for food. They would eat whatever was given to them, for as practitioners they could not choose their given food, which might include meat.

There was a prohibition of *hun*[1] in original Buddhism. This prohibition of hun is from the original Buddhism, but now eating meat is said to be hun. Actually, at that time hun did not refer to meat, but to things such as onions, ginger, and garlic. Why should they be considered hun? At present, many monks also cannot explain it clearly. Because many of them do not truly practice cultivation, they are not clear about a lot of things. What Sakyamuni taught was called "precept, samadhi, wisdom." Precept refers to abandoning all attachments of everyday people. Samadhi means that a practitioner practices cultivation by being completely

---

[1] *hun* (huhn)—food that is forbidden in Buddhism.

in trance and sitting in meditation—one must be totally in trance. Anything that affected one's trance and cultivation would be regarded as serious interference. Whoever ate onions, ginger, or garlic would have a strong odor. At that time, monks usually stayed in a forest or in a cave. Seven or eight people sat in a circle, and they formed many circles to mediate. If someone ate these things, this would produce a very irritating odor that would affect others sitting in trance, seriously interfering with their practice. Thus this rule was made; such food was considered hun, and it was forbidden. Many of the beings cultivated from one's body are quite repulsed by such rich odors. Onions, ginger, and garlic can also stimulate one's desires. If one eats them too much, one can also become addicted to them, and so they were considered hun.

In the past, after reaching very high levels in cultivation and being in the state of kaigong or semi-kaigong, many monks also realized that those rules did not really matter in the course of cultivation practice. If an attachment can be relinquished, that material itself does not have any effect. What really interferes with a person is the mind. Therefore, throughout history the accomplished monks have also found that the matter of whether one eats meat is not a critical issue. The key question is whether the attachment can be removed. If one does not have any attachment, it is fine to eat just about anything to fill the stomach. Since cultivation practices in temples have been a certain way, many people are already accustomed to it. Additionally, it is no longer the simple matter of being a rule, but a chartered regulation in temples that one cannot eat meat at all. People have also become used to this way of cultivation. Let us talk about Monk Jigong[2] who was made very famous by literary works. Monks should not

---

[2] Jigong (jee-gong)—well-known Buddhist monk in the Southern Song Dynasty (1127 A.D.-1279 A.D.).

eat meat, but he ate meat and was thus made quite well known. In fact, since he was expelled from Lingyin Temple, food supplies naturally became his primary concern as his life was in a desperate situation. In order to fill his stomach, he ate whatever he could grab; it would not matter, as long as he just wanted to fill up his stomach and was without attachment to any particular food. At that level of cultivation, he understood this principle. Actually, Jigong only had meat on one or two occasions. As soon as monks eating meat is spoken of, writers become excited. The more shocking the subject, the more interested readers will be. Literary works are based on life and then go beyond it; he was thus publicized. In fact, if the attachment is indeed given up, it does not matter what one eats to fill one's stomach.

In Southeast Asia or in the southern regions of China such as Guangdong and Guangxi,[3] some lay Buddhists will not call themselves Buddhists in a conversation, as if it sounds too old-fashioned. They say that they eat the Buddhist food or that they are vegetarians, which suggests that they are vegetarian Buddhists. They take Buddha cultivation as something so simple. How can being a vegetarian enable one to cultivate Buddhahood? Everyone knows that eating meat is only one attachment and one desire— this is only one attachment. Being a vegetarian only removes this one attachment. One still needs to relinquish jealousy, the competitive mentality, the attachment of zealotry, the mentality of showing off, and various other attachments; there are numerous human attachments. Only by removing all attachments and desires can one complete one's cultivation practice. How can one cultivate Buddhahood by giving up only this attachment of eating meat?

[3] Guangdong (gwang-dong) and Guangxi (gwang-shee)—two provinces in Southern China.

That kind of statement is incorrect.

On the issue of food, besides eating meat one should not be attached to any other food, either. The same is true with other things. Some people say that they just like to eat a particular food—that is also a desire. After reaching a certain level of cultivation, a practitioner will not have this attachment. Of course, our Fa is taught at a very high level and is taught by incorporating different levels. It is impossible for one to reach this step right away. You claim that you just want to eat that particular food, but when your cultivation has really reached the time to give up that attachment, you will not be able to eat it. If you eat it, it will not be tasty, and you will not be able to tell what it tastes like. At the time when I went to work, the cafeteria in the workplace always lost money and was later shut down. After it closed down, everyone brought lunch to work. It was troublesome and a lot of hustle to make meals in the morning. Sometimes, I would buy two steamed buns and a piece of bean curd that was put in soy sauce. In theory, that should be quite a light meal, but eating that all the time was also unacceptable, and the attachment had to be removed. As soon as I saw bean curd again, it would make me feel sick. I could not eat it when I tried it again, lest I develop the attachment. Of course, this will only happen when someone has reached a certain level in cultivation practice. It will not be this way at the beginning.

The Buddha School does not permit drinking alcohol. Have you ever seen a Buddha carrying a wine container? No. I have said that one might not be able to eat meat, but after one gives up the attachment during cultivation practice among everyday people, it is not a problem for one to eat it again later. After quitting drinking alcohol, however, one should not drink again. Doesn't a practitioner have gong in the body? Different forms of gong and some supernormal capabilities are shown on the surface of your body, and they are all pure. As soon as you drink alcohol, they will all leave the body immediately. In a split second, your body will have nothing left, as they all fear that odor. It is quite loathsome if you become addicted to this habit, for drinking alcohol can make one irrational. Why do some Great Taoist cultivation practices require drinking alcohol? It is because they do not cultivate one's zhu yuanshen, and drinking can make one's zhu yuanshen become unconscious.

Some people love alcohol as much as their own lives. Some people enjoy drinking alcohol. Some people are already poisoned by drinking alcohol, and they cannot even pick up their rice bowls without drinking—they cannot do without a drink. As practitioners, we should not be this way. Drinking alcohol is definitely addictive. It is a desire and stimulates one's addictive nerves. The more one drinks, the more one becomes addicted to it. Let us think about it: As practitioners, shouldn't we give up this attachment? This attachment must also be removed. One may think: "It's impossible because I'm responsible for entertaining customers," or "I'm responsible for making business contacts. It's not easy to make a deal without drinking alcohol." I would say that it is not necessarily so. Usually, in doing a business deal, especially in doing business with or in dealing with foreigners, you may ask for a soda, he or she may ask for mineral water, and another person may ask for a beer. Nobody will force you to drink alcohol. You make your own choice and drink as much as you want. Particularly among intellectuals, this case seldom takes place. It is usually like that.

Smoking is also an attachment. Some people say that

smoking can refresh them, but I call it self-deception and deceiving others. When feeling tired from work or from writing something, one may want to take a break by smoking a cigarette. After puffing a cigarette, one feels refreshed. Actually, it is not true. It is because one has taken a break. The human mind can create a false impression and illusion that later can indeed become a concept or false impression that smoking does refresh oneself. It cannot do that at all, nor can it have this effect. Smoking does not do the human body any good. If a person smokes for a long period of time, at the time of autopsy a doctor will find that his or her trachea and lungs are all black.

Don't our practitioners want to purify their bodies? We should constantly purify our bodies and constantly progress toward higher levels. Yet you still put that in your body, so aren't you going the opposite way from us? Furthermore, it is also a strong desire. Some people also know that it is not good, but they just cannot quit. In fact, let me tell you that they do not have correct thoughts to guide themselves, and it will not be easy for them to quit that way. As a practitioner, today you can give it up as an attachment and see if you can quit. I advise everyone that if you truly want to practice cultivation you should quit smoking from now on, and it is guaranteed that you can quit. In the field of this class, no one thinks of smoking a cigarette. If you want to quit, it is guaranteed that you can do it. When you smoke a cigarette again, it will not taste right. If you read this lecture in the book, it will also have this effect. Of course, if you do not want to practice cultivation, we will not take care of it. I think that as a practitioner, you should quit it. I once used this example: Have you ever seen a Buddha or a Tao sitting there with a cigarette in his mouth? How can that be possible? As a practitioner, what's your goal? Shouldn't you quit it? Therefore, I have said that if you want to practice cultivation, you should quit smoking. It harms your body and is a desire as well. That is just the opposite of the requirements for our practitioners.

Jealousy

When I teach the Fa, I often bring up the issue of jealousy. Why is this? It is because jealousy is displayed very strongly in China. It is so strong that it has become natural and one does not even feel it. Why do Chinese people have this strong jealousy? It has its reasons. Chinese people in the past were heavily influenced by Confucianism, and they have developed an introverted character. When they are angry or happy, they do not express it. They believe in self-restraint and tolerance. Because they are accustomed to this way, our nationality as a whole has developed a very introverted character. Certainly, it has its advantages, such as not showing off one's inner strengths. But it also has its disadvantages, and it can bring about negative side effects. Particularly in this Dharma-ending Period, its negative aspects have become more notable and can encourage the deepening of one's jealousy. If someone's good news is made public, others will right away become very jealous. Some people are afraid of mentioning their awards or some benefits from their workplaces or elsewhere, lest others feel uneasy upon learning the news. Westerners call it "Oriental jealousy" or "Asian jealousy." The entire Asian region is more or less this way, owing to the influence of Chinese Confucianism. Particularly in China, it is displayed very strongly.

This jealousy is somehow related to the absolute egalitarianism that was once practiced: After all, if the sky falls,

280

everyone should die together; everyone should have an equal share if there is something good; everyone should have an equal wage increase, regardless of the percentage of the raise. This mentality appears to be fair, with everyone being treated equally. In actuality, how can people be the same? The jobs they do are different, and so are the amount of responsibilities they carry out. There is a principle in this universe called, "no loss, no gain." To gain, one must lose. It is held among everyday people that one does not gain if one does not work for it. More work means more gained, less work means less gained. The more efforts one makes, the more returns one deserves. The absolute egalitarianism practiced in the past claimed that everyone is born equal, and that it is a person's post-natal life that changes him or her. I find this statement too absolute. When anything is made absolute, it becomes incorrect. Why should some people be born male and others female? Why don't they look alike? People are not born the same, as some are born ill or disfigured. From the high level, we can see that one's entire life lies there in another dimension. How can they be the same? People all wish to be equal. If something is not a part of someone's life, how can they be equally made? People are not the same.

The personalities of people in Western countries are comparatively outgoing. One can tell when they are happy or angry. This has its advantages, but it also has its disadvantages and can result in a lack of restraint. Because the two temperaments are different in mindset, they bring about different consequences when doing things. If a Chinese person is praised by his supervisor or given some good things, others' minds will be uneasy. If he gets a larger bonus, he may as well put it in his pocket secretly without letting others know. Nowadays, it is difficult to be a model worker. "You're a model worker. You can do it. You should come to work early in the morning and go home late at night. You can do all this work since you're good at it. We aren't good enough." People will be sarcastic and cynical, and so it is not easy to be a good person.

If this happens in other countries, it will be totally different. If a boss finds out that this worker does a good job today, the boss may give him more of a bonus. He will cheerfully count the bills before others: "Wow, the boss gave me so much money today." He can joyfully tell others about it without consequence. If it happens in China that someone earns an extra bonus, the boss will even tell that person to hide it and not let others see it. In other countries, if a child scores a hundred on a test, he will run home cheerfully and shout: "I scored a hundred today! I've scored a hundred!" The child will run home all the way from school. A neighbor will open her door and say: "Hey, Tom, good kid." Another neighbor may open his window: "Hey, Jack, well done. Good boy." If this happens in China, it will be a disaster. "I've scored a hundred, I've scored a hundred." The child runs home from school. Even before opening his door, a neighbor already begins to curse in his house: "What's so great about getting a hundred? Show off! Who hasn't scored a hundred?" The two mentalities will produce different results. It can evoke one's jealousy, for if someone is doing well, instead of feeling happy for him or her, people's minds will feel uneasy. It can lead to this problem.

A few years ago, absolute egalitarianism was practiced, and it has disordered people's thinking and values. Let me give you a specific example. In the workplace, a person may feel that others are not as capable as he. Whatever he does, he does it well. He finds himself indeed remarkable. He thinks to himself: "I'm qualified to be a factory director or manager, or even a higher position. I think that I could even be Prime Minister." The boss may also say that this person is really capable and can accomplish anything. Colleagues may also express that he is really capable and talented. Nevertheless, there may be another person in the same working group or sharing the same office with him, who is quite incapable of doing anything or is good for nothing. Yet one day this incompetent person gets a promotion instead of him and even becomes his supervisor. He will feel in his heart that it is unfair and complain to his boss and colleagues, feeling very upset and quite jealous.

I am telling you this principle that everyday people are unable to realize. You may think that you are good at everything, but your life does not have it. That person is good at nothing, but his life has it, and he will become a boss. No matter what everyday people think, that is only the viewpoint of everyday people. From the perspective of a higher life, the development of human society progresses according to the specific law of development. Therefore, what one does in life is not arranged based on one's abilities. Buddhism believes in the principle of karmic retribution. One's life is arranged according to one's karma. No matter how capable you are, if you do not have de, perhaps you will have nothing in this life. You think that this person is good at nothing, but he has a lot of de. He can become a high-ranking official or make a big fortune. An ordinary person cannot see this point and always believes that he should do exactly what he is able to. Therefore, he competes and fights all his life with a badly-wounded heart. He might feel very bitter and tired, always finding things unfair. Being unable to eat or sleep well, he feels sad and disappointed. When he gets older, he will end up in poor health and all kinds of illnesses will surface.

Thus, our practitioners should be like this even less so, as a practitioner should follow the course of nature. If something is yours, you will not lose it. If something is not yours, you will not have it even if you fight for it. Of course, that is not absolute. If it were as absolute as that, there would not be the issue of committing wrongdoings. In other words, there are some unstable factors. But as a practitioner, you are in principle protected by Teacher's fashen. Others cannot take away what is yours, even if they want to. We therefore believe in following the course of nature. Sometimes, you think that something should be yours, and others also tell you that it is yours. Actually, it is not. You may believe that it is yours, but in the end it is not yours. From this case, it can be seen whether you can give it up. If you cannot let it go, it is an attachment. This method must be used to get rid of your attachment to self-interest. This is the issue. Because everyday people are not enlightened to this principle, they will all compete and fight before profits.

Among everyday people, jealousy has been displayed very badly. It is also quite notable in the community of cultivators. There is no respect among different qigong practices, such as "your practice is good" or "his practice is good"—both positive and negative comments are made. In my view, they all belong to the level of healing and fitness. Among those mutually disputing practices, most of them belong to chaotic, futi-derived practices, and they disregard xinxing. A person may have practiced qigong for over twenty years without developing any supernormal capabilities, while another person has obtained them soon after beginning the practice. This person will then find it unfair: "I've practiced for over twenty years without developing any supernormal capabilities, and he has developed them. What sort of supernormal capabilities has he got?" This person will be infuriated: "He's got futi and is experiencing cultivation insanity!" When a qigong master teaches a class, someone may also sit there with disrespect: "Oh, what sort of qigong master is he? I'm not even interested in listening to what he says." The qigong master may indeed be unable to talk as well as this person does. Nevertheless, what the qigong master talks about is something only from his own school of practice. This person studies everything and has attended every qigong master's class with a pile of graduation certificates. Indeed, this person knows a lot more than that qigong master. But what's the use? It is all about healing and fitness. The more the person is filled with it, the more chaotic and complex the messages will become, and the harder it will be to practice cultivation—it is all messed up. Genuine cultivation practice teaches following one path, and it should not go astray. This also occurs among true practitioners, for mutual disrespect and not eliminating the competitive mindset can both easily lead to jealousy.

Let me tell a story. In the book <u>Investiture of the Gods</u>,[4] Shen Gongbao[5] found Jiang Ziya[6] to be both old and incompetent. But the Primitive God of Heaven asked Jiang Ziya to confer titles on immortals. Shen Gongbao felt in his heart that it was unfair: "Why is he asked to confer titles on immortals? You see how capable I am. After my head is cut off, I can put it back on my shoulders. Why wasn't I asked to confer titles on immortals?" He was so jealous that he always caused troubles for Jiang Ziya.

---

[4] <u>Investiture of the Gods</u>—a classic work of Chinese fiction.

[5] Shen Gongbao (shun gong-baow)—a jealous character in <u>Investiture of the Gods</u>.

[6] Jiang Ziya (jyang dzz-yah)—a character in <u>Investiture of the Gods</u>.

The original Buddhism in Sakyamuni's time talked about supernormal capabilities. Nowadays in Buddhism, nobody dares to mention supernormal capabilities anymore. If you mention supernatural capabilities, they will say that you have cultivation insanity. "What supernormal capabilities?" They will not recognize them at all. Why is this? At present, even monks do not know what they are all about. Sakyamuni had ten major disciples, of which Mujianlian[7] was said by him to be number one in supernatural capabilities. Sakyamuni also had female disciples, among whom Lianhuase[8] was number one in supernatural capabilities. The same was also true when Buddhism was introduced to China. Throughout history, there have been many accomplished monks. When Boddhidarma came to China, he rode on a stalk of reed to cross a river. As history has developed, however, supernatural capabilities have increasingly been rejected. The main reason is that people such as senior monks, supervisors, or abbots in temples are not necessarily of great inborn quality. Though they are abbots or senior monks, these are only positions of everyday people. They are also practitioners, except that they are professional ones. You practice cultivation at home as amateurs. Whether one succeeds in cultivation all depends on cultivating the heart. The same is true for everyone, and one cannot fall short even a bit. But, a junior monk who cooks meals might not be of poor inborn quality. The more the junior monk suffers, the easier it is for him to become kaigong. The more comfortable the senior monks' lives are, the harder it

---

[7] Mujianlian (moo-j'yen-l'yen)——one of ten major male disciples of Buddha Sakyamuni.

[8] Lianhuase (l'yen-hwa-szz)——one of ten major female disciples of Buddha Sakyamuni.

is for them to become kaigong since there is the issue of karma's transformation. The junior monk always labors hard and tiresomely. It is quicker for him to repay his karma and become enlightened. Perhaps one day he becomes kaigong all of a sudden. With this kaigong, enlightenment, or semi-enlightenment, his supernatural capabilities will all emerge. The monks in the temple will all come to ask him questions, and everyone will respect him. But the abbot will be unable to put up with it: "How can I still be the abbot? What enlightenment? He's experiencing cultivation insanity. Get him out of here." The temple thus expels the junior monk. As time passes, nobody in Chinese Buddhism dares to mention supernormal capabilities. You know how capable Jigong was. He could move the tree trunks from Mt. Emei and throw those logs out from a well[9] one after another. Yet in the end he was still driven out of Lingyin Temple.

The issue of jealousy is very serious as it directly involves the matter of whether you can complete cultivation practice. If jealousy is not abolished, everything that you have cultivated will become fragile. There is this rule: If in the course of cultivation practice jealousy is not given up, one will not attain the Right Fruit—absolutely not. In the past, perhaps everyone heard that Buddha Amitabha spoke of going to a paradise with karma. But that is not going to happen without giving up jealousy. It may be possible that one falls short in some other minor aspects and goes to the paradise with karma for further cultivation. But, it is absolutely impossible if jealousy is not abandoned. Today I am telling practitioners that you should not keep yourselves in the dark without being enlightened to it. The goal that you intend to

---

[9] Mt. Emei (uh-may) is about one thousand miles away from Lingyin (ling-yeen) Temple where the well was located.

achieve is practicing cultivation toward higher levels. The attachment of jealousy must be relinquished, so I have singled out the issue in this lecture.

The Issue of Treating Illness

Speaking of treating illness, I am not teaching you to treat illnesses. No genuine Falun Dafa disciples should treat illnesses for others. Once you treat an illness, all things in your body from Falun Dafa will be taken back by my fashen. Why is this issue taken so seriously? It is because it is a phenomenon that undermines Dafa. You will harm more than your own health. As soon as some people heal an illness, they will itch to do it again. They will grab whoever they see to treat illnesses and show themselves off. Isn't this an attachment? It will seriously hinder one's cultivation practice.

Many phony qigong masters have taken advantage of everyday people's desire to treat patients after learning qigong. They will teach you these things and claim that by emitting qi one can cure illnesses. Isn't this a joke? You have qi, and the other person has qi as well. How can you treat him with your qi? Perhaps his qi cures your illness! There is no constraint between this qi and that qi. When one develops gong in high-level cultivation, what one generates is the high-energy matter, which can indeed heal, repress, and control an illness, but it cannot remove the cause. Therefore, to really heal an illness and completely cure it, one must have supernormal capabilities. There is a specific supernormal capability for curing every illness. With regard to the supernormal capabilities for curing illnesses, I would say that there are over one thousand kinds, and that there are as many supernormal capabilities as illnesses. Without these supernormal capabilities it is useless, no matter how crafty your treatment may be.

In recent years, some people have made the community of cultivators quite chaotic. Among those genuine qigong masters who came to the public for healing and fitness or those who paved the road at the very beginning, who have taught people to treat patients? They always treated your illness or showed you how to practice cultivation and how to keep fit. They taught you a set of exercises, and then you could heal your illness through your own practice. Later, phony qigong masters came to the public and made quite a mess. Whoever wants to treat patients with qigong will attract futi—it is definitely this way. Under the circumstances at that time, some qigong masters also treated patients. That was to cooperate with the cosmic climate at that time. Yet qigong is not a skill of everyday persons, and that phenomenon cannot last forever. It resulted from changes of the cosmic climate at that time; it was only a product of that period of time. Later, some people specialized themselves in teaching others to treat illness, thereby creating a mess. How can an everyday person learn to treat an illness in three or five days? Someone claims: "I can cure this illness or that illness." Let me tell you that these people all carry futi. Do they know what's attached to their backs? They have futi, but they do not feel it, nor do they know it. Still, they may feel very good and think that they are capable.

Genuine qigong masters must go through many years of hard work in their cultivation in order to achieve this goal. When you treat a patient, have you ever thought about whether you have these powerful supernormal capabilities to eliminate this person's karma? Have you ever received any genuine teaching? How can you learn to treat illnesses in three or five days? How can you cure an illness with an ordinary person's hands? Nevertheless, such a phony qigong master has taken advantage of your weaknesses and people's attachments. Don't you seek to cure illnesses? Well, this person will organize a treatment class that specifically teaches you some healing methods, such as the qi needle, the light illuminating method, qi discharging, qi compensation, the so-called acupressure, and the so-called hand-grabbing method. There are a variety of methods aimed at taking your money.

Let us talk about the hand-grabbing method. What we have seen is this situation. Why do people get sick? The fundamental cause of one's being ill and all of one's misfortune is karma and the black substance's karmic field. It is something negative and bad. Those evil beings are also something negative, and they are all black. Thus, they can come because this environment suits them. This is the fundamental cause of one's being ill; it is the most principal source of illnesses. Of course, there are two other forms. One is a very microscopic being in high density that is like a cluster of karma. Another is as if delivered through a pipeline, but this is rarely seen; it is all accumulated from one's ancestors. There are also these cases.

Let us talk about the most common illnesses. Somewhere in the body one may have a tumor, infection, osteophytosis, etc. It is because in another dimension there lies a being in that place. That being is in a very deep dimension. An ordinary qigong master or an ordinary supernatural capability is unable to detect it; they can only see the black qi in one's body. It is correct to say that wherever there is black qi, there is an illness. Yet, the black qi is not the fundamental cause of an illness. It is because there is a being in a deeper dimension, who generates this field. So some people talk about discharging and removing the black qi—go ahead and discharge it as you wish! Shortly afterward, it will be generated again, as some beings are very powerful and can retrieve the qi as soon as it is removed; they can retrieve it on their own. The treatment just does not work no matter how it is applied.

According to one who sees with supernatural capabilities, wherever there is black qi, that place is considered to have pathogenic qi. A doctor of Chinese medicine will find the energy channels blocked in that place, as the qi and blood are not circulating and the energy channels are congested. To a doctor of Western medicine, that place may present the symptom of an ulcer, tumor, osteophytosis, or inflammation, etc. When it manifests in this dimension, it is in this form. After you remove that being, you will find that there is nothing wrong with the body in this dimension. Whether it is protrusion of the lumbar intervertebral discs or osteophytosis, after you remove that thing and clear out that field, you will find it instantly healed. You can take another x-ray and find that the osteophytosis has disappeared. The fundamental reason is that this being was producing an effect.

Some people claim that by teaching you the hand-grabbing method, in three or five days you can cure illnesses. Show me your grabbing method! Human beings are the weakest while that being is quite formidable. It can control your mind and easily manipulate you at will. It can even end your life easily. You claim that you can grab it. How do you grab it? You cannot reach it with your ordinary person's hands. You may grab aimlessly there, and it will ignore you and laugh at you behind your back as well— grabbing aimlessly is quite ridiculous. If you can really touch it, it will harm your hands at once. That will be a real wound! I saw

291

some people before whose two hands looked normal by any examination. Both their bodies and their two hands were not ill, but they could not raise their hands which kept hanging like this. I have come across such a patient: His body in another dimension was injured, and he was truly paralyzed. If that body of yours is injured, aren't you paralyzed? Someone asked me: "Teacher, will I be able to practice qigong? I had a sterilization operation, and I've had something removed from my body." I said that it would not matter since your body in another dimension did not have an operation, and in qigong practice it is that body which is acted upon. Therefore, I just now said that when you try to grab it, it will ignore you if you cannot reach it. If you touch it, it might injure your hand.

To support a major state-run qigong event, I took some disciples to participate in the Oriental Health Expos in Beijing. At both of the two Expos, we were the most outstanding practice. At the first Expo, our Falun Dafa was honored as the "Star Qigong School." At the second Expo, our place was so crowded that we simply could not handle it. There were not many people at other exhibition booths, but our booth was crowded with people. There were three waiting lines: The first line was for those who registered early in the morning for the morning treatment, the second line was waiting to register for the afternoon treatment, and the third line was waiting for my autograph. We do not treat illnesses. Why did we do it? Because this was to support a major, state-run qigong event and to contribute to this course, we participated in it.

I distributed my gong to the disciples who were there with me. Each one got one share that was an energy cluster composed of over a hundred supernormal capabilities. I sealed their hands with gong, but even so, some people's hands were bitten to the point of blistering or bleeding; this even happened quite often. The beings were quite vicious. Do you think you dare to touch them with an ordinary person's hands? Besides, you cannot reach it. It will not work without that kind of supernormal capability. This is because in another dimension it will know whatever you want to do—as soon as you think about it. When you try to grab it, it will run away. Right when the patient goes out the door, it will go back there immediately, and the illness will recur. In order to deal with it, one needs this supernormal capability to nail it there by extending one's hand. Upon nailing it there, we have another supernormal capability that was once called the "Great Soul-Catching Method," and that supernormal capability is even more powerful. It can take out one's yuanshen, and instantly the person will be unable to move. This supernormal capability has its specific purpose, and we just target this thing to grab. Everyone knows that though you find Sun Wukong[10] very big, the Tathagata can use the bowl in his hand to turn Sun Wukong into a very tiny thing by covering him up with it. This supernormal capability can have this effect. No matter how large or tiny this being is, it will be grabbed in the hand instantly and become very tiny.

Additionally, it is not permissible for one's hand to dig into the flesh body of a patient and take something out. That would bring disorder to people's mind in ordinary human society, and that is absolutely prohibited. Even if it were possible, it could not be done this way. The hand one digs with is the hand in another dimension. Suppose that someone has a heart disease. When this hand moves toward the heart to grab that being, the hand in another

---

[10] Sun Wukong—also known as "Monkey King", a character in the classic work of Chinese fiction, <u>Journey to the West.</u>

dimension moves inside the body, and it will be caught instantly. As your outside hand grabs it, both hands close in and will grab it. It is very vicious, sometimes moving in your hands and attempting to drill into them, and sometimes biting and screaming. Though it appears to be very small in your hands, it will become very large if you release it from your hands. This is not something that anyone can touch. Without that supernormal capability, one cannot touch it at all. It is completely unlike how simple people would imagine it.

Of course, this form of qigong treatment might be allowed to exist in the future, as in the past it always existed. But, there must be a condition: This person must be a practitioner. In the course of cultivation practice, out of compassion this person is allowed to do this thing for a few good people. But he cannot completely eliminate their karma since he does not have enough great virtue. Therefore, tribulations will still exist, but the specific diseases will be healed. An ordinary qigong master is not a person who has attained the Tao in cultivation practice. He can only put off illnesses or perhaps transform them. He might transform them into other misfortune, yet he, himself may not even know of this deferral process. If his practice cultivates fu yishi, it is done by his fu yishi. Practitioners in some practices appear to be very famous. Many well-known qigong masters do not have gong because their gong grows in the bodies of fu yishi. That is, some people are permitted to do such things in the course of cultivation practice because they continue to stay at this level. They have been practicing over a decade or for several decades and still cannot go beyond this level. So throughout their lives they always see patients. Because they stay at this level, they are allowed to do that. Falun Dafa disciples are absolutely forbidden to treat patients. You can read this book to a patient. If the patient can accept it, it can heal illness. But the results will differ according to each person's amount of karma.

Hospital Treatment and Qigong Treatment

Let us talk about the relationship between hospital treatment and qigong healing. Some doctors in Western medicine do not recognize qigong, and you can say that the majority of them are this way. Their opinion is that if qigong can heal illness, what do we need hospitals for? "You should replace our hospitals! Since your qigong can heal illness with a hand and without resorting to injections, medication, or hospitalization, wouldn't it be nice if you could replace our hospitals?" This statement is neither rational nor reasonable; some people do not know qigong. In fact, qigong healing cannot resemble the treatments of ordinary people, for it is not a skill of ordinary people—it is something supernatural. So how can something as supernatural as that be allowed to interfere with ordinary human society on a large scale? A Buddha is mighty capable, and he can wipe out all of humankind's illnesses by waving his hand just once. Why doesn't he do it? Besides, there are so many Buddhas. Why don't they show their mercy by curing your illness? It is because ordinary human society is supposed to be this way. Birth, old age, diseases, and death are just such conditions. They all have karmic reasons and are of karmic retribution. You must repay the debt if you have it.

If you cure one's illness, it will be the same as violating that principle, as one would be able to do wrong deeds without repaying them. How can it be possible? As a person in cultivation practice, when you do not have this great ability to thoroughly solve this problem, you are allowed to treat a patient out of compassion. Because your compassion has emerged, you are allowed to do so. But, if you can truly solve this type of problem, it will not be allowed to be done on a large scale. In that case, you would seriously undermine the state of ordinary human society—that is not allowed. Therefore, replacing everyday people's hospitals with qigong will not work at all, as qigong is a supernatural Fa.

If qigong hospitals are allowed to be set up in China and many great qigong masters come out to give treatments, what do you think this will be like? That will not be permitted, because they all maintain the state of ordinary human society. If qigong hospitals, qigong clinics, qigong health centers, and treatment resorts are established, the healing efficacy of qigong masters will drop significantly, and the results of the treatments will at once not be good. Why is it? Since they do this thing among everyday people, their Fa must be as high as that of everyday people. They have to stay at the same level as the state of everyday people. Their healing efficacy must be the same as that of a hospital. So their treatments do not work well, and they also need several so-called "therapy sessions" to heal an illness. It is usually this way.

With or without qigong hospitals, nobody can deny that qigong can heal illnesses. Qigong has been popular in public for so long. Many people have indeed achieved the goal of healing illnesses and keeping fit through the practice. Whether the illness was put off by a qigong master or however it was treated, the illness has now disappeared after all. In other words, nobody can deny that qigong can heal illnesses. Most people who have seen qigong masters are those with difficult and complicated illnesses that cannot be treated at a hospital. They go to qigong masters to try their luck, and the illnesses are eventually healed. Those who can have their illnesses healed at hospitals will not see qigong masters. Particularly at the beginning, people all thought this way. Qigong can therefore heal illnesses, except that it cannot be applied like other things that are done in ordinary human society. While large-scale interference is absolutely not allowed, doing it on a small-scale or its being an uninfluential and quiet practice is permissible. But it will not completely heal the illness—this is also certain. The best way to heal one's illness is to practice qigong on one's own.

There are also some qigong masters who claim that hospitals cannot cure illnesses, and that the efficacy of hospital treatments is just like such and such. How should we speak of this? Of course, it involves reasons from many areas. In my view, the principal one is that human moral values have hit a low point, leading to a variety of odd diseases that hospitals cannot cure. Taking medicine is not effective, either. There are a lot of phony drugs as well. It is all because of the extent to which human society has become corrupt. Nobody should blame others for it, as everyone has added fuel to the flame. Consequently, everyone will come across tribulations in cultivation practice.

Some illnesses cannot be detected at a hospital, even though people are actually ill. Some people are diagnosed with illnesses that do not have names, since they have never been seen before. Hospitals call all of them "modern diseases." Can hospitals heal illnesses? Of course, they can. If hospitals could not heal illnesses, why would people believe in them and go there for treatments? Hospitals are still able to heal illnesses, but their means of treatment belong to the level of everyday people while illnesses are supernatural. Some illnesses are quite serious, and so hospitals require early treatment if one has such an illness. If it becomes too serious, hospitals will be helpless, as overdoses of medicine can poison a person. Present medical treatments are at the same level as our science and technology—they are all at the level of everyday people. Thus, they only have such healing efficacy. One issue that should be clarified is that average qigong treatments and hospital treatments only defer to the remaining half of life or later those tribulations that are the fundamental cause of illnesses. The karma is not removed at all.

Let us talk about Chinese medicine. Chinese medicine is very close to qigong healing. In ancient China, supernatural capabilities were common to virtually all Chinese medical doctors, such as those great medical scientists: Sun Simiao, Huatuo, Li Shizhen, and Bian Que.[11] They all had supernatural capabilities that were all documented in medical texts. Yet, now these excellent parts are often criticized. What Chinese medicine has inherited are only those prescriptions or experiences from research. Ancient Chinese medicine was very advanced, and the extent of its progress was beyond present medical science. Some people may think that modern medicine is so advanced with its CT scans to examine the inside of the human body and its ultrasound, photography, and X-rays. Though modern equipment may be quite advanced, in my view it is still inferior to ancient Chinese medicine.

Huatuo saw a tumor in Caocao's[12] brain and wanted to

---

[11] Sun Simiao (sun szz-meow), Huatuo (hwa-twoah), Li Shizhen (lee shr-jhun), Bian Que (b'yen chueh)—well-known doctors of Chinese medicine in history.

[12] Caocao (tsaow-tsaow)—emperor of one of the three kingdoms (220 A.D.-265 A.D.).

operate on it. Caocao thought that Huatuo meant to murder him, and so he imprisoned Huatuo. As a result, Huatuo died in prison. When Caocao's illness recurred, he remembered Huatuo and looked for him, but Huatuo was already dead. Later, Caocao indeed died of this illness. Why did Huatuo know it? He had seen it. This is our human supernatural capability which all great doctors in the past had. After tianmu is open, one can see from one side, simultaneously, four sides of a human body. One can see from the front to the rear, and the left to the right. One can see one layer after another or see beyond this dimension the fundamental cause of an illness. Are modern medical means able to do that? Far from it. It will take another thousand years! CT scans, ultrasound, and X-rays can also examine the inner human body, but the equipment is too bulky, and such large things are not portable; nor will they work without electricity. This tianmu, however, can go wherever one goes, and it does not need a power supply. How can they be compared?

Some people talk about how marvelous modern medicine is. I would say that it might not be so, as ancient Chinese herbs could, upon application, indeed heal illnesses. There are a lot of things that have not been passed down, but many have not been lost and are still in use among people. When I taught a class in Qiqihar,[13] I saw a person who had a vendor stand on the street and was pulling teeth for people. One could easily tell that this person came from the South, as he was not dressed like a Northeasterner. He would not refuse anyone who came to him. He would pull a tooth for anybody who came, and he had there a pile of pulled teeth. His purpose was not to pull teeth, but to sell his liquid drug. The liquid drug emitted very thick yellow fumes.

---

[13] Qiqihar (chee-chee-har)—a city in northeastern China.

While pulling a tooth, he would open the drug bottle and put it on the patient's cheek toward the area of the bad tooth. The patient would be asked to inhale the fumes of the yellow liquid drug, which was barely consumed. The drug bottle would be sealed and put aside. The man would take out a matchstick from his pocket. While talking about his drug, he would push the bad tooth with the matchstick and it would come out. It was not painful. The tooth would have just a few bloodstains, but there would be no bleeding. Think about it, everyone: A matchstick can be broken if it is used with much force, but he used it to pull a tooth with only a little contact.

I have said that in China there are still some things being passed down among people, which Western medicine's precision instruments cannot match. Let us see whose treatment is better. His matchstick can pull a tooth. If a doctor in Western medicine wants to pull a tooth, the doctor will first inject the patient with anesthetics here and there. Injections are quite painful, and one must wait until the anesthetic works. Then the doctor will pull the tooth with a pair of pliers. After a lot of time and effort, if the doctor is not careful, the root may break inside the tooth bed. Then the doctor will use a hammer and a drill to dig for it, which can make the patient palpitate with fear and anxiety. Later, a precision instrument will be used for the drilling. Some people are in so much pain from the drilling that they almost jump. The tooth will ooze quite a bit of blood, and the patient will spit out blood for a while. Whose treatment would you say is better? Whose is more advanced? We should look not only at the tools' appearance, but also at their effectiveness. Ancient Chinese medicine was quite progressive, and present-day Western medicine will not be able to catch up with it for many years to come.

Ancient Chinese science is different from our present science that we have learned from the West, as it took another path that could bring about a different state. Therefore, we cannot understand ancient Chinese science and technology through our current way of understanding things. Because ancient Chinese science focused directly on the human body, life, and the universe, and it studied these subjects directly, it took a different approach. At that time, when students went to school, they were required to sit in meditation and good posture. When they picked up their brush-pens, they would regulate their breathing and qi. All professions believed in emptying the mind and regulating the breathing, as this was the state throughout society.

Someone has said: "Would we have cars and trains if we followed ancient Chinese science? Would we have today's modernization?" I would say that you cannot understand another circumstance from the perspective of this environment. There should be a revolution in your thinking. Without television sets, people would have them in their foreheads, and they could watch anything they want to see. They would also have supernormal capabilities. Without trains and planes, people would be able to levitate into the air from where they sit, without using an elevator. It would bring about a different state of societal development, and it would not necessarily be confined to this framework. The flying saucers of extraterrestrials can travel back and forth at an inconceivable speed and become large or small. They have taken another alternative method of development, which is another scientific approach.

LECTURE EIGHT

Bigu[1]

Some people have brought up the issue of bigu. There is this phenomenon of bigu. It does not only exist in the community of cultivators, but also among a good number of people in our entire human society. Some people do not eat or drink for several years or over a decade, yet they live very well. There are some people who speak of bigu as an indicator of a certain level, while others take it as a sign of body purification. It is also claimed by some to be a high-level cultivation process.

In fact, it is none of the above. What is it, then? Bigu actually refers to a special cultivation method in a specific environment. Under what circumstance is it used? In ancient China, particularly prior to the establishment of religions, many practitioners employed the form of secret practice or solitary cultivation in remote mountains or caves far away from human settlements. Once they chose to do it this way, it would involve the issue of food supplies. If one did not use the bigu method, one could not practice cultivation at all and would die there of hunger or thirst. I went from Chongqing[2] to Wuhan to teach the Fa, and I took a boat heading east on the Yangtze River. I saw some caves on both sides of the Three Gorges in the mid sections of the

---

[1] Bigu (bee-goo)—"no grain"; an ancient term for abstinence from food and water.

[2] Chongqing (chong-ching)—the most populated city in Southwestern China.

mountains; many well-known mountains also have these things. In the past, after climbing into a cave with the help of a rope, a practitioner would cut off the rope to practice in the cave. If this person could not succeed in cultivation, he would die inside it. Without food or water, it was under this very special circumstance that he resorted to this particular cultivation method.

Many practices have gone through this inheriting process, and so they include bigu. A lot of practices do not include bigu. Today, the majority of the practices that have been made public do not incorporate bigu. We have said that one should be single-minded in one practice, and that you should not do whatever you humanly desire to. You might think that bigu is good and pursue it. What do you want it for? Some people think that it is good and become curious, and perhaps they think that their skills are good enough to show off. There are people with all kinds of mentalities. Even if this method is used in cultivation practice, one must consume one's own energy to sustain this physical body. Therefore, it is not worth the effort. You know that particularly after the founding of religions, one has been supplied with food and tea during the period of sitting in trance or solitary cultivation in a temple. It does not involve this issue. In particular, we practice cultivation amidst ordinary human society. You do not need to employ this method at all. In addition, if your school of practice does not include it, you should not casually do something at will. If you really want to practice bigu, however, you may go ahead. As far as I know, usually when a master teaches a high-level practice and genuinely takes a disciple, or if one's school of practice has bigu, this phenomenon may take place. Nevertheless, one cannot promote it in public; one typically takes the disciple away to practice it secretly or alone.

Now there are also qigong masters teaching bigu. Has bigu taken place? Not really, in the end. Who has succeeded with it? I have seen many people hospitalized, and quite a few people's lives are in jeopardy. Then, why is there this situation? Doesn't the phenomenon of bigu exist? Yes, it does. However, there is one point: Nobody is allowed to casually undermine the state of our ordinary human society—it is not allowed to be disrupted. Not to mention how many people in the whole country would not need to eat and drink, I would say that it would make things much easier if people in the Changchun areas did not need to eat and drink! We would not need to worry about making meals. Farmers sweat so hard in the fields, and now nobody would need to eat. That would really make things much easier, as people would only work without having to eat. How could that be allowed? Would that be a human society? It is definitely forbidden, as such large-scale interference with ordinary human society is not allowed.

When some qigong masters teach bigu, many people's lives are endangered. Some people are simply attached to seeking bigu, yet this attachment has not been removed, among many other attachments of everyday people. Such a person's mouth will be watering when he sees some delicious food. Once this desire surges, he cannot control it and will be anxious to eat the food. When his appetite arises, he will want to eat; otherwise he will feel hungry. However, he will throw up if he eats. Since he cannot eat, he will become very nervous and quite scared. Many people are hospitalized and, in actuality, many people's lives are endangered. There are people who look for me and ask me to take care of these messy cases, and I am not willing to do it. Some qigong masters simply do things irresponsibly. Nobody is willing to take care of these problems for them.

Furthermore, if you get into trouble in practicing bigu, isn't it from your own pursuit? We have said that these phenomena do exist, but they are not the so-called "high-level state" or so-called "special reactions." It is only a practice method used under a special circumstance, so it cannot be promoted widely. A number of people go after bigu and classify it as so-called bigu or semi-bigu, and rank it into different levels. Some people claim that they only need to drink water, while others claim that they only need to eat fruit. All these are phony bigu, and as time passes, they are all bound to fail. A genuine practitioner will stay in a cave without drinking or eating—that is real bigu.

Stealing Qi

When speaking of stealing qi, some people will look pale as if a tiger was mentioned, and they will be too scared to practice qigong. Because of gossip about the phenomena of cultivation insanity, stealing qi, and so on, in the community of cultivators many people are too scared to practice qigong or approach qigong. If it were not for these views, perhaps more people would be practicing qigong. Yet, there are qigong masters with poor xinxing who specially teach these things. That makes the community of cultivators quite chaotic. Actually, it is not as terrible as they have described. We have said that qi is only qi, although you may call it the "mixed primary qi" and this qi or that qi. As long as a person's body has qi, he is at the level of healing and fitness and is not yet a practitioner. As long as he has qi, it means that his body has not yet been highly purified and so still has pathogenic qi—this is for sure. The person who steals qi is also at the level of qi. Among our practitioners, who would want that impure qi? The qi in a non-practitioner's body is rather impure, though it can become brighter through qigong practice. So the place of an illness will show a very big cluster of high-density black substance. By continuing the practice, if the person has indeed healed the illness and become fit, his qi will gradually turn yellow. If he keeps practicing further, the illness will really be cured, and his qi will disappear as well. He will enter the state of the Milky-White Body.

That is to say, if one has qi, one still has illnesses. We are practitioners—what do we need qi for in the practice? Our own bodies need to be purified. Why should we need that impure qi? Definitely not. A person who wants qi is still at the level of qi. Being at that level of qi, he cannot distinguish good qi from bad qi, as he does not have that ability. The genuine qi in your body's dantian cannot be taken away by him since that primary qi can only be removed by someone with high-level abilities. As for the impure qi in your body, let him steal it—it is not a big deal. During practice, if I want to fill myself with qi, by just giving it a thought, my belly will be full of it shortly.

The Tao School teaches the standing exercise of *tianzi zhuang*[3] while the Buddha School teaches pouring qi into the top of the head. There is a lot of qi in the universe for you to fill yourself with everyday. With the laogong point and the *baihui* point[4] open, you may fill yourself up with qi through your hands while focusing on dantian. You will be full of it in a while. No matter how much you are filled with qi, what use does it have?

---

[3] *tianzi zhuang* (tyen-dzz jwahng)—a form of standing qigong exercise in the Tao School.

[4] *baihui* (buy-hway)—acupuncture point located at the crown of one's head.

306

When some people have practiced qi a lot, their fingers and bodies feel like they are swollen. When others walk up to such a person, they will feel a field around him: "Wow, you've practiced really well." I would say that it is nothing. Where's your gong? It is still a practice of qi, which cannot replace gong no matter how much qi one has. The purpose of practicing qi is to substitute the qi inside one's body with good qi from outside, and to purify the body. What does one accumulate qi for? At this level, without any fundamental change, qi is still not gong. No matter how much qi you have stolen, you are still nothing but a big bag of qi. What use does it have? It is not yet transformed into the high-energy matter. So what should you be afraid of? Let him steal the qi if he really wants to.

Think about it, everyone: If your body has qi, it has illnesses. Then, when the person steals your qi, isn't he stealing your pathogenic qi as well? He cannot differentiate these things at all, since one who wants qi is also at the level of qi and will not have any capabilities. A person who has gong does not want qi—that is for sure. If you do not believe it, we can conduct an experiment. If a person really wants to steal your qi, you can stand there and let him steal it. You can focus your mind on filling your body with qi from the universe here while he is stealing your qi behind you. You will see what a good deal it is, as it will help you speed up your body purification, and you will not have to fill up and discharge qi from your body. Because he has a bad intention and steals something from others, though he has stolen something not good, he has also committed a deed that loses de. Therefore, he will give you de. It forms a circuit whereby while he takes your qi here, he gives you de over there. The person who steals qi does not know this—if he knew it, he would not dare to do it!

All those people who steal qi have bluish faces, and they are all this way. Many people who go to the parks for qigong practice aspire to remove illnesses, and they have all kinds of diseases. When one is healing an illness, one must try to discharge the pathogenic qi. Yet the person who steals qi will not discharge qi and will collect all kinds of pathogenic qi all over his body. Even his internal body becomes very dark. As he always loses de, his appearance is all black. With a large field of karma and great loss of de, he will become black inside out. Were the person who steals qi to find himself experiencing this change and realize that he is giving de to others by doing this foolish thing, he would not do it at all.

Some people have blown qi out of proportion: "If you're in America, you can receive the qi that I emit." "You can wait on the other side of the wall, and you'll receive the qi that I emit." Some people are very sensitive and can feel it when the qi is emitted. But qi does not travel in this dimension. It moves in another dimension where there is no such wall. Why can't you feel anything when a qigong master emits qi on level ground? There is a screen there in the other dimension. Thus, qi does not have as much penetrative power as people have described.

What really works is gong. When a practitioner can emit gong, he or she no longer has any qi and can give off high-energy matter, which is seen in the form of light by tianmu. When it reaches another person, it makes that person feel warm; it can restrain an ordinary person. Nevertheless, it still cannot completely achieve the goal of curing illnesses, for it only has a repressing effect. In order to truly cure illnesses, there must be supernormal capabilities. There is a specific supernormal capability for each disease. At the very microscopic level, each microscopic particle of gong assumes your own image. It can recognize people and has intelligence, as it is high-energy matter. If someone steals it, how can it stay there? It will not stay there and cannot be placed there, as it is not that person's own property. As to all those true practitioners, after they develop gong they are looked after by their masters. Your master is watching what you do. When you try to take things from another person, that person's master will not let it happen, either.

Collecting Qi

In teaching cultivation practice at higher levels, stealing qi and collecting qi are not issues that we will help resolve for everyone. This is because I still have this intention of restoring the reputation of cultivation practices and doing some good deeds. I will disclose such bad phenomena, which nobody addressed in the past. I want all of you to know it so that some people will not commit bad deeds all the time. Some people who do not know the truth of qigong are always scared to talk about it.

There is plenty of qi in the universe. Some people talk about the heavenly yang qi and the earthly yin qi. As you are also an element of the universe, you may go ahead and collect the qi. But some people do not collect the qi in the universe. They specialize in teaching people to collect qi from plants. They have even summarized their experience: How and when to collect this qi, the qi of a poplar tree is white, or the qi of a pine tree is yellow. Someone also claims: "There was a tree in front of our house. It died because I collected its qi." What kind of ability is that? Isn't that a bad deed? It is known to all that when we truly practice cultivation, we want positive messages and assimilation to the characteristic of the universe. Shouldn't you practice Shan? In order to assimilate to the characteristic of the universe, Zhen-Shan-Ren, one must practice Shan. If you always commit bad deeds, how can you increase gong? How can your illness be cured? Isn't this the opposite of what our practitioners should do? That is also killing lives and committing bad deeds! Someone may say: "The more you say, the more inconceivable it is—killing an animal is killing a life, and killing a plant is also killing a life." Actually, it is so. Buddhism has talked about samsara. You might have been reincarnated into a plant during samsara. That is how it is said in Buddhism. Here we do not talk about it that way, but we tell everyone that trees are also lives. Not only do they have lives, but they also have very high-level thought activity.

For instance, there is a person in America who is specialized in electronic studies and teaches others how to use lie detectors. One day, an idea suddenly hit him. He put both ends of a lie detector to a dragon pot plant and poured water to its root. He then found that the lie detector's electronic pen had quickly drawn a curve. This curve was identical to that drawn when the human brain produces a brief second of excitement or happiness. At that moment, he was shocked. How could a plant have feelings? He almost wanted to yell in the streets: "Plants have feelings!" Enlightened by this occurrence, he continued to do research in this area and conducted many experiments.

One time he placed two plants together and asked his student to stomp one plant to death in front of the other plant. Then he took the other plant into a room and connected it to a lie detector. He asked five of his students to enter the room in turn from the outside. The plant had no reactions when the first four students entered the room. When the fifth student—who had ruined the plant—came into the room, before he even walked up to the plant, the electronic pen quickly drew a curve that only appears when a person is frightened. He was really shocked! This occurrence implies a very important issue: We have always believed that a human being is a high-level life with sensory functions that can distinguish things and a brain that can analyze things. How can plants distinguish things? Doesn't this indicate that they have sensory organs as well? In the past, if someone said that plants had sensory organs, thinking minds, feelings, and could recognize people, this person would have been called superstitious. In addition to these, plants seem to have surpassed our people today in certain regards.

One day he connected a lie detector to a plant and wondered: "What kind of experiment should I do? Let me burn its leaves with fire and see how it reacts." With this thought—even before the leaves were burned—the electronic pen quickly drew a curve the same as that created only when someone cries for help. This super sensory function was in the past called mind reading; it is a latent human function and an innate ability. Yet, all of humankind is corrupted today. To regain them, you must practice cultivation from the start and return to your original, true self or to your original nature. Yet the plant has them, and it knows what is on your mind. It sounds quite inconceivable, but it was an actual scientific experiment. He has conducted different experiments, including testing the capability of long-distance remote controls. Upon publication, his papers caused quite a stir throughout the world.

Botanists in different countries including those in our country have all begun their research in this field, and it is no longer something superstitious. The other day I said that what our

311

humankind today has experienced, invented, and discovered is sufficient to change our present textbooks. Due to the influence of conventional mentalities, however, people are reluctant to acknowledge them. Nobody is systematically organizing these things, either.

In a park in the Northeast, I noticed that a group of pine trees were dead. No one knows what kind of qigong some people were practicing there: They would roll all over the ground and afterwards collect qi from the trees with their feet one way and with their hands another. Soon after, all the pine trees over there turned yellow and died. Was what they did a good deed or a bad one? From our practitioners' perspective, that was killing lives. You are a practitioner. Thus, to gradually assimilate to the universe's characteristic and release those bad things of yours, you must be a good person. Even from an everyday person's perspective, it was not a good deed, either. It was abusive of public property, and it sabotaged the green vegetation and the balance of the ecological system. It is not a good deed from any perspective. There is plenty of qi in the universe, and you may collect it as much as you want. Some people have a lot of energy. Upon practicing at a certain level, they can indeed with one wave of their arms collect plants' qi in a large area. Still, that is nothing but qi. No matter how much one collects it, what use does it serve? When some people go to a park, they do not do anything else. One claims: "I don't need to practice qigong. It's good enough to collect qi while I walk around, and my practice is then over. It's adequate to just get qi." They think that qi is gong. When people walk up to this person, they will feel that his body is quite chilly. Doesn't the plant qi have the yin nature? A practitioner must maintain the balance of yin and yang. Although this person's body smells like pine oil, he may still think he does

312

well in his practice.

Whoever Practices Cultivation Will Attain Gong

The issue of who practices gong and who attains gong is a very important one. When I am asked about the advantages of Falun Dafa, I say that Falun Dafa can enable gong to cultivate practitioners and so reduce the amount of time in practice. It solves the problem of one's not having time to practice and yet still being cultivated constantly. Meanwhile, ours is a genuine cultivation practice of mind and body. Our physical bodies will undergo great changes. Falun Dafa has another superb feature which, until today, I had not previously mentioned. Because it involves a major issue of historical significance and has quite an impact on the community of cultivators, nobody in history has dared to disclose it, nor is anyone allowed to unveil it. Yet, I have no choice but to make it known.

Some disciples have said: "Every sentence that Master Li Hongzhi has said is a heavenly secret and a disclosure of the heavenly secrets." We are, however, truly bringing people toward higher levels, which is to save people. Being responsible to everyone is a responsibility we are able to assume. Thus, it is not disclosing heavenly secrets. If one talks about it irresponsibly, that is a disclosure of heavenly secrets. Today we will make public this issue of who practices gong and who attains gong. In my view, all practices today—including throughout history the practices in the Buddha School, the Tao School, and the Qimen School—have cultivated one's fu yuanshen, and it has been fu yuanshen that obtains gong. The zhu yuanshen that we are mentioning here refers to our own minds. One should be aware of what one is thinking about or doing—that is your real self. But, you do not know at all what your fu yuanshen does. Though you and it are born simultaneously with the same name, same appearance, and control the same body, it is not you in a strict sense.

There is a principle in the universe: Whoever that loses gains. Whoever practices cultivation obtains gong. Throughout history, all practices have taught people to be in trance during practice, and that one should not think of anything. Then one should be in a deep trance until, in the end, one loses awareness of everything. Some people sit in mediation for three hours as though only a brief second had just passed. Others may admire this person's ability for being in trance. Did he actually practice? He himself does not know it whatsoever. In particular, the Tao School teaches that *shishen*[5] dies while yuanshen is born. What "shishen" refers to we call "zhu yuanshen," and the "yuanshen" it refers to we call "fu yuanshen." If your shishen really dies, you will indeed be dead, and you really will not have a zhu yuanshen. Someone from another practice told me: "Teacher, when I practice I'm unable to recognize anyone at home." Yet another person told me: "I won't practice like others who do it early in the morning and late at night. After I go home, I lie down on a couch and go out of myself to practice. While lying there I'll watch myself practice." I found it very sad, but it also was not sad.

Why do they save fu yuanshen? Lu Dongbin[6] once made a statement: "I'd rather save an animal than a human being." Indeed, it is too difficult for people to be enlightened since everyday

---

[5] *shishen* (shr-shuhn)—one's main soul.

[6] Lu Dongbin (lyu dong-bin)—one of the Eight Deities in the Tao School.

people are deluded by ordinary human society. With practical benefits before them, they cannot give up the attachment. If you do not believe it, upon the conclusion of this class, some people will walk out of this auditorium as everyday people again. If anyone offends them or bumps into them, they will not put up with it. After a period of time, they will not conduct themselves as practitioners at all. Many Taoists in history have realized this point: Human beings are very difficult to save, for their zhu yuanshen are extremely lost. Some people have good enlightenment quality and will understand it right away with a hint. Some people will not believe you no matter what you say. They think that you are telling tall tales. We are talking so much about cultivating one's xinxing, yet this person still behaves as usual once he is among everyday people. He thinks that the actual and tangible benefits within his reach are practical, and he will pursue them; the Fa from Teacher also sounds reasonable, but cannot be followed. The human zhu yuanshen is most difficult to save, while fu yuanshen can see scenes in other dimensions. They therefore think: "Why should I save your zhu yuanshen? Your fu yuanshen is also you. Isn't it the same if I save it? It's all you, and it doesn't matter who gets it—it will all be obtained by you."

Let me describe specifically the methods of their practices. If one has the supernormal capability of clairvoyance, one will probably see this scene: When you sit in meditation, as soon as you are in trance, someone with the same appearance as yours will suddenly leave your body. If you try to differentiate, where is your own self? You are sitting right here. After you watch that person leave your body, the master will take this person to practice cultivation in a dimension transformed by the master. It may be in the form of a bygone society, today's society, or a society in another dimension. The person will be taught the practice and go through numerous hardships for one or two hours daily. When the person returns from the practice, you will also wake up from trance. This is what is observable.

It will be even more sad if one cannot see or know anything and wakes up after two hours in trance. As a way of practice, some people fall asleep for two or three hours and completely give themselves away to others. This is done intermittently with the sitting meditation for a certain amount of time daily. Another type is completed at one time. Everyone may have heard of Boddhidarma, who sat before a wall for nine years. In the past, there were many monks who would sit for decades. In history, the record for the longest sitting time is over ninety years. Some even sat longer than this. Even with thick dust deposited on their eyelids and grass growing on their bodies, they would continue sitting there. Some in the Tao School also teach it. In particular, some practices in the Qimen School require one to fall asleep. One can sleep for decades without exiting the trance state, and one will not wake up. But who has practiced? The person's fu yuanshen has gone out to practice. If he can see it, he will find the master taking his fu yuanshen off to practice. Fu yuanshen can also owe much karma, and the master does not have the ability to eliminate all of the karma. Therefore, the master will tell it: "You should practice hard here. I'll be away and come back in a short while. You wait for me."

The master knows exactly what will happen, but it still must do it this way. Eventually a demon will come to scare the person or transform into a beauty to seduce it—there will be all kinds of things. The demon then realizes that it indeed is not affected in the least. This is because it is relatively easier for fu yuanshen to practice cultivation, as it can know the truth. Being desperate, the

316

demon will make an attempt on its life for revenge, and indeed kill it. With that, its debt is repaid all at once. After death, fu yuanshen will emerge like a waft of smoke drifting about and will be reincarnated in a very poor family. The child will begin to suffer from an early age. When it grows mature, the master will come back. Of course, the child cannot recognize him. Using supernormal capabilities, the master will unlock its saved memory. It will at once recall everything. "Isn't this my master?" The master will tell it: "Now, it's time to start the practice." Thus, after many years the master will pass the teachings to it.

After the instruction, the master will again tell it: "You still have many attachments to remove. You should go out to wander about." Wandering around in society is rather torturous. It must beg for food and meet different kinds of people who will scold, insult, or take advantage of it. It might encounter all kinds of things. It will treat itself as a practitioner and balance well relations with others, always maintaining and upgrading xinxing. It will not be moved by the temptations of different benefits among everyday people. After many years, it will return from wandering around. The master will say: "You've already attained the Tao and have completed cultivation. If you don't have anything to do, you may pack up and get ready to leave. If there's still something to do, you may go ahead to finish that everyday people's business." After many years, fu yuanshen returns. Upon fu yuanshen's return, zhu yuanshen also comes out of the trance state, and zhu yishi wakes up.

Yet, this person has not actually practiced cultivation. That fu yuanshen has practiced it, so fu yuanshen will obtain gong. But zhu yuanshen has also suffered. After all, the person has devoted his entire youth to sitting there, and this lifetime as an everyday person is all over. So what will happen? After awakening from trance, this person will feel that he has developed gong through his practice and has obtained supernormal capabilities. If he wants to treat a patient or do something, he will be able to, as fu yuanshen will try to satisfy him. Because this person is zhu yuanshen, after all, zhu yuanshen controls the body and makes decisions. In addition, he has spent so many years sitting here that this lifetime has elapsed. When this person dies, fu yuanshen will walk away. Each will go one's own separate way. According to Buddhism, this person will still go through samsara. Since a great enlightened person has been successfully cultivated in his body, this person has also accumulated a lot of de. So what will happen? He might become a high-ranking official or make a big fortune in his next life. It can only be this way. Didn't his cultivation end up in vain?

It has taken us much effort to get permission to articulate this issue. I have unveiled the eternal mystery—it was the secret of secrets that absolutely could not be disclosed. I have revealed the root of all different cultivation practices throughout history. Didn't I say that it deeply involved historical considerations? These are the reasons. Think about it: Which practice or school does not practice cultivation this way? You practice back and forth, but without obtaining gong. Aren't you sad? So who's to blame? Human beings are so lost that they are not enlightened to it, no matter what hints they are given. If something is said at a high level, they will find it inconceivable. If something is said at a low level, they do not get it. Even when I address it this way, some people still want me to cure their illnesses. I really do not know what to say to them. We teach cultivation practice, and we can only take care of those who practice cultivation toward the high levels.

318

In our school of practice, it is zhu yishi that obtains gong. Then, will zhu yishi obtain gong if you say so? Who gives permission? It is not like that, for there must be a prerequisite. Everyone knows that our school of practice does not shun ordinary human society in cultivation practice, nor does it avoid or run away from conflicts. In this complex environment of everyday people, you should be clear-minded and knowingly lose in terms of interests. When your self-interest is taken by others, you will not go to compete and fight for it like others. With different xinxing interference, you will suffer losses. In this difficult environment, you will temper your will and upgrade your xinxing. Under the influence of different ill thoughts from everyday people, you will be able to reach above and beyond.

Think about it, everyone: Isn't it you who suffers knowingly? Isn't it your zhu yuanshen that sacrifices? As to what you have lost among everyday people, haven't you knowingly lost it? Then this gong should belong to you, as whoever loses, gains. Therefore, this is why our school does not avoid practicing cultivation in this complex environment of everyday people. Why do we practice cultivation amidst the conflicts of everyday people? It is because we ourselves are going to obtain gong. The future professional practitioners in temples will practice cultivation by wandering around among everyday people.

Some people have asked: "Don't other practices at present also practice among everyday people?" But, those practices are promoting healing and fitness. Nobody has truly, publicly taught practices toward the high levels except for taking a single disciple privately. Those who genuinely teach their disciples have already taken them away to give them private instruction. Over the years, who has talked about these things in public? Nobody has done this. Our school of practice has taught this way, because ours is just such a cultivation practice, and we will obtain gong precisely in this way. Meanwhile, our school of practice gives hundreds and thousands of things all to your zhu yuanshen to truly enable you to attain gong yourself. I have said that I have done something unprecedented and opened the widest door. Some people have understood these words of mine, as what I have said is really not inconceivable. As a person, I have a habit: If I have a yard and I say only an inch of it, you may still claim that I am boasting, but what was said is in fact only a tiny portion. Because of the great gap in levels, I cannot disclose to you a bit of higher Dafa.

Our school practices cultivation this way, enabling you, yourself to truly attain gong. That is unprecedented since the beginning of heaven and earth—you may examine history. It is good because you will obtain gong yourself, but it is also very difficult. Amidst the complex environment of everyday people and its interpersonal xinxing frictions, it is most difficult for you to rise above and beyond. It is difficult, as you will knowingly lose your vested interests among everyday people. Are you moved or not by your vested interests, by the mind games that people play against each other, or when your relatives or friends suffer— how are you to weigh them? It is so difficult to be a practitioner! Someone said to me: "Teacher, it's enough to be a good person among everyday people. Who can succeed in cultivation?" After hearing that, I felt really disappointed! I did not say a word to him. There are all kinds of xinxing. However much one can be enlightened to is however much one understands; whoever understands will attain.

Lao Zi said: "Tao is the way that can be followed, but it isn't an ordinary way." Tao will not be precious if one can pick it up everywhere on the ground and succeed in practicing it. Our school of practice teaches you to attain gong through conflicts. Therefore, we should accord with everyday people as much as possible. Materially, you will not really be made to lose anything. But in this material environment you need to upgrade your xinxing. It is convenient because of this. Our school of practice is the most convenient, as one can practice it among everyday people instead of becoming a monk or nun. It is also most difficult because of this, as one will practice cultivation in this most complex environment of everyday people. Moreover, it is the best because of this, for it enables one to attain gong oneself. This is the most crucial point in our school of practice, and today I have disclosed it to everyone. Of course, when zhu yuanshen attains gong, fu yuanshen also obtains it. Why is this? When all messages, living beings, and cells in your body are attaining gong, fu yuanshen is certainly obtaining it as well; however, its gong level will not be as high as yours at any time. You are the master while it is the guard of Fa.

Speaking of this, I would also like to add that there are many people in the community of cultivators, who have always attempted to practice toward the high levels. They have traveled everywhere and spent a lot of money. They have not found the well-known masters after having been all over the country. Being well-known does not necessarily mean that one really knows things well. In the end, these people have traveled back and forth, spending much money and effort for nothing. Today we have made public to you this great practice. I have already delivered it to your doorstep. It is up to you whether you can practice cultivation and make it. If you can do it, you may continue your cultivation. If you cannot do it or cannot practice cultivation, from now on you should not think about practicing cultivation at all. Except for demons that will deceive you, nobody else will teach you, and in the future you will not be able to practice cultivation. If I cannot save you, nobody else can. As a matter of fact, finding a true master from an orthodox Fa to teach you is harder than climbing to heaven. There is nobody at all who cares. In the Dharma-ending Period, even very high levels are also in the End of Havoc. Nobody is taking care of everyday people. This is the most convenient school of practice. In addition, it is practiced directly according to the characteristic of the universe. It is the quickest, most direct path, and it precisely targets one's mind.

Heavenly Circulation

In the Tao School, the great and small heavenly circulations are taught. We will explain what the "heavenly circulation" is. The heavenly circulation that we usually refer to is the connecting of the two energy channels[7] of *ren* and *du*. This heavenly circulation is a skin-deep heavenly circulation which accounts for nothing but healing and fitness. This is called the small heavenly circulation. Another heavenly circulation that is neither called "the small heavenly circulation" nor "the great heavenly circulation" is a form of heavenly circulation during meditation. This one travels in a circle inside one's body from niwan to dantian, ascending there as an interior circulation—this is the actual heavenly circulation for cultivation practice in meditation. After this heavenly circulation forms, it will become a very powerful energy current which then brings hundreds of energy

---

[7] energy channels—in Chinese medicine, they are said to be conduits of qi which comprise an intricate network for energy circulation.

channels in motion via one energy channel, so as to open up all other energy channels. The Tao School teaches the heavenly circulation, but Buddhism does not. What does Buddhism teach? When Sakyamuni taught his Dharma, he did not teach gong, nor did he talk about it. Yet, his practice also has his own form of transformation in cultivation practice. How does the energy channel move in Buddhism? It starts at and goes through the baihui point. Then it develops from the top of one's head to the lower body in a spiral form and, in the end, through this method it drives hundreds of energy channels into motion and opens them up.

The central energy channel in the Tantric religion also serves this purpose. Someone has said: "There isn't a central energy channel. So why can the Tantric religion develop this central energy channel?" In fact, when all energy channels in the human body are put together, they amount to hundreds or tens of thousands in number. They intersect vertically and horizontally just like blood vessels, and they even outnumber blood vessels; there are no blood vessels between the internal organs, but there are energy channels. They will be connected vertically and horizontally from the top of one's head to different parts of the body. Perhaps they are not straight initially, and they will be opened up for the connection. They will then gradually expand and slowly form a straight energy channel. With this energy channel as the axis, it rotates by itself to spur into motion several conceptual wheels in level rotations. Its goal is also to open up all energy channels in the body.

The cultivation practice in our Falun Dafa avoids using this method of one energy channel bringing hundreds of energy channels into motion. From the very beginning, we require that hundreds of energy channels be opened up and make simultaneous rotations. All at once, we practice at a very high level and avoid the low-level things. For some people to open up all the hundreds of energy channels with one energy channel, a whole lifetime may be insufficient. Some people must practice cultivation for decades, and it is very difficult. Many practices have said that one lifetime is not enough to succeed in cultivation, while there are many practitioners in high-level practices, who can prolong their lives—don't they talk about cultivating life? They can prolong their lives to practice cultivation, which will take a very long time.

The small heavenly circulation is basically for healing and fitness, while the great heavenly circulation is practicing for gong—that is when one truly practices cultivation. The great heavenly circulation that the Tao School refers to does not come as powerfully as ours, which opens up hundreds of energy channels all at once. The rotation of the great heavenly circulation in the Tao School refers to that of several energy channels that will travel once from the Three Yin and Three Yang[8] channels of one's hands to the bottom of one's feet, to both legs, to the hair, and all over the entire body. That is the great heavenly circulation in motion. As soon as the great heavenly circulation is in motion, this is practicing gong. Therefore, some qigong masters do not teach the great heavenly circulation, for what they teach are only things for healing and fitness. Some people have also spoken about the great heavenly circulation, but they have not installed anything in your body, and you cannot open them up on your own. Without the system installed, how can things be easily opened up by relying on one's mind-intent? It is like doing aerobics—how can that

---

[8] Three Yin and Three Yang—a collective name for the three yin/yang meridians of both the hand and the foot.

open them up? Cultivation depends on the efforts of the individual while transforming gong is done by the master. Only after the internal "mechanism" is fully given to you, can there be this effect.

Throughout history the Tao School has considered the human body a small universe: It believes that the exterior of the universe is as big as its interior, and that its exterior looks the same as its interior. This view seems inconceivable and not easily understood. This universe is so big—how can it be compared with a human body? We are making this point: Our present physics studies elements of matter from molecules, atoms, electrons, protons, and quarks to neutrinos, but what size is further down the line? A microscope cannot detect it at that point, so what will the very microscopic particle be further down the line? It is not known. In fact, what our physics now understands is simply so far away from the smallest microscopic particles of the universe. Once one does not have this flesh body, one's eyes will be able to see things with magnified vision and will see the microscopic level. The higher one's level, the greater the microscopic level one can see.

At his level, Sakyamuni brought up the theory of three thousand worlds, which is to say that in this Milky Way there are also people with flesh bodies like those of our human race. He also mentioned that a grain of sand contains three thousand worlds, and this agrees with the understanding of our modern physics. What's the difference between the rotation pattern of electrons orbiting nuclei and that of Earth orbiting the sun? Therefore, Sakyamuni said that at the microscopic level, a grain of sand contains three thousand worlds. It is just like a universe with life and matter within. If it is true, think about it: Is there sand in the world of that grain of sand? Are there three thousand worlds in the sand from that grain of sand? Then is there sand in the three thousand worlds in the sand of the sand? If the search continues on downward, it will be endless. Therefore, even at the level of Tathagata, Sakyamuni made this statement: "It's immense, without an exterior, and it's tiny, without an interior." It is so immense that he could not see the perimeter of the universe, yet so tiny that he could not detect the most microscopic particle from the origin of matter.

One qigong master has said: "In a sweat pore there is a city with moving trains and cars." It sounds quite inconceivable, but we find this statement not inconceivable if we really understand and study it from the scientific perspective. The other day when I spoke about opening tianmu, many people during the opening of their tianmu found this situation: They were racing out along a tunnel in their foreheads as though they could not reach its end. Everyday during their practice, they feel like they are racing out along this big road, with mountains and rivers on both sides. While running, they pass through cities and see quite a lot of people, and they may think that it is an illusion. What's the matter? What is seen is quite clear and not an illusion. I have said that if one's body is really that immense at the microscopic level, it is not an illusion. This is because the Tao School has always considered the human body a universe. If it is indeed a universe, the distance from the forehead to the pineal body will be more than 108 thousand li. You may charge toward the outside, but it is a very remote distance.

If the great heavenly circulation is fully opened in the course of cultivation practice, it will bring the practitioner a supernormal capability. What supernormal capability? It is known to everyone that the great heavenly circulation is also called "the meridian heavenly circulation," "the *qiankun*[9] rotation," or "the *heche*[10] rotation." At a very low level, the rotation of the great heavenly circulation will form an energy current, which will gradually become more condensed, transforming toward higher levels and becoming a large, high-density energy belt. This energy belt will have a rotating motion. In its rotation, we can, with a very low-level tianmu, find that it can make qi exchange places inside one's body. The qi from the heart may move to the intestines, or the qi from the liver may travel to the stomach ... At the microscopic level we can see that what it carries is something very large. If this energy belt is released outside one's body, it is the ability of teleportation. One with very powerful gong can move something very big, and this is called the Great Teleportation. One with very weak gong can move something very small, and this is called the Small Teleportation. These are the types of teleportation and their generation.

The great heavenly circulation directly involves practicing gong. Thus, it brings about different conditions and forms of gong. It will also bring us a very special state. What state is it? Everyone may have read this phrase called *"bairi feisheng"*[11] in ancient books such as <u>Shenxian Zhuan</u>,[12] <u>Dan Jing</u>, <u>Tao Tsang</u>, or <u>Xingming Guizhi</u>. It means that a person can levitate in broad daylight. In fact, let me tell you that a person can levitate once the great heavenly circulation is opened—it is just that simple. Some people will think that there are quite a few people whose

---

[9] *qiankun* (chyen-kuhn)—"heaven and earth."

[10] *heche* (huh-chuh)—"river vehicle."

[11] *bairi feisheng* (buy-rhe fay-shung)—Taoist term for "levitation in broad daylight."

[12] <u>Shenxian Zhuan</u> (shuhn-shyen jwan)—a Chinese biography of Taoist deities.

great heavenly circulations have opened after so many years of practice. I would even say that it is not inconceivable for tens of thousands of people to have reached this level, because the great heavenly circulation is, after all, only the beginning step in cultivation practice.

Then, why hasn't anyone seen these people levitate or seen them take off into the air? The state of ordinary human society cannot be disturbed, nor can the form of ordinary human society be casually disrupted or altered. How can it be allowed for everybody to fly in the air? Will that be an ordinary human society? This is one primary aspect. From another perspective, human beings do not live among everyday people to be human, but to return to their original, true selves. So there is an issue of being enlightened to it. If one sees that many people can indeed levitate, one will also want to practice cultivation, and there will not be the issue of enlightening. Therefore, if you can levitate through cultivation, you should not casually show it to others or demonstrate it to others, as they also need to practice cultivation. Consequently, after your great heavenly circulation is opened, you will not be able to levitate if your finger tip, toe tip, or a certain part of your body is locked.

When our great heavenly circulations are about to open, a situation will occur wherein some people will lean forward during the sitting meditation. Because the circulation in one's back is opened better, one's back will feel very light while the body's front will feel heavy. Some people lean backward and feel their backs are heavy while the fronts of their bodies feel light. If all of your body is opened well, you will feel as if you are being lifted up, like levitating off the ground. Once you can truly levitate, you will not be allowed to levitate—but this is not absolute. Those

328

who develop supernormal capabilities are usually at both ends: Children do not have attachments, nor do elderly people—especially elderly women. They can easily develop and preserve this capability. For men, especially young men, once they have a capability, they cannot help having the mindset of showing off. At the same time, they might use it as a means for competition among everyday people. It is thus not allowed to exist and will be locked up as soon as it is developed during practice. If one part of the body is locked, this person will not be able to levitate. This is not to say that you will be absolutely forbidden to have this state. You might be allowed to try it, and some people are able to keep it.

These situations occur wherever I give lectures. When I taught a class in Shandong, there were practitioners from Beijing and Jinan.[13] Someone asked: "Teacher, what's happened to me? While walking, I feel like I'm leaving the ground. I also feel like I'm levitating while sleeping at home. Even the bedding covers take off like a balloon." When I taught a class in Guiyang,[14] there was an elderly practitioner from Guizhou who was an elderly woman. She had two beds in her room, with one bed by one wall and the other bed next to another wall. When she was sitting in meditation on the bed, she felt herself levitating, and when she opened her eyes she found herself having drifted to the other bed. She thought to herself, "I should return to my bed," and so she flew back again.

There was a practitioner in Qingdao[15] who sat in meditation on a bed during lunch break when no one was around in his office.

---

[13] Jinan (jee-nahn)—capital of Shandong Province.

[14] Guiyang (gway-yahng)—capital of Guizhou Province.

[15] Qingdao (ching-dow)—a seaport city in Shandong Province.

As soon as he sat there, he levitated and moved harshly up and down, as high as a meter. He would come down after rising up, and this kept occurring. The bedding cover was even bounced to the floor. He was a little bit excited and somewhat scared. This up and down movement lasted the whole lunch period. Finally, the office bell rang, and he thought to himself: "I shouldn't let others see this. They'd wonder 'what's going on?' I should quickly stop." He stopped the practice. This is why elderly people can conduct themselves well. If this had happened to a young person, when the office bell rang he would think: "You should all come to see me levitate." This is where one cannot easily control one's mentality of showing off: "See how well I've practiced—I can levitate." Once one shows it off, the capability will be gone, as it is not allowed to exist this way. There are many such cases among practitioners everywhere.

We require that hundreds of energy channels be opened from the very beginning. By this day, eighty to ninety percent of our practitioners have reached the state where their bodies are very light and free of illness. At the same time, we have said that in this class you are not only pushed to this state where your body is completely purified, but also many things have been installed in your body so that in this class you can develop gong. It is the same as my raising you up and then sending you further ahead. I have been teaching the Fa to everyone in the class, and everyone's xinxing has been changing constantly as well. Upon walking outside this auditorium, many of you will feel like different people, and your outlook will be guaranteed to change. You will know how to conduct yourselves in the future, and you will no longer be so befuddled. It is guaranteed to be this way. Therefore, your xinxing has already caught up.

Speaking of the great heavenly circulation, though you are not allowed to levitate, you will feel that your body is light, as though treading on air. In the past, you would be tired if you walked a few steps, but now it is very easy no matter how far you walk. You feel as if being pushed while riding a bike, and you are not tired when going upstairs—no matter how many floors there are. It is guaranteed to be this way. Those who read this book and practice cultivation on their own can also reach this state, as expected. I am a person who will not say what he does not want to say, but what I say must be true. Especially under this circumstance, if I do not tell the truth in teaching the Fa, if I make inconceivable statements, or if I speak aimlessly and casually, I will be teaching an evil Fa. It is not easy for me to do this thing, as the whole universe is watching. It is not permitted once one deviates.

An everyday person will only know this great heavenly circulation, and that will be it. In fact, this is not enough. For the body to be replaced and transformed completely by the high-energy matter as soon as possible, there must be another heavenly circulation that drives into motion all the energy channels in your body. It is called "the *maoyou*[16] heavenly circulation," and this is probably known by very few people. This term is occasionally mentioned in books, but nobody has explained it or told you. It is only discussed in theories, as it is the secret of secrets. We will disclose all of it to you here. It can start from baihui point (or also from the huiyin point), and it comes out to move along the borderline between yin and yang. It then moves from the ear down to the shoulder, going along each finger, the side of your body, and then coming down to your foot's sole. Then it moves up one

---

[16] *maoyou* (maow-yo)—the borderline between yin and yang sides of the body.

thigh and down the other, going across your other foot's sole and coming up the other side of your body. It again moves along each finger and reaches the top of your head, completing a full circle. This is the maoyou heavenly circulation. Others can write a book about it, and I have summed it up in a few words. I think that it should not be considered a heavenly secret, yet others find these things very precious and will not discuss them except when truly teaching their disciples. Although I have disclosed it, none of you should use mind-intent to guide or control it in the practice. If you do, you are not practicing our Falun Dafa. Genuine practice toward higher levels is in a state of wuwei and free of any mind activities. Everything is installed in your body, ready-made. They are automatically formed, and these internal mechanisms cultivate you; they will make self-rotations when the time is due. One day during practice your head might swing from side to side. If your head swings to this side, it is rotating this way. If your head swings to the other side, it is rotating that way. It rotates both ways.

When the great or the small heavenly circulations have been opened, one's head will nod during the sitting meditation, and this is the sign of energy passing through. The same is true with the Falun heavenly circulation that we practice; we just practice it this way. In fact, when you are not practicing, it rotates by itself. It will constantly rotate forever; when you practice, you are reinforcing the mechanisms. Haven't we talked about the Fa cultivating practitioners? Normally, you will discover that your heavenly circulation is always rotating. Though you are not practicing, this layer of the energy mechanism or the external energy mechanism installed outside your body is driving your body in practice—it is all automatic. It can also rotate in reverse, as it rotates both ways and is constantly opening your energy channels.

So what's the goal of opening the heavenly circulation? Opening the heavenly circulation is not itself the purpose of the practice. Even if your heavenly circulation is opened, I would say that it is still nothing. If one's cultivation continues further, through the method of the heavenly circulation one aims at opening hundreds of energy channels via one energy channel, and one can thereby open all the body's energy channels. We have already started to do this. With further practice, one will find in the rotation of the great heavenly circulation that the energy channels will become very wide like a finger and quite broad inside. Because the energy has also become very powerful, after the energy current forms, it will become very wide and bright. This is still nothing. When will the practice be good enough? Hundreds of one's energy channels must gradually become wider, with energy getting stronger and brighter. In the end, thousands of energy channels will join together and turn one's body into one without any energy channels or acupuncture points; they will join together to make one whole body. This is the ultimate purpose of opening energy channels. Its goal is to have the human body completely transformed by the high-energy matter.

At this point, one's body will basically be transformed by the high-energy matter. In other words, one has reached the highest level of Shi-Jian-Fa cultivation. The human flesh body will have been cultivated to the ultimate limit. At this time, one will experience another situation. What kind of situation? This person will have developed a lot of gong. In cultivating an everyday person's body or in the course of Shi-Jian-Fa cultivation, all human supernormal capabilities (potential capabilities) and everything will be developed. However, while practicing among everyday people, most of them are locked up. In addition, one's gongzhu will grow very high. All forms of gong will be reinforced by the mighty gong, becoming quite powerful. Yet, they can only function in this dimension of ours, and cannot act on anything in other dimensions since they are supernormal capabilities cultivated from our ordinary human flesh bodies. Nonetheless, they will already be very substantial. In different dimensions, and in terms of the body's forms of existence in different dimensions, there will be quite a lot of changes. The things this body carries in each level of the dimensions will be quite substantial and appear very scary. Some people have eyes all over their bodies, and all the sweat pores in their bodies will become eyes. There will be eyes within this person's entire dimensional field. Because it is gong from the Buddha School, some people will carry the image of Bodhisattva or Buddha all over their bodies. All forms of gong will have reached a very substantial extent. In addition, many living beings will manifest themselves.

At this time, a situation called "*sanhua juding*"[17] will occur. It is a very conspicuous state that is also eye-catching. One is able to see it with a low-level tianmu. One will have three flowers above the head. One is a lotus flower, but it is not the lotus flower in our physical dimension. The other two flowers are also from another dimension and are extraordinarily beautiful. These three flowers take turns rotating above one's head. They will rotate clockwise or counter-clockwise, and each flower can also rotate by itself. Each flower will have a big pole as thick as the diameter of the flower. These three big poles will reach all the way to the top of the sky, but they are not gongzhu—they are just in this form and are extraordinarily wonderful. If you can see them, you

---

[17] *sanhua juding* (sahn-hwa jew-ding)— "three flowers gathered above a practitioner's head."

will be shocked as well. When one's cultivation reaches this stage, one's body will be white and pure, and the skin will be fair and delicate. At this point, one will have reached the highest form of Shi-Jian-Fa cultivation, yet this is not the ultimate end. One still needs to continue cultivation practice and move forward.

The next step forward is the interim level between Shi-Jian-Fa and Chu-Shi-Jian-Fa, called the state of the Pure-White Body (also known as the "crystal white body"). When cultivation of the physical body has reached the highest form of Shi-Jian-Fa, it is only that the human flesh body has transformed into the highest form. When the whole body is truly in this form, it is completely composed of the high-energy matter. Why is it called the Pure-White Body? It is because this body has already reached the absolute purity of the highest degree. When it is seen with tianmu, the entire body is transparent—just like transparent glass. When you look at it there is nothing, as it will exhibit this state. Put simply, this body is already a Buddha-body. This is because the body composed of the high-energy matter is already different from our physical bodies. At this point, all supernormal capabilities and supernatural skills will be abandoned at once. They will be placed in a very deep dimension, as they are useless and will no longer serve any function. One day in the future when you succeed in cultivation, you may look back and review your journey of cultivation practice by taking them out for a look. At this time, only two things will be left: Gongzhu still remains, and the cultivated yuanying will have grown very large. Yet, both exist in a deep dimension that cannot be seen by a person with an average level of tianmu. All one can see is that this person's body is transparent.

Because the state of the Pure-White Body is only an interim

335

level, with further cultivation practice one will truly begin Chu-Shi-Jian-Fa cultivation, also known as the cultivation of Buddha-body. The whole body will be composed of gong. By now one's xinxing will have become stable. One will begin cultivation practice with a fresh start and develop supernormal capabilities all over again, and they should no longer be called "supernormal capabilities." They should be called "the divine power of Buddha Fa," as they can act on all dimensions with their boundless power. As you continue to practice cultivation in the future, you, yourself will know things at higher levels, how to practice cultivation, and cultivation practice's forms of existence.

Attachment of Zealotry

I will address an issue that belongs to the attachment of zealotry. Many people have practiced qigong for a very long time. There are also people who have never practiced it, but who have pursued and pondered the truth and meaning of human life. Once they learn our Falun Dafa, they will understand at once many questions in life that they have wished to understand but could not answer. Perhaps along with their minds being elevated, they will become very excited—this is for sure. I know that a genuine practitioner will know its weight and cherish it. Yet, this problem often occurs: Due to human excitement, one will develop the unnecessary mentality of zealotry. It causes one to behave abnormally in formalities, in interacting with others in ordinary human society, or in the environment of ordinary human society. I say that this is unacceptable.

The majority of people in our school will practice cultivation in ordinary human society, so you should not distance yourself

336

from ordinary human society and you must practice cultivation with a clear mind. The relationships between one another should remain normal. Of course, you have a very high xinxing level and a righteous mentality. You will upgrade your own xinxing and your own level; you do not commit wrongdoings and only do good deeds—these are only such a manifestation. Some people conduct themselves as though they are either mentally abnormal or they have seen enough of this secular world. They say things that others cannot comprehend. Others will say: "How come a person who learns Falun Dafa becomes like this? It seems he has a mental problem." Actually, it is not so. He is simply too excited and so appears to be irrational without common sense. Think about it, everyone: Your acting like this is also wrong, and you have gone to the other extreme—again it is an attachment. You should give it up and practice cultivation while living normally like everyone else among everyday people. If while among everyday people others consider you infatuated, they will not deal with you and will keep a distance from you. Nobody will provide you with opportunities to improve xinxing, nor treat you as a normal person—I would say that this is not right! Therefore, everyone must be sure to pay attention to this issue and conduct himself or herself well.

Our practice is unlike ordinary practices that make one absent-minded, in trance, or infatuated. Our practice requires you to cultivate yourselves with a clear mind. Someone always says: "Teacher, once I close my eyes my body will swing." I would say that it is not necessarily so. You have already developed a habit of abandoning your zhu yishi. Once you close your eyes you will put zhu yishi to rest, and it will disappear. You have already developed this habit. While sitting here, why doesn't your body swing? If you maintain the state in which your eyes are

337

open, will your body swing with eyes slightly closed? Absolutely not. You think that qigong should be practiced this way and you have formed such a concept. Once you close your eyes, you will disappear without knowing where you are. We have said that your zhu yishi must be conscious, because this practice cultivates your own self. You should make progress with a conscious mind. We also have meditation exercises. How do we practice meditation? We require of everyone that no matter how deeply you meditate, you must know that you are practicing here. You are absolutely forbidden to be in a state of trance wherein you know nothing. Then, what specific state will occur? When you sit there, you should feel wonderful and very comfortable as though you are sitting inside an egg shell; you will be aware of yourself practicing the exercise, but you feel that your whole body cannot move. This is what must occur in our practice. There is another situation whereby in the sitting meditation one finds that one's legs, body, arms, and hands have disappeared, with only the head remaining. As one practices further, one will find that even one's head disappears, and there only remains one's own mind and a little thought that is aware of oneself practicing here. It is sufficient if we can achieve this state. Why is this? When one practices in this state, the body is being fully transformed, and it is the optimum state. We thus require you to achieve this state of tranquility. However, you should not fall asleep or lose consciousness, otherwise good things might be practiced by someone else.

All of our practitioners should be sure to never behave very abnormally among everyday people. If you play a bad role among everyday people, others may say: "Why do those people who learn Falun Dafa all behave this way?" It is the same as undermining the reputation of Falun Dafa, so make sure to pay attention to this issue. In other matters or in the course of cultivation practice, one should be sure to not develop the attachment of zealotry—this mentality can be very easily taken advantage of by demons.

Xiu Kou[18]

Xiu kou was also required by religions in the past. However, the xiu kou to which religions referred applied mainly to some professional practitioners—monks and Taoists who would not open their mouths to talk. Because they were professional practitioners, they intended to abandon human attachments to a greater extent. They believed that once one thinks, it is karma. Religions have classified karma as "good karma" and "sinful karma." Regardless of whether it is good karma or sinful karma, from either the emptiness approach in the Buddha School or the nothingness teaching in the Tao School, it should not be produced. Therefore, they claimed that they would not do anything since they could not see the karmic relationship of affairs, that is, whether those matters were good or bad, or what karmic relationships existed. An ordinary practitioner who has not reached such a high level cannot see these things, so he will worry that though something appears to be good on the surface, it could be a bad thing once it is done. Therefore, one does his best to practice wuwei and will not do anything so that one can avoid producing karma. This is because once karma is produce, one must eliminate it and suffer for it. For instance, for our practitioners it is already predetermined at what stage they will become enlightened. If you unnecessarily insert something

---

[18] xiu kou (shyo-ko)—"cultivation of speech."

halfway along, it will cause difficulties to your entire cultivation practice. One thus practices wuwei.

The Buddha School requires xiu kou, which is to say that one's speech is dictated by one's mind. Accordingly, this mind has intentions. If one's mind wants itself to think a little bit, express something, do something, or direct one's sensory organs and four limbs, it may be an attachment among everyday people. For example, there are conflicts among one another, such as "you're good, but he isn't good," or "your cultivation is good, but his isn't." These are conflicts themselves. Let us talk about something that is common, such as "I want to do this or that," or "this matter should now be done this way or that way." Perhaps, it will unintentionally hurt someone. Because interpersonal conflicts are all very complex, one may unintentionally produce karma. As a consequence, one absolutely wants to seal off one's mouth and say nothing. In the past, religions took xiu kou very seriously, and this is what has been taught in religion.

The majority of our Falun Dafa practitioners (that is, except for those professional practitioners) practice cultivation among everyday people. They therefore cannot avoid leading a normal life in ordinary human society and interacting with society. Everyone has a job and must do it well. Some people must do their work by talking. So isn't it a conflict? It is not a conflict. Why isn't it a conflict? The xiu kou that we refer to is very different from that of others. Because of differences in cultivation ways, the requirements are also different. We should all speak according to a practitioner's xinxing rather than create conflicts or say something improper. As practitioners, we must measure ourselves with the standard of the Fa to determine whether we should say certain things. What should be said will not present a problem if one complies with the xinxing standard for practitioners according to the Fa. In addition, we must talk about and spread the Fa, so it is impossible not to talk. The xiu kou that we teach refers to: that which involves fame and personal gain that cannot be given up among everyday people, that which has nothing to do with the actual work of practitioners in society, the senseless gossiping among practitioners in the same school of practice, attachments that cause one to show off, hearsay or circulating rumors, or those discussions on some social issues that one is excited about. I hold that these are all attachments of everyday people. I think that in these areas we should watch what we say—that is the xiu kou we refer to. Monks in the past took these things very seriously, because once one started to think one will create karma. Therefore, they would cultivate "body, speech, and mind." The cultivation of body they spoke of meant that one would not commit bad deeds. Cultivation of speech meant that one would not talk. Cultivation of mind meant that one would not even think. In the past, there were strict requirements for these things in professional cultivation in temples. We should conduct ourselves according to a practitioner's xinxing standard. It should be fine as long as one grasps what should or should not be said.

LECTURE NINE

Qigong and Physical Exercises

At an ordinary level, people easily take qigong to be directly related to physical exercises. Of course, at a low level, qigong and physical exercises are the same with respect to attaining a healthy body. Yet, its specific exercise methods and adopted means differ greatly from those of physical exercises. To obtain a healthy body through physical exercises, one must increase the amount of exercise and intensify physical training. Qigong practice, however, is just the opposite, as it does not require one to move. If there is any movement, it is gentle, slow, and curved. It is even motionless and still—this differs greatly from physical exercises in terms of form. From the high-level perspective, qigong is not limited to only healing and fitness, for it embodies something of higher levels and deeper content. Qigong is not this little smattering of things at the level of ordinary people. It is supernormal and has different manifestations at different levels. It is such a thing that goes far beyond everyday people.

With regard to the nature of the exercises, they also differ tremendously. To get the body ready for this modern level of competition and to meet its criteria, an athlete, especially an athlete today, is required to increase the amount of exercise. Therefore, one must always keep the body in prime shape. To achieve this goal, one must increase the amount of exercise to make blood circulate adequately in the body, enhance one's metabolism, and always keep the body in an improving state. Why should metabolism be enhanced? It is because an athlete's body must be always improving and in its best condition for competition. The human body is composed of numerous cells. These all have the following sort of process: The newly divided cell's life is very vigorous, and the cell manifests a state of growth. When it grows to the ultimate point, it cannot grow anymore and can only decline until its end. A new cell will then replace it. For instance, let us use the twelve hours of daytime to describe it. A cell divides at 6 A.M. and shows a state of growth. When it reaches 8 A.M., 9 A.M., or 10 A.M., these are all very good periods. By the time noon arrives, it can no longer move up, and can only go down hill. At this point, the cell still has the remaining half of its life, but this remaining half is unsuitable for an athlete's competition condition.

What should be done, then? One must intensify the training and increase blood circulation, and then, the newly divided cells can replace the old ones. It takes this path. That is to say, before the cell's entire journey is over or when only half its life is through, it will be replaced. The body will thus always maintain strength and make improvements. Yet, human cells cannot divide like this without limit, as the number of cell divisions is finite. Suppose that a cell can only divide one hundred times in one's life. Actually, it can divide more than a million times. And suppose that when a cell divides a hundred times for a normal person, he can live one hundred years. But now this cell has only lived half of its life, so he can only live for fifty years. Yet, we have not seen any major problems occurring to athletes, because athletes today have to retire before the age of thirty. In particular, now the competition level is very high, and the number of retired athletes is also large. An athlete can thus resume a normal life and will not appear very much affected. Theoretically, it is essentially this way. Physical exercise can enable one to keep a healthy body, but it will shorten one's life. From the appearance, an athlete in his teens looks like one in his twenties, while one in his twenties looks like one in his thirties. An athlete usually gives the impression of early aging. If there is an advantage, there will be—from the dialectical perspective—a disadvantage. In actuality, one takes this path.

Qigong practice is just the opposite of physical exercises. It does not require strenuous movements. If there is any movement, it is gentle, slow, and curved. It is so gentle and slow that it becomes even motionless or still. You know that the cultivation method of sitting in trance requires the state of stillness. Everything such as the heartbeat and blood circulation will slow down. In India, there are many yoga masters who can sit in water or be buried in the earth for many days. They can make themselves completely still and even control their heartbeats. Suppose that one's cells divide once a day. A practitioner can cause his body's cells to divide once every two days, once every week, once every half a month, or even once in a longer period of time. He has already extended his life, then. This only refers to those practices that just cultivate the mind without cultivating the body, as they can also achieve this and prolong one's life. Someone may think: "Isn't one's life or lifetime pre-determined? How can one live longer without cultivating the body?" True. If a practitioner's level reaches beyond the Three Realms, his life will be extended, but on the surface he will look very old.

A true practice that cultivates the body will constantly accumulate the collected high-energy matter in the cells of one's body and constantly increase its density to gradually repress and slowly replace those everyday person's cells. At this time there will be a qualitative change, and this person will stay young forever. Of course, the process of cultivation is a very slow and gradual one, and one must sacrifice quite a lot. It is not very easy for one to temper oneself physically and mentally. Can one remain calm in a xinxing conflict with others? Will one be unaffected when personal, vested interests are at stake? It is very difficult to do this, so it is not that as long as one wants to achieve this goal, one can achieve it. Only when one's xinxing and de have been cultivated to this level can one achieve this goal.

Many people have been taking qigong to be an ordinary physical exercise, when in fact the differences are so great that they are not the same at all. Only when practicing qi at the lowest level, which is for healing and fitness to ensure a healthy body, is this lowest-level goal in common with that of physical exercises. At the high level, however, they are entirely different things. The body purification in qigong also has its purpose and, furthermore, practitioners are required to comply with supernormal principles instead of everyday people's principles. But physical exercises are only something for everyday people.

Mind-intent

With regard to mind-intent, this refers to our human mind activities. In the community of cultivators, how are mind activities in the brain viewed? How does it look at different forms of human thinking (mind-intent)? And how do they manifest? Modern medicine still cannot solve many questions in its study of the human brain, because it is not as easy as studying the surface of our bodies. At deeper levels, different dimensions assume different forms. But it is also unlike what some qigong masters have said. Some qigong masters do not even know themselves what is going on, nor can they explain it clearly. They think that once they use their minds and develop a thought, they will be able to do something. They claim that those things are done by the thoughts or their mind-intent. Actually, those things are not done by their mind-intent at all.

First of all, let us talk about the origin of one's thoughts. In ancient China, there was the phrase "heart-thinking." Why was it called heart-thinking? Ancient Chinese science was very advanced since its research directly targeted things such as the human body, life, and the universe. Some people indeed feel that it is their hearts that think, while others feel that it is their brains that think. Why is there this situation? It is quite reasonable when some people talk about heart-thinking. This is because we have found that an everyday person's yuanshen is very tiny, and the actual messages from the human brain are not a function of the human brain itself—they are not generated by the brain, but by one's yuanshen. One's yuanshen does not stay only in the niwan palace. The niwan palace in the Tao School is the pineal body that our modern medicine has come to understand. If one's yuanshen is in the niwan palace, one will really feel that the brain is thinking about something or sending forth messages. If it is in one's heart, one will really feel that the heart is thinking about something.

A human body is a small universe. Many living beings in a practitioner's body might be able to exchange locations. When yuanshen changes its location, if it moves to one's stomach, one will feel that the stomach is indeed thinking about something. If yuanshen moves to one's calf or heel, one will actually feel that the calf or heel is thinking about something. It is guaranteed to be so, though it may sound quite inconceivable. When your cultivation level is not very high, you will find that this phenomenon exists. If a human body does not have yuanshen and things such as temperament, character, and personality, it is only a piece of meat and not a complete person with individuality. So what functions does the human brain have? As I see it, in the form of this physical dimension, the human brain is only a processing factory. The actual message is sent forth by yuanshen. What is transmitted, however, is not a language, but a message of the universe that represents a certain meaning. Upon receiving such a command, our brains will process this into our present language or other such forms of expression; we express it through hand gestures, eye contact, and such entire movements. The brain has only this effect. The actual commands and thoughts come from one's yuanshen. People usually believe that they are direct and independent functions of the brain. In fact, yuanshen is sometimes in the heart, so some people can indeed feel their hearts thinking.

At present, those people who conduct research on the human body believe that what the human brain transmits is something like an electric wave. We will not address at the outset what is actually transmitted, but they have acknowledged that it is a material existence. Thus, it is not superstitious. What effects does this material have? Some qigong masters claim: "I can use my mind-intent to perform teleportation, open your tianmu, cure your illness, etc." Actually, as for some qigong masters, they do not even know, nor are they clear about what supernormal capabilities they possess. They only know that they can do whatever they want, as long as they think about it. In reality, it is their mind-intent at work: Supernormal capabilities are directed by the brain's mind-intent, and they carry out specific tasks under the command of mind-intent. Yet, mind-intent cannot do anything itself. When a practitioner does something specific, it is his or her supernormal capabilities that do the work.

Supernormal capabilities are potential capabilities of the human body. With the development of our human society, the human mind has become increasingly sophisticated, attaching more importance to "reality" and becoming more dependent on so-called modern tools. Consequently, human inborn capabilities have become increasingly degenerate. The Tao School teaches returning to the original, true self. In the course of cultivation practice, you must seek the truth, and in the end return to your original, true self and your inherent nature. Only then, can you reveal these inborn abilities of yours. Nowadays, we call them "supernatural capabilities" when they are all actually human inborn capabilities. Human society appears to be progressing, but in fact it is regressing and moving further away from the characteristic of the universe. The other day I mentioned that Zhang Guolao rode backward on a donkey, but people might not have understood what this meant. He discovered that going forward is moving backward, and that humankind has been moving further away from the characteristic of the universe. In the universe's course of evolution and especially after joining the big wave of the present commodity economy, many people have become very morally corrupt, and they are moving further away from Zhen-Shan-Ren, the characteristic of the universe. Those who drift along with the current of everyday people cannot realize the extent of humanity's moral corruption. Therefore, some people even consider everything to be good. Only those people whose xinxing has been upgraded through cultivation will realize, by looking back, that human moral values have decayed to this terrible extent.

One qigong master has said: "I can develop your supernormal capabilities." What supernormal capabilities can he develop? Without energy, one's supernormal capabilities will not work.

How can you develop them without it? When one's supernormal capabilities are not formed and sustained by one's own energy, how can you develop them? It is absolutely impossible. What this master said about developing supernormal capabilities is nothing, but connecting your developed supernormal capabilities with your brain. They will perform at the command of your brain's mind-intent. This is what he does in terms of developing supernormal capabilities. Actually, he has not developed any of your supernormal capabilities, but has just done this little bit of work.

For a practitioner, one's mind-intent dictates supernormal capabilities to do things. For an everyday person, one's mind-intent directs the four limbs and the sensory organs to work, just like the production office in a factory: The director's office issues orders to each department of specific functions to carry out duties. It is also like the military headquarters: The commander's office gives the order and directs the entire army to carry out a mission. When I was out of town giving lectures, I frequently discussed this issue with administrators in local qigong societies. They were all very surprised: "We've been studying how much potential energy and consciousness the human mind has." In reality, it is not so. They were wrong from the very beginning. I have said that to study the science of the human body, one must revolutionize one's thinking. To understand those supernormal things, one cannot apply everyday people's deductive methods and their ways of viewing issues.

Speaking of mind-intent, it has several forms. For example, some people bring up vague awareness, the subconscious, inspiration, dreams, etc. Speaking of dreams, no qigong master is willing to explain them. Because at birth you were also born simultaneously in many dimensions of the universe, these other selves of yours make up a complete, integrated entity with you and interrelate to each other, being mentally connected. Additionally, in the body you have your own zhu yuanshen, fu yuanshen, and images of other different beings. As forms of existence in other dimensions, every cell and all internal organs carry your image's message. Thus, it is extremely complex. In a dream, things may be this way one moment and some other way in another. Where do they come from, anyway? It is said in medical science that this is because one's cerebral cortex has experienced changes. This is a reaction manifested in this physical form. In fact, it is the result of receiving messages from another dimension. Therefore, you feel muddle-headed in a dream. This has nothing to do with you, and you do not need to pay attention to it. There is one kind of dream that concerns you directly. We should not call such a dream a "dream." Your main consciousness or zhu yuanshen may have seen in a dream that a family member has come up to you, you may indeed have experienced something, or you may have seen or done something. In these cases, it is that your zhu yuanshen has actually done or seen something in another physical dimension, as your consciousness was clear and real. These things actually do exist, except that they occur in another physical dimension and they are done in another time-space. How can you call it a dream? It is not. Your physical body here is actually asleep, so you may as well call it a dream. Only such dreams have something to do with you directly.

Speaking of human inspiration, the subconscious, vague awareness, and so on, I would say that these terms are not invented by scientists. They are terms crafted by writers and are based upon the conventions of everyday people—they are unscientific. What is the "vague awareness" that people refer to? It is difficult to explain clearly and it is too vague, since various human messages are too complex, and they appear to be some strands of vague memories. As for the subconscious that people refer to, we can explain it easily. According to the definition of the subconscious, it usually refers to one's doing something without knowing. Typically, people say that one does something subconsciously rather than intentionally. This subconscious is exactly the same as the fu yishi that we have mentioned. When one's zhu yishi relaxes and does not control the brain, one does not have a clear consciousness, as if one falls asleep. Either in a dream or in an unconscious state, one will be easily controlled by fu yishi or fu yuanshen. At that time, fu yishi is able to do certain things, which is to say that you will be doing things without a clear mind. Yet these things often tend to be done pretty well, since fu yishi can see from another dimension the nature of the matter and will not be misled by our ordinary human society. Therefore, after one realizes what one has done, one will look back: "How could I do it so badly? I wouldn't do it this way with a clear mind." You may now say that it is not good, but when you look back ten days or half a month later, you will say: "Wow! It was done so well! How did I do it then?" These things often take place. Because fu yishi does not care what happens at that time, it will, however, have a good effect in the future. There are also some things that do not have any consequences and only have some effects at that moment. When fu yishi does these things, it may do a very good job right then.

There is another form: Namely, those of you with very good inborn quality can easily be controlled by higher beings in doing things. Of course, this is another issue, and it will not be addressed here. We mainly discuss thoughts that come from our own selves.

As for "inspiration," it too is a term invented by writers. It is generally believed that inspiration, as an accumulation of one's lifelong knowledge, appears in a second like a shining spark. I would say that according to the perspective of materialism, the more knowledge one accumulates in life, the sharper one's mind should be in its application. At the time when one applies it, it should come out continuously, and there should not be an issue of inspiration. All the so-called inspiration, when it comes, is not in this state. Usually when a person uses the brain, he keeps using it until he feels that his knowledge is exhausted and as though he is at his wit's end. He will be unable to continue writing a paper, be short of ideas in composing a piece of music, or be unable to complete a scientific research project. At this point, a person is usually tired, with the brain wasted and cigarette butts scattered on the floor. He gets stuck, has a headache, and still cannot come up with any ideas. In the end, under what conditions does inspiration appear? If he is tired, he will think: "Forget it. I'll take a break." Because the more his zhu yishi controls his brain the less other lives can step in, with this break and the relaxation of his mind, all of a sudden he can unintentionally recall something from his brain. Most inspiration comes this way.

Why does inspiration come at this time? Because when one's brain is controlled by zhu yishi, the more it uses the brain, the greater control it has, and the less fu yishi can step in. When one is thinking, has a headache, and suffers, fu yishi also suffers and has a very painful headache. As a part of this body and being born simultaneously from the same mother's womb, it also controls a portion of this body. When one's zhu yishi relaxes, fu yishi will project what it knows into the brain. Because it can see the nature of a matter in another dimension, the work will, accordingly, be done, a paper written, or the music composed.

Some people will say: "In that case, we should make use of fu yishi." This is like what someone asked in a note just now: "How do we contact fu yishi?" You cannot get in touch with it because your practice has just begun and you do not have any abilities. You are better off not making any contact, as your intention is bound to be an attachment. Some people may think: "Can we use fu yishi to create for us more wealth and accelerate the development of human society?" No! Why is this? It is because what your fu yishi knows is also very limited. With the complexity of dimensions and so many levels, the structure of the universe is quite complex. Fu yishi can only know what is in its dimension and will not know anything beyond its dimension. In addition, there are many different vertical levels and dimensions. The development of humankind can be controlled only by higher lives at a very lofty level, and it progresses according to the law of development.

Our ordinary human society progresses according to the law of history's development. You may wish it to develop in a certain way and to achieve a certain goal, but that higher life does not consider it this way. Did people in ancient times think of today's aircraft, trains, and bikes? I would say that it is unlikely they did not. Because history did not evolve to that stage, they could not invent them. On the surface, or from the perspective of conventional theories and present human knowledge, it is because human science at that time had not yet reached this level and so they could not invent them. In fact, how human science should develop is also paced according to the arrangement of history. If you want to humanly realize a certain goal, it cannot be achieved. Of course, there are people whose fu yishi can easily play a role. One writer claims: "I can write tens of thousands of words a day for my book without getting tired at all. If I want, I can write it very quickly, and others will still find it really good once they read it." Why is it so? This is the result of joint efforts from his zhu yishi and fu yishi, as his fu yishi can also assume half the job. But it is not so all the time. Most fu yishi do not get involved at all. It is not good if you want it to do something, for you will get the opposite results.

A Clear and Clean Mind

Many people cannot achieve a tranquil mind during practice, and they go everywhere to ask qigong masters: "Teacher, I can't attain tranquility no matter how I practice. Once I settle down, I'll think of everything, including odd thoughts and ideas." It is like overturning rivers and seas with everything surfacing, and one cannot attain tranquility whatsoever. Why is one unable to attain tranquility? Some people cannot understand it and believe that there must be some secret tricks. They will find well-known masters: "Please teach me some advanced tricks so that I can have a mind of tranquility." In my view, that is looking for external help. If you want to improve yourself, you should search your inner self and work hard on your heart—only then can you truly ascend and achieve tranquility in sitting meditation. The ability to achieve tranquility is gong, and the depth of ding indicates one's level.

How can an everyday person attain tranquility at will? One cannot do it at all unless one has very good inborn quality. In other words, the fundamental reason for one's being unable to achieve tranquility is not an issue of techniques, but that your mind and heart are not clean. In ordinary human society and in interpersonal conflicts, you compete and fight for personal gain, all kinds of human sentimentality, and your attachments to desires. If you do not let go of these things and take them lightly, how can you easily achieve tranquility? While practicing qigong, someone claims: "I just don't believe it. I've got to calm down and stop thinking." As soon as that is said, all thoughts will pop up again, as it is your mind that is not clean. You are therefore unable to have a tranquil mind.

Some people might disagree with my stance: "Don't some qigong masters teach people to use certain techniques? One can concentrate, visualize something, focus one's mind on dantian, look internally at dantian, chant the Buddha's name, and so on." These are types of techniques. Yet they are not merely techniques, but also manifestations of one's accomplishment. Accordingly, such an accomplishment directly involves our xinxing cultivation and our improvement in level. Moreover, one cannot attain tranquility by using such techniques alone. If you do not believe it, you can give it a try. With different strong desires and attachments and without being able to give up everything, you may try and see if you can achieve tranquility. Some people say that it will work to chant the Buddha's name. Can you attain tranquility by chanting the Buddha's name? Someone claims: "It's easy to practice Buddha Amitabha's school of practice. It'll work just by chanting the Buddha's name." Why don't you try such chanting? I would call it an accomplishment. You say that it is easy, but I say that it is not easy, as no school of practice is easy.

Everyone knows that Sakyamuni taught "samadhi." What did he teach prior to samadhi? He mentioned "precept" and abandoning all desires and addictions until everything disappears—then one can achieve samadhi. Isn't it such a principle? But "samadhi" is also an accomplishment, as you are unable to completely achieve "precept" all at once. With the gradual abandonment of all bad things, one's ability to concentrate will also improve from shallow to deep. When one chants the Buddha's name, one must do it single-mindedly with nothing else in mind until other portions of the brain become numb and one becomes unaware of anything, with one thought replacing thousands of others, or until each word of "Buddha Amitabha" shows up before one's eyes. Isn't this an accomplishment? Can one do this at the very beginning? One cannot. If one cannot do it, one will certainly be unable to achieve tranquility. If you do not believe it, you can give it a try. While chanting the Buddha's name repeatedly with one's mouth, one's mind thinks about everything: "Why does my boss in the workplace dislike me so much? My bonus for this month is so little." The more one thinks about it, the angrier one becomes, while one's mouth is still chanting the Buddha's name. Do you think this person can practice qigong? Isn't this a matter of accomplishment? Isn't it an issue of your mind being unclean? Some people's tianmu are open, and they can look internally at dantian. As to the dan that accumulates in one's lower abdominal area, the purer this energy matter is, the brighter it becomes. The less pure it is, the more opaque and more dark it is. Can one attain tranquility just by looking internally at that dan in the dantian? One cannot attain it. It is not up to the technique itself. The key is that one's mind and thoughts are not clear and clean. When you look internally at dantian, the dan looks bright and pretty. In a second, this dan transforms into an apartment: "This room will be for my son when he gets married. That room is for my daughter. As an old couple, we'll live in the other room, and the room in the center will be a living room. It's just great! Will this apartment be assigned to me? I have to think

356

of a way to get it. What should be done?" People are just attached to these things. Do you think that you can achieve tranquility this way? It has been said: "When I come to this ordinary human society, it's just like checking into a hotel for a few days. Then I leave in a hurry." Some people are just obsessed with this place and have forgotten their own homes.

In genuine cultivation practice one must cultivate one's own heart and inner self. One should search inside oneself rather than outside. Some schools of practice say that Buddha is in one's heart, and this also has some truth. Some people have misunderstood this statement and say that Buddha is in their hearts, as though they themselves are Buddhas or their hearts have Buddha—they have understood it this way. Isn't that wrong? How can it be understood like that? It means that you must cultivate your heart if you are to succeed in cultivation—it tells this principle. How can there be a Buddha in your body? You must practice cultivation to succeed.

The reason that you cannot achieve tranquility is that your mind is not empty and you have not reached that high a level. It should move from shallow to deep in accordance with the level of your improvement. When you give up attachments, your level will be upgraded, and your ability to concentrate will also improve. If you want to achieve tranquility through some techniques or methods, I would call this searching for external help. In qigong practice, however, going awry and following an evil way simply refer to people searching for external help. With Buddhism in particular, if you search for external help, you are said to have taken a demonic way. In genuine cultivation practice one must cultivate the heart: Only when you upgrade your xinxing can your mind be clean and free of pursuits. Only when your xinxing is upgraded may you assimilate to the characteristic of the universe and remove different human desires, attachments, and other bad things. Only then will you be able to abandon the bad things in yourself and ascend so that you will not be restricted by the characteristic of the universe. Then, the substance of de can be transformed into gong. Don't they complement each other? It is just such a principle!

This is the reason why one is unable to achieve tranquility, as one subjectively cannot meet a practitioner's standard. At present, there is also an objective situation that seriously interferes with your practicing cultivation toward higher levels, and it seriously affects practitioners. Everyone knows that with the reforms and openness, the economy has become flexible and policies are also less restrictive. Many new technologies have been introduced, and people's living standard has improved. All everyday people think that it is a good thing. But things should be looked at dialectically, in both ways. With the reforms and openness, bad things of different forms have also been imported. If a piece of literary work is not written with some pornography, the book seems unable to sell since the issue of sales quantity is involved. If movies and television programs do not show footage of bedroom scenes, in terms of the audience ratings no one seems to watch them. As for artwork, nobody can tell whether it is genuine art or something else. There were no such things in our ancient Chinese traditional arts. The traditions of our Chinese nationality were not invented or created by any one person. In addressing prehistoric culture, I mentioned that everything has its origin. Human moral values have been distorted and changed. The standard that measures good and bad has all changed. That is the affairs of everyday people. Yet this universe's characteristic, Zhen-Shan-Ren, remains unchanged as the sole criterion to differentiate good and bad persons. As a practitioner, if you want to rise above and beyond, you must use this criterion—not the standard of everyday people—to assess things. Thus, there is this objective interference. There is more to it, such as homosexuality, sexual freedom, and drug abuse.

When human society has developed to this step today, think about it: What will happen if it goes on like this? Can it be allowed to exist like this forever? If humankind does not do something about it, heaven will. Whenever humankind experiences catastrophes, it is always under such conditions. With so many lectures, I have not brought up the issue of humankind's great catastrophes. This hot topic has been discussed in religions and by many people. I am raising this question to everyone, so think about it, everyone: In our ordinary human society, the human moral standard has undergone such a change! Tensions among one another have reached such an extent! Don't you think that it's come to an extremely dangerous point? Therefore, this present, objectively existing environment also seriously interferes with our practitioners' cultivation toward higher levels. Nude pictures are displayed right over there, hanging in the middle of the street. Once you look up, you will see them.

Lao Zi once made this statement: "When a wise person hears the Tao, this person will practice it diligently." When a wise person learns of the Tao, this person will think that it is not easy to obtain the orthodox Fa. Why wait and not start the practice today? The complex environment, in my view, is instead a good thing. The more complex it is, the greater the persons it will produce. If one can elevate oneself above and beyond it, one's cultivation will be the most solid.

For a practitioner who is truly determined to practice cultivation, I would say that it turns out to be a good thing. Without conflicts arising or opportunities to improve your xinxing, you cannot make progress. If everyone is nice to each other, how do you practice cultivation? As for one who is an average practitioner, one is "an average person who hears the Tao," and one for whom it will be fine to either practice or not practice cultivation; perhaps this person will not succeed. Some people who are here listening find what Teacher says reasonable. Upon returning to ordinary human society, they will still think that those immediate gains are more practical and real. They are real. Not only you, but also many Western millionaires and wealthy people have discovered that there is nothing left after death. Material wealth does not come with birth, nor will it go with you after death—they are very hollow. Yet, why is gong so precious? This is because it is attached to the body of your yuanshen, and it comes with you at birth and goes with you after death. We have said that one's yuanshen does not become extinct, and this is not a superstition. After the cells in our physical bodies have degenerated, the particles smaller than cells in other physical dimensions have not become extinct. Only a shell has come off.

All of what I have just addressed belongs to the issue of one's xinxing. Sakyamuni once made this statement, as did Boddhidarma: "This oriental land of China is a place where people of great virtues are produced." Throughout history, many monks and a lot of Chinese people have been very proud about this; it seems to suggest that they can cultivate high-level gong, and thus many people are pleased and feel flattered: "After all, it has to be our Chinese people. The land of China can produce people of great inborn qualities and great virtues." In fact, many people have not understood the meaning behind it. Why does the land of

China produce people of great virtues and high-level gong? Many people do not understand the genuine meaning of what those high-level people have said, nor do they understand the realm or mindset of those people at higher levels and in lofty realms. Of course, we have said that we will not point out what it means. Think about it, everyone: Only by being among the most complex group of people and in the most complex environment can one cultivate the high-level gong—it implies this.

Inborn Quality

One's inborn quality is determined by the amount of the substance de in one's body of another dimension. With less de and more black substance, one's karmic field will be large. In that case, one is of poor inborn quality. With a lot of de or the white substance, one's karmic field will be small. Accordingly, this person is of good inborn quality. One's white substance and black substance can be mutually transformed. How are they converted? Doing good deeds produces the white substance, as the white substance is obtained through enduring hardships, suffering miseries, or doing good deeds. The black substance is produced by doing wrong and bad deeds, and it is karma. It undergoes such a transformational process. Meanwhile, it also has a carry-over relationship. Because it follows one's yuanshen directly, it is not something from one lifetime, but is accumulated from a remote age. Therefore, people talk about the accumulation of karma and the buildup of de. In addition, they can be passed down from ancestors. Sometimes, I recall what ancient Chinese people or elderly people have said: "One's ancestors have accumulated de. Accumulate de or lose de." That was said so correctly! It is very right, indeed.

A person's good or poor inborn quality can determine whether his enlightenment quality is good or poor. One with poor inborn quality can also become one with very poor enlightenment quality. Why is this? It is because one with good inborn quality has a lot of the white substance that is assimilated to our universe and to the characteristic Zhen-Shan-Ren without any barrier. The characteristic of the universe can manifest directly in your body and be in immediate contact with your body. But black substance is just the opposite. As it is obtained by doing wrong deeds, it goes the opposite way from our universe's characteristic. Therefore, this black substance becomes separated from the characteristic of our universe. When this black substance accumulates to a great amount, it will form a field surrounding one's body and wrap one up inside. The larger the field, the higher its density and thickness, and this will make one's enlightenment quality become worse. This is because one is unable to receive the universe's characteristic of Zhen-Shan-Ren, as one has acquired the black substance by doing wrong deeds. Usually, it is harder for such a person to believe in cultivation practice. The poorer his enlightenment quality, the greater the karmic resistance he will encounter. The more hardships he suffers, the less he will believe it and the harder it will be for him to practice cultivation.

It is easier for someone with a lot of the white substance to practice cultivation. This is because in the course of cultivation, as long as this person is assimilated to the characteristic of the universe and his xinxing improves, his de will be transformed directly into gong. For someone with a lot of the black substance, however, there is an additional procedure. It is like a product that a factory makes: Others all come with ready-made material, while this person comes with raw material that needs to be processed.

It has to go through this process. Therefore, he must first suffer hardships and eliminate karma, so as to transform it into the white substance, forming this substance of de. Only then can he develop the high-level gong. But such a person usually does not have a good inborn enlightenment quality. If you ask him to suffer more, he will believe it less and it will be harder for him to endure it. Therefore, it is difficult for someone with a lot of the black substance to practice cultivation. In the past, the Tao School or a school of practice that taught only one disciple required that the master search for a disciple instead of vice versa. It was also determined by how much of these things this disciple's body carried.

Inborn quality determines one's enlightenment quality, but this is not absolute. Some people do not have very good inborn quality, but their home environment is very good; many family members practice cultivation. Some of them are also religious believers and believe very much in the matter of cultivation practice. In this environment, one can be made to believe in it, and this enables enlightenment quality to improve. So it is not absolute. Some people have very good inborn quality, but due to their being educated with that tiny bit of knowledge from our practical society, and especially because of the absolute methods in ideological education a few years ago, they have been made very narrow-minded and will not believe anything beyond their knowledge. This can seriously affect their enlightenment quality.

For example, I taught tianmu opening on the second day of a class. Right away, one person with good inborn quality had his tianmu opened at a very high level. He saw numerous scenes that many other people could not see. He told others: "Wow, I saw

363

Falun falling like snow flakes on the audience's bodies throughout the whole auditorium. I saw what Teacher Li's real body looks like, Teacher Li's halo, what Falun looks like, and how many fashen there are." He saw that Teacher was giving lectures at different levels and how Falun were adjusting practitioners' bodies. He also saw that during the lecture it was Teacher's *gongshen*[1] that was giving a lecture at each different level. In addition, he saw the heavenly beauties casting flowers about, and so on. He saw some things as wonderful as this, indicating that his inborn quality was quite good. As he went on and on, in the end he said: "I don't believe these things." Some of these things have already been verified by science, and many things can also be explained by modern science; we have discussed some of them as well. This is because what qigong understands is indeed beyond the understanding of modern science—this is for sure. In this view, one's inborn quality does not entirely determine one's enlightenment quality.

Enlightenment

What is "enlightenment?" "Enlightenment" is a term from religion. In Buddhism, it refers to a practitioner's understanding of the Buddhist Dharma, the enlightenment in terms of understanding, and the ultimate enlightenment. It means the enlightenment of wisdom. Nevertheless, it is already applied to everyday people nowadays. It suggests that this person is very smart and can read what is on his boss' mind. He can learn things quickly and know how to please his boss. People call that good enlightenment quality, and it is usually understood this way. Once

---

[1] *gongshen* (gong-shuhn)—a body made of gong.

364

you rise slightly higher above the level of everyday people, however, you will find that the principles at this level, as understood by everyday people, are usually wrong. This is not at all the enlightenment that we refer to. Instead, the enlightenment quality of a smart person is not good, because a person who is overly smart will only do superficial work in order to be appreciated by his boss or supervisor. In that case, won't the actual work be done by somebody else? Accordingly, this person will owe others. Because he is smart and knows how to please others, he will gain more profits while others will suffer more losses. Because he is smart, he will not suffer any losses, nor will he easily lose anything. Consequently, others must suffer losses. The more he cares for this tiny bit of practical gain, the more narrow-minded he becomes, and the more he feels that material gains of everyday people are something one cannot drop. Furthermore, he finds himself being very practical, and he will not suffer any losses.

Some people even envy this person! I am telling you not to envy him. You do not know what a tiring life he leads: He cannot eat or sleep well; he fears losing self-interest even in dreams, and he will go all out for personal gain. Wouldn't you say that he leads a tiring life, as his entire life is dedicated to that? We say that when you take a step back in a conflict, you will find the seas and the skies boundless, and it will certainly be another situation. A person like that will not give in, however, and leads the most tiring life. You should not learn from him. It is said in the community of cultivators: "Such a person is completely lost. He is totally lost among everyday people over material benefits." It will not be so easy to ask him to preserve de! If you ask him to practice cultivation, he will not believe you: "Practice cultivation? As practitioners, you won't fight back when you're beaten or sworn at. When others give you a hard time, instead of treating it the same way as they do in your mind, you turn around to express your gratitude. You've all become Ah Q! All of you are mentally ill!" As for such a person, there is no way for him to understand cultivation practice. He will say that you are inconceivable and foolish. Wouldn't you say that he is difficult to save?

This is not the enlightenment that we refer to. Rather, it is what this person calls "foolish" in terms of self-interest, and that is the enlightenment we have talked about. Of course, such a person is not really foolish. We simply treat the issue of personal, vested interests with indifference, while in other areas we are very wise. In terms of conducting scientific research projects or carrying out assignments from our supervisors or other duties, we are very clear-minded and perform them very well. Only in terms of our personal benefits or our interpersonal conflicts will we care less. Who will call you foolish? Nobody will say that you are foolish—it's guaranteed to be so.

Let us talk about a truly foolish person, for this principle is totally reversed at higher levels. A foolish person is unlikely to do major wrongdoings among everyday people, nor is he likely to compete and fight for self-interest. He does not seek fame nor lose de, but others will give him de. Beating him up and swearing at him will both give de to him, and this substance is extremely valuable. In our universe, there is this principle: no loss, no gain. To gain, one must lose. When others see this very foolish person, they will all verbally abuse him: "You're such a fool." With this verbal abuse, a piece of de will be thrown over there. By taking advantage of him, you are the gaining side, so you must lose something. If one walks over and kicks him: "You're such a big idiot." Well, a big chunk of de will again be tossed to him. When someone bullies or kicks him, he will only smile: "Come on. You're giving me de all the same, and I'm not going to reject a bit of it!" Then, according to the principles at higher levels, think about it, who's smart? Isn't this person smart? He is the smartest one, as he does not lose any de. When you toss de to this person, he does not reject a bit of it whatsoever. He will take all of it and accept it with a smile. He may be foolish in this life, but not in the next—his yuanshen is not foolish. It is said in religion that with a lot of de, a person will become a high-ranking official or make a big fortune in the next lifetime; both of these are exchanged for one's de.

We have said that de can be directly transformed into gong. Doesn't the height of your cultivation level come from transforming this de? It can be transformed directly into gong. Isn't the gong that determines one's level and energy potency transformed with this substance? Wouldn't you say that it's very precious? It can come with birth and go with death. It is said in Buddhism that your cultivation level is your Fruit Status. However much you sacrifice, however much you will gain—it is just such a principle. It is said in religion that with de one can become a high-ranking official or make a big fortune in the next life. With little de, one will have a hard time even begging for food because there is no de to exchange. No loss, no gain! Without any de, one would become extinct in terms of both body and soul; one would be really dead.

In the past, there was a qigong master whose level was very high when he first came to the public. This qigong master later became obsessed with fame and interests. His master took away his fu yuanshen since he also belonged to those people who cultivate fu yuanshen. When his fu yuanshen was still around, he was controlled by his fu yuanshen. For instance, one day his workplace gave out an apartment unit. The supervisor said: "All those in need of the apartment come here to describe your conditions and explain why each of you needs the apartment." Everyone provided their own reasons while this person did not say a word. In the end, the supervisor found that this person had a greater need for it than others, and that the apartment should be given to him. Other people claimed: "No, the apartment shouldn't be given to him. It should be given to me because I need the apartment badly." This person said: "Then you can go ahead and take it." An everyday person would see him as foolish. Some people knew that he was a practitioner and asked him: "As a practitioner, you don't want anything. What do you want?" He responded: "Whatever others don't want, I'd like to have that." Actually, he was not foolish at all and was quite bright. Only in terms of personal, vested interests, would he be like this. He believed in following the course of nature. Others asked him again: "What doesn't a person want these days?" He replied: "No one wants the piece of stone on the ground, which is kicked here and there. So I'll pick it up." Everyday people find it inconceivable and cannot understand a practitioner. They cannot understand it, as their spiritual realms are far apart and the gap between their levels is also too great. Of course, he was not about to pick up that stone. He told a principle that an everyday person cannot comprehend: "I won't seek anything among everyday people." Let us talk about the stone. You know that it is written in Buddhist scriptures: "In the Paradise of Ultimate Bliss, the trees are made of gold, and so are the ground, birds, flowers, and houses. Even the Buddha-body is golden and shiny." One cannot find a piece of stone there. The currency used over there is said to be stones. He would not go there and carry a piece of stone, but he told this principle that an everyday person cannot comprehend. Indeed, practitioners will say: "Ordinary people have their pursuits, and we don't seek them. As for what ordinary people have, we also aren't interested. Yet what we have is something that ordinary people cannot obtain, even if they want to."

Actually, the enlightenment we just addressed is still one that concerns the course of cultivation practice, and this is exactly opposite to that of everyday people. The enlightenment that we really refer to is a matter of whether in the course of cultivation practice one can be enlightened to and accept the Fa taught by the master or the Tao taught by the Taoist master, whether one treats oneself as a practitioner upon encountering tribulations, and whether one can follow the Fa while practicing cultivation. As for some people, no matter how you tell them about it, they still will not believe and will think that it is more practical to be everyday persons. They will hold on to their stubborn beliefs rather than relinquish them, and this renders them unable to believe. Some people only want to heal illnesses. Once I mention here that qigong is not used to heal illnesses whatsoever, their minds will react negatively and, therefore, they will not believe what is taught later.

Some people just cannot improve their enlightenment quality. They casually make marks in my book. Those of our practitioners with tianmu open can each see that this book looks very colorful, golden, and shiny. Each word bears the image of my fashen. If I tell lies, I will be deceiving everyone. That mark you made looks very dark. How do you dare to casually make marks in it? What are we doing here? Aren't we bringing you to practice cultivation toward higher levels? There are things you should also think about. This book can guide your cultivation practice. Don't you think it's precious? Can you truly practice cultivation by worshipping

369

the Buddha? You are very reverent and dare not even lightly touch that Buddha statue for which you burn incense daily, yet you dare to ruin the Dafa that can truly guide your cultivation practice.

Speaking of the issue of one's enlightenment quality, this refers to the depth of your understanding of something that occurs at different levels in the course of cultivation practice, or of a certain Fa that the master has taught. Yet, this still is not the fundamental enlightenment that we refer to. The fundamental enlightenment that we talk about refers to this: In one's lifetime, from the outset of cultivation practice one will constantly move up and let go of human attachments and various desires, and one's gong will also constantly grow until the final step in cultivation practice. When this de substance has completely transformed into gong and this person's cultivation journey designed by the master has come to an end, "Boom!" all locks will be exploded open at that very second. His tianmu will reach the highest point of his level, and he can see at his level the truth of different dimensions, the forms of existence for different lives and matter in different time-spaces, and the truth of our universe. All of his divine powers will emerge, and he can contact different kinds of lives. By this time, isn't this person a great enlightened person or a person enlightened through cultivation practice? When translated into ancient Indian language, he is a Buddha.

The enlightenment that we refer to is this fundamental enlightenment that belongs to the sudden enlightenment form. Sudden enlightenment means that a person is locked during his lifelong cultivation, and he does not know how high his gong level is or in what form his cultivated gong appears. He does not feel anything at all, and all the cells in his body are even locked. The gong that he has cultivated is locked until the final step, and

370

only then can it be released. Only someone with great inborn quality can do it, as this cultivation practice is quite painful. One must begin by being a good person. One should always improve xinxing, always suffer hardships, ascend constantly in cultivation, and always seek to upgrade xinxing, even though one cannot see one's own gong. Cultivating is most difficult for such a person, and he or she must be someone with great inborn quality. This person will practice cultivation for many years without knowing anything.

There is another form of enlightenment called gradual enlightenment. From the very beginning, many people have felt the rotation of Falun. At the same time, I have also opened everyone's tianmu. For various reasons, some people will be able to see things in the future, if not now. They will be able to go from seeing things vaguely to seeing more clearly, and they will go from having been unable to use it to knowing how to use it. One's level will constantly rise. As your xinxing improves and different attachments are abandoned, all your different supernormal capabilities will develop. The entire transformation process of cultivation practice and the transformation process of the body will all occur under the circumstance that you can see or feel them. The changes will continue until the final step when you can fully understand the truth of the universe, and when you have reached the highest expected point in cultivation. The transformation of benti and the reinforcement of supernormal capabilities will have each reached a certain degree and will gradually achieve this goal. This is gradual enlightenment. This cultivation method of gradual enlightenment also is not easy. With supernormal capabilities, some people cannot give up their attachments and will easily show off or do some bad deeds. You will thus lose gong, and your cultivation practice will be in vain and end up in ruins. Some people can observe and see the manifestation of different lives at different levels. One may ask you to do this or that. That person may ask you to practice his things and take you as his disciple, but he cannot help you achieve the Right Fruit since he, too, has not attained the Right Fruit.

Additionally, all beings in higher dimensions are immortals who can become very large and fully display their supernatural powers. If your mind is not upright, won't you follow them? Once you follow them, your cultivation practice will end up in vain. Even if that being is a genuine Buddha or a genuine Tao, you still must start cultivation practice all over again. Aren't they still immortals no matter from which levels of heaven they come? Only when one reaches a very high level of cultivation and achieves the goal can one completely rise above and beyond. To an ordinary person, however, an immortal can surely appear tall, giant, and very capable. Yet that being might not have attained the Right Fruit, either. With the interference of various messages and the distraction of various scenes, can you remain undisturbed? Therefore, it is also difficult to practice cultivation with tianmu open, and it is harder to control your xinxing well. Fortunately, however, many of our practitioners will have their supernormal capabilities unlocked half-way through their cultivation process, and they will then reach the state of gradual enlightenment. Everyone's tianmu will be opened, but many people's supernormal capabilities are not allowed to come forth. When your xinxing gradually reaches a certain level and you can conduct yourself well with a steady mind, they will be exploded open all at once. At a certain level, you will enter the state of gradual enlightenment, and at this time it will be easier for you to conduct yourself well.

Different supernormal capabilities will all come forth. You will move up in cultivation on your own until, in the end, all of them are unlocked. You will be allowed to have them half-way through your cultivation practice. Many of our practitioners belong to this group, so you should not be anxious to see things.

Everyone may have heard that Zen Buddhism also speaks of the differences between sudden enlightenment and gradual enlightenment. Huineng, the sixth patriarch in Zen Buddhism, taught sudden enlightenment while Shenxiu[2] from the Northern School of Zen Buddhism taught gradual enlightenment. The dispute between the two on Buddhist studies has lasted a very long time in history. I call it meaningless. Why? It is because what they referred to was only the understanding of a principle in the process of cultivation practice. As to this principle, some may understand it all at once, while others may comprehend and understand it gradually. Does it matter how one understands? It is better if one can understand it all at once, but it is also fine if one gradually understands it. Aren't both enlightened? Both are enlightened, so neither is wrong.

People with Great Inborn Quality

What is a person with "great inborn quality?" There are still differences between somebody with great inborn quality and somebody with good or poor inborn quality. It is extremely difficult to find someone with great inborn quality, as it will take a very long historical period for such a person to be born. Of

---

[2] Shenxiu (shuhn-shyo)—founder of the Northern School of Zen Buddhism in the Tang Dynasty.

course, a person with great inborn quality must first have a great amount of de and a very large field of this white substance—this is certain. Meanwhile, this person should also be able to endure the toughest hardships of all. He must have a mind of great forbearance, too, and be able to sacrifice. He must be able to preserve de as well, have good enlightenment quality, and so on.

What is the toughest hardship of all? It is believed in Buddhism that to be human is to suffer—as long as you are human beings, you must suffer. It believes that lives in all other dimensions do not have our ordinary human bodies. They therefore will not become ill, nor will there be the problems of birth, old age, illness, and death. There would not be such suffering to begin with. People in other dimensions can levitate, as they are weightless and very wonderful. Because of this body, everyday people will encounter this problem: They cannot stand being cold, hot, thirsty, hungry, or tired, and yet they will still have birth, old age, illness, and death. In any case, one will not be comfortable.

I read in a newspaper that at the time of the earthquake in Tangshan,[3] many people died from the earthquake, but some were rescued. A special society survey was conducted with this group of people. They were asked: "How did you feel in the state of death?" Surprisingly, these people all spoke in agreement of the same unique situation. Namely, at the very moment of death they did not feel scared; on the contrary, they suddenly felt a sense of relief, with some sort of subconscious excitement. Some people felt free from the bondage of the body and could levitate very lightly and wonderfully; they were also able to see their own bodies. Some people could also see lives in other dimensions,

---

[3] Tangshan (tahng-shahn)—a city in Hebei Province.

374

and still others had gone somewhere else. All of them mentioned a sense of relief at that very moment, and of some sort of subconscious excitement without any feeling of suffering. This suggests that with this human flesh body, one will suffer, but since everyone comes from the mother's womb this way, nobody knows this is suffering.

I have mentioned that one must suffer the toughest hardships of all. The other day I said that humankind's time-space concept is different from that in another, larger time-space. Here, one shichen is two hours, which is a year in that space. If a person practices cultivation in this harsh condition, he will be considered truly remarkable. When this person develops the heart for the Tao and wants to practice cultivation, he is just simply great. With such hardships, he still has not lost his original nature and wants to return to the origin through cultivation practice. Why can practitioners be helped unconditionally? It is just because of this. When this person sits in meditation for one night in this dimension of everyday people, upon seeing this, others will say that he is really remarkable as he has already sat there for six years. This is because one shichen of ours equals one year over there. Our humankind's dimension is an extremely unique one.

How does one endure the toughest hardships of all? For instance, one day a person goes to work and the workplace is not doing well. This situation can no longer continue as people are not doing their jobs. The workplace will be reformed and use contract workers. Surplus staff will be laid off, and this person is one of those whose rice bowls are suddenly taken away. How will he feel? There are no other places to earn an income. How can he make a living? He does not have any other skills, so he sadly goes home. As soon as he arrives home, an elderly parent at home is ill and in serious condition. Getting worried, he will hurry to take the elderly parent to a hospital. He will go through a lot of trouble to borrow money for the hospitalization. He will then return home to prepare something for the elderly parent. As soon as he comes home, a school teacher will come knocking at the door: "Your child has injured someone in a fight, and you should hurry up and take a look." Soon after he takes care of that matter and comes back home, just as he is sitting down, a phone call will come, telling him: "Your spouse is having an affair with someone." Of course, you will not run into such a scenario. An ordinary person cannot stand suffering such hardships and will think: "What am I living for? Why don't I find a rope to hang myself and put an end to everything?" I am just saying that one must be able to suffer the toughest hardships of all. Of course, they might not assume this form. Nevertheless, conflicts among one another, frictions in xinxing, and competition for personal gain are things no easier than those problems. Many people just live to prove their points and will hang themselves when they cannot deal with things anymore. Therefore, we must practice cultivation in this complex environment and be able to endure the toughest hardships of all. Meanwhile, we must have a mind of great forbearance.

What is a "mind of great forbearance?" As a practitioner, the first thing you should be able to do is to not fight back when you are beaten or sworn at—you must be tolerant. Otherwise, what kind of practitioner will you be? Someone says: "It's really hard to be tolerant, and I've got a bad temper." If your temper is not good, you should change it, for a practitioner must be tolerant. Some people will lose their temper in disciplining children and yell at them, making quite a scene. You should not be that way in disciplining children, nor should you yourselves get really upset.

You should educate children with reason so that you can really teach them well. If you cannot even get over a trifle and lose your temper easily, how can you expect to increase your gong? Someone says: "If someone kicks me while I'm walking down the street and no one around knows me, I can tolerate it." I say that this is not good enough. Perhaps in the future you may be slapped in the face twice, and you will lose face in front of someone whom you least want to see it. It is to see how you will deal with this issue and whether you can endure it. If you can tolerate it and yet it preys on your mind, it is still not good enough. As you know, when a person reaches the Arhat level, in his heart he is not concerned about anything. He does not care at all in his heart for any ordinary human matter, and he will always be smiling and in good spirits. No matter how much loss he suffers, he will still be smiling and in good spirits without any concern. If you can really do this, you have already reached the entry-level Fruit Status of Arhatship.

Someone has said: "If tolerance is practiced to such an extent, everyday people will all say that we are too cowardly and too easily taken advantage of." I do not call it being cowardly. Think about it, everyone: Even among everyday people, the middle-aged or older people and those with high-level education also exercise self-restraint and refrain from disputing with others, let alone our practitioners. How can it be taken as being cowardly? I say that it is the manifestation of great forbearance and an expression of strong will. Only a practitioner can have this mind of great forbearance. There is such a saying: "When an ordinary person is humiliated, he'll draw his sword to fight." For an ordinary person, it is only natural that if you swear at me I will swear at you, and that if you hit me I will hit you back as well. That is an ordinary person. Can he be called a practitioner? As a practitioner, without strong will and self-restraint, you will not be able to do this.

You know that in ancient times there was a man called Han Xin,[4] who was said to be very capable as a senior general for Liu Bang[5] and the backbone of the country. Why did he have those great achievements? It was said that Han Xin was an unusual person, even at a young age. There is a story about Han Xin, which says that he suffered the humiliation of crawling between someone's legs. Han Xin liked to practice martial arts in his youth, and a martial artist would usually carry a sword. One day as he was walking down the street, a local ruffian blocked his way with his hands on his waist: "What do you carry that sword for? Do you dare to kill someone? If you do, cut off my head." As he was talking, he stuck out his head. Han Xin thought: "Why should I cut off your head?" At that time killing someone would also be reported to the government and one would have to repay the life. How could one kill somebody at will? When the ruffian saw that Han Xin did not dare to kill him, he said: "If you don't dare to kill me, you'll have to crawl between my legs." Han Xin indeed crawled between his two legs. This showed that Han Xin had a mind of great forbearance. Because he was different from everyday people, he could accomplish those great achievements. It is an ordinary person's motto that one should live to prove one's point. Think about it, everyone: Living to prove one's point—isn't it tiring? Isn't it painful? Is it worthwhile? Han Xin was an everyday person after all. As practitioners, we should be much better than he. Our goal is to rise above and beyond the

---

[4] Han Xin (hahn-sheen)—the leading general for Liu Bang.

[5] Liu Bang (leo bahng)—the emperor and founder of the Han Dynasty (206 B.C.-23 A.D.).

level of ordinary people and to strive toward higher levels. We will not run into that situation. Yet the humiliations and embarrassment that a practitioner suffers among everyday people are not necessarily easier than that. Xinxing tensions among one another are not any easier than that and will be even worse, as they are also quite tough.

Meanwhile, a practitioner should also be able to make sacrifices, abandoning different attachments and desires of everyday people. It is impossible to be able to do it all at once, so we can make it gradually. If you could make it today, you would now be a Buddha. Cultivation practice takes time, but you should not slack off. You may say: "Teacher has said that cultivation practice takes time—let's do it slowly." That will not do! You must be strict with yourself. In cultivation of the Buddha Fa, you should strive forward vigorously.

You must also be able to preserve de, maintain your xinxing, and not do things at will. You should not casually do whatever you want, and you must be able to maintain your xinxing. Among everyday people, this statement is often heard: "Doing good deeds accumulates de." A practitioner does not practice to accumulate de, as we believe in preserving de. Why do we believe in preserving de? It is because we have seen this situation: Accumulating de is what everyday people believe, as they want to accumulate de and do good deeds so that they can live well in the next life. But we do not have this issue. If you succeed in cultivation practice, you will attain the Tao and there will not be the issue of your next life. When we talk about preserving de here, it has another shade of meaning. Namely, these two substances carried in our bodies are not accumulated in one lifetime—they are inherited from a remote age. Though you could ride a bike all over the city, you might not run into some good deeds to perform. Though you could go about things this way everyday, you might not encounter such opportunities.

It carries still another shade of meaning: In trying to accumulate de, you may think that something is a good deed, but if you do it, it may turn out to be a wrong deed. When you think that something is a wrong deed, but if you interfere with it, it may turn out to be a good thing. Why? It is because you cannot see its karmic relationship. Laws regulate the affairs of everyday people, which is not a problem. Being a practitioner is supernormal, so as a supernormal person, you must conduct yourself with supernormal principles instead of measuring yourself with those of everyday people. If you do not know the karmic relationship of a matter, you can easily commit an error when handling it. Therefore, we teach wuwei, and you should not do something just because you want to. Some people say: "I just want to discipline bad people." I would say that you are best off becoming a policeman. But, we are not asking you to stay out of things when you encounter a murder or a fire. I am telling everyone that when an interpersonal conflict occurs or when one kicks or hits someone else, it is likely that these people owed each other in the past, and they are clearing the debt. If you step in to stop it, they will not be able to clear the debt and must wait to do it again the next time. This means that if you cannot see the karmic relationship, you can easily do bad deeds and lose de as a consequence.

It does not matter if an everyday person gets involved in the affairs of everyday people, as he or she will apply the principles of everyday people to size things up. You must use the supernormal principles to look at things. It is a xinxing issue if you do not help stop a murder or a fire when you see it. How will you otherwise demonstrate that you are a good person? If you do not help stop a murder or a fire, with what else will you get involved? Yet, there is one point to be made: These things really do not have anything to do with our practitioners. They might not be arranged for you to run into. We have said that preserving de enables you to avoid making mistakes. Perhaps if you do a little of something, you may do a bad deed, and then you will lose de. Once you lose de, how can you upgrade your level? How can you achieve your ultimate goal? It involves such issues. In addition, one must have good enlightenment quality. Good inborn quality can make one have good enlightenment quality. The impact of environment can also have an effect.

We have also said that if every one of us cultivates the inner self, examines our own xinxing to look for the causes of wrongdoing so as to do better next time, and considers others first when taking any action, human society will become better and the moral values will return to a higher standard. The spiritual civilization will also become better, and so will public security. Perhaps there will not be any police. No one will need to be governed, as everyone will discipline himself or herself and search their inner self. Wouldn't you say this would be great? Everyone knows that laws are becoming more comprehensive and impeccable. Yet why are there people who still do bad deeds? Why don't they comply with the laws? It is because you cannot govern their hearts. When they are not seen, they will still do bad deeds. If everyone cultivates the inner self, it will be totally different. There will not be a need for you to fight injustice.

This Fa can only be taught to this level. It is up to your own cultivation to attain what is at higher levels. The questions raised by some people have become more specific. If I explain all the questions in your life, what will be left for you to cultivate? You must practice cultivation and become enlightened on your own. If I tell you everything, nothing will remain for you to cultivate. Fortunately, Dafa has already been made public, and you can do things according to Dafa.

*   *   *

I think that my time for teaching the Fa has virtually come to a close. Therefore, I want to leave genuine things for everyone so that there is Fa to guide everyone in future cultivation practice. Throughout the entire course of teaching this Fa, I have been responsible to everyone and, at the same time, to society. In fact, we have also been following this principle. Whether it is done well or poorly, I will not comment and will leave it to public opinion. My intention is to make this Dafa public and have more of our people benefited, enabling those who truly want to practice cultivation to advance in their cultivation practice by following the Fa. At the same time as teaching the Fa, we have also explained the principles of being a person, and hope that if after the class you cannot follow this Dafa to practice cultivation, you will at least become a good person. This way, you will benefit our society. In fact, you already know how to be a good person. After the class, you will also become a good person.

In the course of teaching the Fa, there have also been things that have not gone smoothly, and different kinds of interference have been quite enormous. Because of the great support from the hosting organization, administrators in different professions, and the efforts from staff members, our classes have been quite a success.

All of what I have addressed in the lectures is for guiding everyone to practice cultivation toward higher levels. In the past, no one taught these things in their instruction. What we have taught is very explicit and has incorporated modern science and contemporary science of the human body. In addition, what has been taught is at a very high level. It is primarily intended to enable everyone to truly obtain the Fa in the future and ascend through cultivation practice—this is my starting point. In the course of teaching the Fa and gong, many people have also found the Fa very good, but very difficult to follow. Actually, I think it depends on the person as to whether it is difficult or not. For an everyday person who does not want to practice cultivation, he will find cultivation practice simply too difficult, inconceivable, or impossible. As an everyday person, he does not want to practice cultivation and will find it very difficult. Lao Zi said: "When a wise person hears the Tao, this person will practice it diligently. When an average person hears it, this person will practice it on and off. When a low-level person hears it, this person will laugh at it loudly. If this person doesn't laugh at it loudly, it's not the Tao." To a genuine practitioner, I would say that it is very easy and not something too high to reach. In fact, many veteran practitioners sitting here or who are not present have already reached very high levels in their cultivation practice. I have not told you so, lest you develop some attachment or become complacent, as that will affect the development of your gongli. As a genuinely—determined practitioner, one will be able to endure everything and give up or care less for any attachment in the face of different vested interests. As long as one can do this, it will not be difficult. Those people find it difficult because they cannot let go of these things. Cultivation practice itself is not

383

difficult, nor is upgrading one's level itself difficult. It is because they cannot give up the human mind that they call it difficult. This is because it is very difficult to relinquish something in the face of practical gain. The vested interests are right here, so how can you abandon this attachment? It is actually because of this that one will find it difficult. When an interpersonal conflict occurs, if you cannot practice forbearance or treat yourself as a practitioner in dealing with it, I would say this is unacceptable. When I practiced cultivation in the past, many great masters told me these words, and they said: "When it's difficult to endure, you can endure it. When it's impossible to do, you can do it." In fact, that is how it is. After you return home, everyone can give it a try. When you are overcoming a real hardship or tribulation, you should give it a try. When it is difficult to endure, you try to endure. When it looks impossible and is said to be impossible, you give it a try and see if it is possible. If you can really make it, you will indeed find: "After passing the shady willow trees, there will be bright flowers and another village ahead!"

Because I have talked so much, it will be very difficult for everyone to remember with so many things mentioned. I will mainly make a few requirements: I hope that all of you will treat yourselves as practitioners in future cultivation practice and truly continue your cultivation practice. I hope that both veteran and new practitioners will be able to practice cultivation in Dafa and succeed in it! I hope that after going home everyone will make the best use of his or her time for genuine cultivation practice.

....

On the surface, <u>Zhuan Falun</u> is not elegant in terms of language. It may even not comply with modern grammar. If I were to use modern grammar to organize this book of Dafa, however, a serious problem would arise wherein though the structure of the book's language might be standard and elegant, it would not encompass a more profound and higher content. This is because modern, standardized terminology cannot express the guidance of Dafa at different higher levels and the manifestation of the Fa at each level; nor is it able to bring about practitioners' transformation of benti and gong, or other such fundamental changes.

....

Li Hongzhi
January 5, 1996

Glossary

Ah Q (ah cue) 阿Q   A foolish character in a Chinese novel.

Arhat 羅漢   Enlightened being with Fruit Status in the Buddha School and one who is beyond the "Three Realms."

asura 修羅道   "Malevolent spirits" (from Sanskrit).

Bagua (bah-gwa) 八卦   As a prehistoric diagram, it discloses the changes of the course of nature.

baihui (buy-hway) 百會   An acupuncture point located at the crown of one's head.

bairi feisheng (buy-rhe fay-shung) 白日飛升   A Taoist term for "levitation in broad daylight."

benti (bun-tee) 本體   One's physical body and the bodies in other dimensions.

Bian Que (b'yen-chueh) 扁鵲   A well-known doctor of Chinese medicine in history.

Big Lotus Flower Hand Sign 大蓮花手印   A hand posture for kaiguang.

bigu (bee-goo) 闢谷   "No grain"; an ancient term for abstinence from food and water.

Bodhisattva 菩薩   Enlightened being with Fruit Status in the Buddha School, and one who is higher than an Arhat and lower than a Tathagata.

386

Bodhisattva Avalokitesvara 觀音菩薩　Known for her compassion, she is one of the two senior Bodhisattvas in the Paradise of Ultimate Bliss.

Caocao (tsaow-tsaow) 曹操　Emperor of one of the Three Kingdoms (220 A.D.-265 A.D.).

Changchun (chahng-choon) 長春　Capital city of Jilin Province.

chi (chr) 尺　A Chinese unit of length (=1/3 meter).

Chongqing (chong-ching) 重慶　The most populated city in Southwestern China.

Chu-Shi-Jian-Fa 出世間法　"Beyond-Triple-World-Fa."

Da Ji (dah jee) 妲己　A wicked concubine of the last emperor in the Shang Dynasty (1765 B.C.-1122 B.C.). She is believed to have been possessed by a fox spirit and to have caused the fall of the Shang Dynasty.

Dafa (dah-fah) 大法　"Great law"; principles.

dan (dahn) 丹　Energy cluster in a cultivator's body, collected from other dimensions.

Dan Jing (dahn jing) 丹經　A classic Chinese text of cultivation practice.

dantian (dahn tien) 丹田　"Field of dan"; the lower abdominal area.

de (duh) 德　"Virtue"; a white substance.

Dharma 法　Buddha Sakyamuni's teachings.

Dharma-ending Period　According to Buddha Sakyamuni, Dharma-ending Period begins five hundred years after he passed away, and his Dharma could no longer save people thereafter.

Diamond Sutra 金剛經　A Buddhist scripture.

digging into a bull's horn 鑽牛角尖   A Chinese expression for going down a dead end.

ding (ding) 定   A state of empty, yet conscious mind.

the Eight Deities 八仙   Well-known Taos in Chinese history.

energy channels 脈   In Chinese medicine, they are said to be conduits of qi which comprise an intricate network for energy circulation.

Fa (fah) 法   Law and principles in the Buddha School.

fashen (fah-shun) 法身   "Law body"; a body made of gong and Fa.

fengshui (fung-shway) 風水   Chinese geomancy, a practice of reading landscapes.

Five Elements 五行   Metal, wood, water, fire, and earth.

fowei (fwuo-way) 佛位   The Buddha status.

Fruit Status 果位   One's level of attainment in the Buddha School, e.g. Arhat, Bodhisattva, Tathagata, etc.

futi (foo-tee) 附體   Spirit or animal that possesses a human body; spirit or animal possession.

fu yishi (foo yee-shr) 副意識   Secondary consciousness; fu yuanshen or secondary soul(s).

fu yuanshen (foo yu-en-shun) 副元神   Secondary soul(s); fu yishi or secondary consciousness.

"Great Cultural Revolution"   A communist political movement that denounced traditional values and culture (1966-1976).

gong (gong) 功   1. Cultivation energy; 2. practice that cultivates such energy.

gongli (gong-lee) 功力   "Energy potency."

gongshen (gong-shuhn) 功身   A body made of gong.

gongzhu (gong-jew) 功柱   An energy pole that grows above a practitioner's head.

Great Jade Emperor 玉皇大帝   In Chinese mythology, the deity that supervises the Three Realms.

guan (gwan) 關   "Pass."

guanding (gwan-ding) 灌頂   Pouring energy into the top of one's head; initiation ritual.

Guangdong (gwang-dong) 廣東   A province in Southern China.

Guangxi (gwang-shee) 廣西   A province in Southern China.

Guanyin (gwan-yeen) **sect** 觀音法門   A cult named after Bodhisattva Avalokitesvara, the "Goddess of Mercy."

Guiyang (gway-yahng) 貴陽   Capital of Guizhou Province.

Guizhou (gway-jhoe) 貴州   A province in Southwestern China.

Han (hahn) 漢   The majority ethnicity of Chinese people.

Han Xin (hahn-sheen) 韓信   A leading general for Liu Bang in the Han Dynasty (206 B.C.-23 A.D.).

heche (huh-chuh) 河車   "River vehicle."

hegu (huh-goo) 合谷   An acupuncture point on the dorsum of the hand.

Hetu (huh-too) 河圖   As a prehistoric diagram, it discloses the changes of the course of nature.

389

Hinayana 小乘佛教   "The Small Vehicle Buddhism."

Huangdi Neijing (hwang-dee nay-jing) 黃帝內經   Yellow Emperor's scripture for internal cultivation.

Huatuo (hwa-twoah) 華陀   A well-known doctor of Chinese medicine in history.

huiyin (hway-yeen) 會陰 An acupuncture point in the center of the perineum.

hun (huhn) 葷   Food that is forbidden in Buddhism.

Investiture of the Gods 封神演義   A classic work of Chinese fiction.

Iron Sand Palm, Cinnabar Palm, Vajra Leg, Arhat Foot   Types of Chinese martial arts techniques.

Jiang Ziya (jyang dzz-yah) 姜子牙   A character in Investiture of the Gods.

jie (jyeh) 劫   A number for hundreds of millions of years.

Jigong (jee-gong) 濟公   A well-known Buddhist monk in the Southern Song Dynasty (1127 A.D.-1279 A.D.).

Jinan (jee-nahn) 濟南   Capital of Shandong Province.

kaigong (kye-gong) 開功 The final release of cultivation energy; full enlightenment.

kaiguang (kye-gwang) 開光   "Light-opening"; in Buddhism, it is a consecration ritual to invite a Buddha to a Buddha statue or a Buddha portrait.

karma 業力   A black substance resulted from previous wrongdoing.

Lady Queen Mother 王母娘娘 In Chinese mythology, the highest-level female deity within the Three Realms.

Lao Zi (laow-dzz) 老子 Founder of the Tao School.

laogong (laow-gong) 勞宮 An acupuncture point at the center of the palm.

Last Havoc The community of cutivators holds that the universe has three phases of evolution (The Beginning Havoc, The Middle Havoc, The Last Havoc), and that now is the final period of The Last Havoc.

Lei Feng (lay-fung) 雷鋒 A Chinese moral exemplar in the 1960's.

li (lee) 里 A Chinese unit for distance (=0.5 km). In Chinese, "108 thousand li" is a common expression to describe a very far distance.

Li Shizhen (lee shr-jhun) 李時珍 A well-known doctor of Chinese medicine in history.

Lianhuase (l'yen-hwa-suh) 蓮花色 One of ten major female disciples of Buddha Sakyamuni.

Liu Bang (leo bahng) 劉邦 Emperor and founder of the Han Dynasty (206 B.C.-23 A.D.).

Lu Dongbin (lyu dong-bin) 呂洞賓 One of the Eight Deities in the Tao School.

Luoshu (luo-shew) 洛書 As a prehistoric diagram, it discloses the changes of the course of nature.

Mah Jong 麻將 A traditional Chinese game played by four people.

Mahayana 大乘佛教 "The Great Vehicle Buddhism."

maoyou (maow-yo) 卯酉　The borderline between yin and yang sides of the body.

Milky-White Body 奶白體　A purified body without qi.

Ming Dynasty 明朝　Period between 1368 A.D. and 1644 A.D. in Chinese history.

mingmen (ming-mun) 命門　"Gate of life"; an acupuncture point on the lower back and on the posterior midline.

mo ding (muh ding) 摸頂　As claimed by some qigong masters, touching the top of one's head to give energy.

Mujianlian (moo-j'yen-l'yen)　One of ten major male disciples of Buddha Sakyamuni.

Nanjing (nahn-jing) 南京　Capital of Jiangsu Province.

nirvana　(From Sanskrit) departing the human world without this physical body, the method of completing cultivation in Buddha Sakyamuni's School.

niwan palace 泥丸宮　A Taoist term for the pineal body.

pangmen zuodao (pahng-mun zuoh-dow) 旁門左道　"The side door and clumsy way."

Pure-White Body 淨白體　A transparent body at the highest level of Shi-Jian-Fa cultivation.

qi (chee) 氣　In Chinese culture, it is believed to be "vital energy"; but compared with gong, it is a lower form of energy .

qiankun (chyen-kuhn) 乾坤　"Heaven and earth."

Qianmen (chyen-mun) 前門　One of the major shopping districts in Beijing.

qigong (chee-gong) 氣功　A form of traditional Chinese practice which cultivates qi or "vital energy."

qiji (chee-jee) 氣機　"Energy mechanism."

Qimen (chee-mun) **School** 奇門功法　"Unconventional school".

Qin Hui (chin hway) 秦檜　A wicked official of the royal court in the Southern Song Dynasty (1127 A.D.-1279 A.D.).

Qingdao (ching-dow) 青島　A seaport city in Shandong Province.

Qiqihar (chee-chee-har) 齊齊哈爾　A city in Northeastern China.

Ren 忍　Endurance, forbearance, tolerance.

Right Fruit 正果　Attainment of Fruit Status in the Buddha School.

Sakyamuni 釋迦牟尼　The historical Buddha, Guatama Siddhartha.

samadhi 定　In Buddhism, "meditation in trance."

samsara 六道輪回　The six paths of reincarnation in Buddhism. (One may become a human being, an animal, a plant, or other forms of matter through reincarnation.)

sanhua juding (sahn-hwa jew-ding) 三花聚頂　"Three flowers gathered above a practitioner's head."

sarira 舍利子　Relics of a monk after cremation.

setting up a bodily crucible and furnace to make dan using gathered medicinal herbs　A Taoist metaphor for internal alchemy.

Shan (shahn) 善　Kindness, benevolence, compassion.

393

shangen (shahn-guhn) 山根　　An acupuncture point located between one's eyebrows.

Shen Gongbao (shun gong-baow) 申公豹　A jealous character in <u>Investiture of the Gods.</u>

<u>Shenxian Zhuan</u> (shuhn-shyen jwan) 神仙傳　A Chinese biography of Taoist deities.

Shenxiu (shuhn-shyo) 神秀　Founder of the Northern School of Zen Buddhism in the Tang Dynasty.

Shi-Jian-Fa (shr-jyen-fah) 世間法　"In-Triple-World-Fa"; Buddhism holds that one must go through samsara if one has not reached beyond the Triple-World-Fa or the Three Realms.

shichen (shr-chuhn) 時辰 A Chinese unit of time for two hours.

shishen (shr-shuhn) 識神 One's main soul.

Suming Tong (sue-ming tong) 宿命通　Precognition and retrocognition.

Sun Simiao (sun szz-meow) 孫思邈　A well-known doctor of Chinese medicine in history.

Sun Wukong 孫悟空　Also known as "Monkey King", a character in the classic work of Chinese fiction, <u>Journey to the West</u>.

svastikam　　"Wheel of light" from Sanskrit, the symbol dates back over 2,500 years and has been unearthed in cultural relics in Greece, Peru, India, and China. For centuries it has connoted good fortune, represented the sun, and been held in positive regard.

Taiji (tie-jee) 太極   The symbol of the Tao School.

Taiyuan (tie-yu-en) 太原 Capital city of Shangxi Province.

Tang (tahng) **Dynasty** 唐朝   One of the most prosperous periods in Chinese history (618 A.D.-907 A.D.).

Tangshan (tahng-shahn) 唐山   A city in Hebei Province.

Tantrism 密宗   An esoteric cultivation way in Buddhism.

tanzhong (tahn-jong) 檀中   An acupuncture point on the anterior midline of the chest.

Tao (daow) 道   1. Also known as "Dao," a Taoist term for "the Way of nature and the universe"; 2. enlightened being who has achieved this Tao.

Tao Tsang (daow-zang) 道藏   A classic Chinese text of cultivation practice.

Tathagata 如來   Enlightened being with Fruit Status in the Buddha School who is above the levels of Bodhisattva and Arhat.

the world of ten directions 十方世界   A Buddhist conception of the universe.

tian (t'yen) 田   "Field."

Tiananmen 天安門   The Gate of Heavenly Peace in front of the Forbidden City in Beijing.

tianmu (t'yen-moo) 天目 "Heavenly eye," also known as the "third eye."

tianzi zhuang (tyen-dzz jwahng) 天字椿   A form of standing qigong exercise in the Tao School.

Wuhan (woo-hahn) 武漢 Capital of Hubei Province.

wuwei (woo-way) 無爲   "Non-action"; "without intention."

Xinjiang (sheen-jyang) 新疆   A province in Northwestern China.

Xingming Guizhi (shing-ming gwee-jhr) 性命圭旨   A classic Chinese
text for cultivation practice.

xinxing (sheen-shing) 心性   Mind or heart nature; moral character.

xiu kou (shyo-ko) 修口   "Cultivation of speech."

Xuanguan Shewei (shwen-gwan shuh-way) 玄關設位   "Placement of
the mysterious pass."

xuanguan yiqiao (shwen-gwan yee-chyow) 玄關一竅   One aperture of
the mysterious pass.

yin (yeen) 陰 and **yang** (yahng) 陽   The Tao School believes that
everything contains opposite forces of yin and
yang which are mutually exclusive, yet
interdependent, e.g. female (yin) vs. male (yang).

yinghai (ying-high) 嬰孩 Cultivated infant(s).

yuan (yu-en) 元   A unit of Chinese currency (approx. =
USD$0.12).

yuanshen (yu-en-shun) 元神   "Essential soul."

yuanying (yu-en-ying) 元嬰   A Taoist term for "the immortal infant."

yuzhen (yu-jhun) 玉枕   An acupuncture point in the lower rear side of
one's head.

zhang (jahng) 丈   A Chinese unit of length (=3 1/3 meters).

Zhang Guolao (jahng gwo-laow) 張果老   One of the Eight Deities in the
Tao School.

Zhen (jhun) 眞   Truth, truthfulness.

Zhen-Shan-Ren 眞善忍 Truthfulness-benevolence-forbearance.

Zhouyi (jo-ee) 周易 As a prehistoric diagram, it discloses the changes of the course of nature.

zhu yishi (jew yee-shi) 主意識 One's main consciousness; zhu yuanshen or main soul.

zhu yuanshen (jew yu-en-shun) 主元神 One's main soul; zhu yishi or main consciousness.

zhuyou ke (jew-yo kuh) 祝由科 The practice of supplication.

List of Falun Dafa Books in English

Zhuan Falun
China Falun Gong
Falun Dafa—Essentials for Further Advancement
Falun Dafa Lectures in the United States

Coming Soon...
Falun Dafa Explication
Zhuan Falun Exposition
The Great Perfection Way of Falun Dafa
Zhuan Falun (Vol. II)
Falun Dafa Lecture in Sydney
Falun Dafa Lecture at the First Conference in North America
Falun Dafa Lecture at the Conference in Europe
Falun Dafa Lecture at the Assistants Meeting in Changchun
Falun Dafa Lecture at the Conference in Singapore
Falun Dafa Lecture at the Conference in Switzerland
Hong Yin (Master Li Hongzhi's poems)

For more information on Falun Dafa books and materials, please visit The Universe Publishing Company's website at
http://www.universepublishing.com

Free Instruction and Workshops Worldwide

Falun Dafa practitioners provide free instruction and workshops worldwide. Books in different languages are available on Internet for free download. For further information, please visit the following websites:

http://www.falundafa.org (USA)
http://www.falundafa.ca (Canada)
http://www.falundafa.au (Australia)

or call toll free: **1-877-FALUN99 (North America)**

Falun Dafa Books and Tapes Order Form

TO: **The Universe Publishing Company**
        P. O. Box 2026
        New York, NY 10013
        Tel: (212) 343-3056 Fax: (212) 343-9512
        E-mail:order@universepublishing.com
        WebSite: www.universepublishing.com

Name: **E-mail (if any):**
Telephone: **Fax (if any):**
Address:

Shipping Address (if different from above):

ISBN and Description	Unit Price	Qty.	Total
1-58613-100-1 China Falun Gong (English)	$12.95	____	_____
1-58613-101-X Zhuan Falun (English)	$12.95	____	_____
1-58613-403-5 Falun Dafa Exercise Instruction Video Tape (English, 60min.)	$12.00	____	_____

                                    SubTotal: _____

NY Sales Tax 8.25% (For New York Residents Only): _____

(Individuals add $2 per item for shipping) Shipping: _____

                                  Grand Total: _____

Please make your check or money order payable to:
    The Universe Publishing Company
    P. O. Box 2026
    New York, NY 10013